THE ROMANCE OF THE HAREM

Victorian Literature and Culture Series

Karen Chase, Jerome J. McGann, *and* Herbert Tucker, *General Editors*

DANIEL ALBRIGHT
Tennyson: *The Muses' Tug-of-War*

DAVID G. RIEDE
Matthew Arnold and the Betrayal of Language

ANTHONY WINNER
Culture and Irony: *Studies in Joseph Conrad's Major Novels*

JAMES RICHARDSON
Vanishing Lives: *Style and Self in Tennyson, D. G. Rossetti, Swinburne, and Yeats*

JEROME J. McGANN, EDITOR
Victorian Connections

ANTONY H. HARRISON
Victorian Poets and Romantic Poems: *Intertextuality and Ideology*

E. WARWICK SLINN
The Discourse of Self in Victorian Poetry

LINDA K. HUGHES and MICHAEL LUND
The Victorian Serial

ANNA LEONOWENS
The Romance of the Harem
Edited and with an Introduction by Susan Morgan

THE ROMANCE
OF THE HAREM

Anna Leonowens

*Edited and with an
Introduction by
Susan Morgan*

UNIVERSITY PRESS OF VIRGINIA

Charlottesville and London

THE UNIVERSITY PRESS OF VIRGINIA
Copyright © 1991 by the Rector and Visitors
of the University of Virginia

First published 1991

Library of Congress Cataloging-in-Publication Data
Leonowens, Anna Harriette, 1834–1914.
The romance of the harem / Anna Leonowens ; edited and with an
introduction by Susan Morgan.
    p.   cm. — (Victorian literature and culture series)
Includes bibliographical references.
ISBN 0–8139–1327–6. — ISBN 0–8139–1328–4 (pbk.)
1. Thailand—History—1782–1945—Fiction.   I. Morgan, Susan,
1943– .   II. Title.   III. Series.
PR4883.L64R66   1991
823'.8—dc20   90-25964
                                                                   CIP

Printed in the United States of America

To Usana, and to all my women friends

Contents

Introduction

IT IS HARD TO KNOW which is more bizarre: Anna Leonowens's own life or her book about the lives of the women in the royal harem of Siam in the 1860s. It is even harder to know how much of the accounts she has given us about either her life or the lives in the harem is factually true. Around *The Romance of the Harem* and around its author shimmer the gaudily alluring veils of misinformation, contradiction, obscurity, and denunciation.

From its first publication in Boston in December 1872, *The Romance of the Harem* has had its admirers and its avid detractors—and no one in between. American reviewers who seemed to know nothing of Siam found the book both interestingly written and morally useful. The *New York Times* review on February 14, 1873, opened by saying that "this tropical book disarms criticism" (p. 9). The major American review, appearing in the May 15, 1873, issue of the *Nation,* was also graciously upbeat. Yet the anonymous reviewer is careful to begin by pointing out that the tales in *The Romance of the Harem* "deserve the name of romances, so wild and strange are they in incident and atmosphere." In terms reminiscent of some of Nathaniel Hawthorne's introductions to his novels, the reviewer goes on to make his central point, that these tales are "all revealing the dark places of the earth, full of the habitations of cruelty, but revealing also some of the greatest and brightest qualities of human nature" (p. 338). Another, much briefer, anonymous review in the *Atlantic Monthly* in May 1873 also implied that the tales in *The Romance of the Harem* are true. The writer went on to offer a useful summary of the traditional definition of the function of travel literature: "it is by the reading of such books as this, which intimately acquaint us with the remote life of other lands and religions, that we are to learn how true to one humanity are the traits of all the different peoples, and to feel the essential unity of the race" (p. 625).

Other responses were neither gracious nor upbeat. Those reviewers, again anonymous, who appeared themselves to have some familiarity with Siam, were intensely critical of *The Romance of the Harem.* In England, where the book was published at the beginning of 1873, the major review appeared in the February 15, 1873, issue of the *Athenaeum.* The writer, reviewing the book by the title under which it was released by Trubner & Co., *The Romance of Siamese Harem Life,* clearly hated the book. He (I presume) launched the review by reminding the reader that Leonowens's previous book, *The English Governess at the Siamese Court,* was full of errors (he may well have been the writer of the hostile review of that book in the *Athenaeum* of December 24, 1870) and by pointing out that the illustrations in the present volume are unacknowledged or are falsely identified.[1] The review went on to announce that "it is our duty to point to a few instances of manifest, we might almost say inexcusable error" (p. 205), and spent the rest of quite a long discussion doing just that.

Even in America, in spite of the pleasant published reviews, Leonowens must have received some substantial challenges to the truth of her writings. In a letter to the *New York Times,* March 3, 1875, she answers the reviewer of someone else's book who had charged that she never actually made the trip to the newly discovered ruins of Angkor Wat in Cambodia, which she had written an account of.[2] Leonowens cites the evidence of her passports, then more generally defends the accuracy of her methods by claiming that her written account is based on "several hundred pages of manuscript, notes, and translations made during the journey" (p. 6).

In the twentieth century the responses to Leonowens's writing by those few Western scholars of Siam who have deigned to pay any attention to it have also been resoundingly negative. They have labeled Leonowens's account of her experiences in the harem as at best a fantasy, at worst a fraud. Ian Grimble, who did a BBC (British Broadcasting Corporation) production on Leonowens on

May 6, 1970, described her as "a mischief maker, a squalid little girl, . . . one of those awful little English governesses, a sex-starved widow."[3] Her two most thorough, and relentless, critics have been A. B. Griswold and W. S. Bristowe. Was Griswold right in his 1957 evaluation that Leonowens herself hovered "on the fringes of reality, often escaping into make-believe," or that "she had no sense of proportion but an acute sense of melodrama"?[4] What of the exposé Bristowe offered in 1976 in his biography of Louis Leonowens, Anna's son, that Anna Leonowens was a virtual con artist who lied about everything in her background? Bristowe went so far as to surmise that Leonowens's revisions of her personal history become explicable as an attempt to cover the fact that she was of mixed blood and so was not all white. As he put it, Leonowens "may have had what was called 'a touch of the tar-brush' in her veins."[5]

Certainly, these traditional Western experts on Siam, as Thailand was called in the nineteenth-century, have offered evaluations that discredit Leonowens's writing. Leonowens's own experiences in Siam formed the basis on which her books laid claim to some authority. The experts have been emphatic in their insistence that her work does not have a right to make that claim. The opinion from everybody who knows anything about Thailand seems to have been that she does not. They have denounced Leonowens as an amateur, an outsider, a fake. The image of Leonowens that her critics have projected is that of a lower-class conniver of dubious respectability, ungrateful to her royal employer, crippled by ignorance, and blinded by narrow-minded religious prejudices. To steal a phrase from Joseph Conrad's *Lord Jim,* they have insisted that Leonowens is not "one of us." She has been disqualified from membership not only on the grounds of her lack of knowledge and her lack of rationality, but also on that more fundamental ground of perhaps not being truly, which is to say wholly, Western. So there we have it. Leonowens is uninformed, irrational, a liar, and probably not even white.

The clannish scorn of traditional Western intellectuals who have written about the East is a tempting reason for being drawn to Leonowens's work, but in itself it is insufficient. Why, then, should we read this obscure travel account, with its dubious and often inaccurate or uncheckable facts and its author of shady repute?

Who was Anna Leonowens? Here is the story passed through Anna's own accounts and those of her family, immortalized in its bare outlines by all the standard dictionaries of biography and amplified in Margaret Landon's creative biography. Anna Harriette Crawford, who grew up in Carnarvon, Wales, until she finished school at fifteen, was the child of an uprooted couple. Born in Carnarvon on November 5, 1834, she was just six years old when her parents kissed her goodbye, left her to be raised by Mrs. Walpole (a relative who ran a school), and sailed to India. Captain Thomas Maxwell Crawford was ordered to India with his regiment, and his wife went with him. Anna never saw her father again, for he was killed in a Sikh uprising when she was not quite seven. Her mother stayed on in India, and it would be almost ten years before Anna saw her again.

In 1849, when Anna Crawford was fifteen, she sailed to India. Her mother had remarried, and Anna now had a tyrannical step-father (whose name has never been discovered). In Bombay this teenage girl met Major Thomas Louis Leonowens and, after an educational tour of the Middle East with the Reverend George Percy Badger and his wife, Anna returned to Major Leonowens and married him in 1851. Their first child died in India, their second in Australia. By 1853 they had gone back for a time to England, probably to have their children in a healthier climate than the East. A daughter, Avis, was born in October 1853, and exactly a year later, a son, Louis. In 1856 the family returned to the East, to Singapore, and in 1858 Thomas Leonowens died there, of heat prostration after a tiger hunt. Mrs. Leonowens started a school for the children of her husband's brother officers, but earning a living was a struggle. In 1862 she took a job as governess to the children of the king of Siam. Sending Avis, now seven-and-a-half, back to a boarding school in England, Anna Leonowens, along with Louis, now six-and-a-half, sailed to Bangkok in March 1862.

But there is another, more lurid, version of the story. In 1976, in a chapter called "Anna Unveiled," W. S. Bristowe published what he titled "The True Story of Anna Leonowens." He had pieced the story together after checking birth and marriage records, army lists, and burial records in England, India, Wales, Singapore, and Penang.[6] Anna Leonowens was born in India (not in Wales), on November 6, 1831 (not 1834), the second daughter of a poor army sergeant named Edwards (not a captain named Crawford), who died three months before she was born. Her mother, who may have been the child of a mixed marriage, married another soldier (a corporal, soon demoted to a private) when Anna was two months old. Anna and her sister, Eliza, were sent back to school in England. In 1845 they returned to India as teenagers. Eliza had just turned fifteen when she married a thirty-eight-year-old sergeant.

As she claimed, Anna met the thirty-year-old Reverend Mr. Badger upon her return to India at age fourteen, and accompanied him to the Middle East when his job as assistant chaplain transferred him there. But he had no wife (and when he did marry a few years later, the girl was three years younger than Anna). The Reverend Mr. Badger and Anna traveled unchaperoned. Anna stayed with him in the Middle East for a while, returned to India, and married Thomas Leon Owens—*Mr.* Owens—on Christmas Day, 1849, when she had just turned eighteen. Tom and Anna Owens seem to have moved a few times. No birth records have been found for their surviving children, Avis and Louis. A first daughter named Selina was born in India in 1851, and must have died. A second child may have been born in Australia and died, but no records have been found. Avis was probably born in 1854 and Louis in 1855. Tom Owens died in Malaya in May 1859. On the death record he is described as thirty-two years old, and the "Hotel Master" in Penang (one of the British "Straits Settlements," along with Singapore and Malacca). In death his name changed; it is given as Thomas Leonowens.

What is at stake in the difference between these two versions of Anna Leonowens's life before becoming a governess in Siam is, of course, primarily class, but also reputation, and possibly race.

What we must also decide is how our knowledge of these two versions can shape our approaches to Leonowens's books.

Was Anna Leonowens herself of mixed blood? Bristowe's suggestion that Anna's mother may have been the product of a union between an English soldier and an Indian woman is quite possible, even plausible. It fits with what we know happened to a great many unmarried English soldiers when they got to India and provides at least one motive for the discrepancies in Leonowens's own version. Nonetheless, however credible this suggestion is, we should not forget that it is also a complete invention. No one actually knows now who Anna's maternal grandmother was. No one has any facts about her except that her name was Anne and she married Anna's grandfather after he arrived in India.

It is not invention that there was mixed blood in Anna's family, but it occurred in the generation that came after hers. In Anna Leonowens's autobiographical writings she never mentions her sister, Eliza. Eliza's first child, Anna's niece, did marry around 1862 a man of mixed Indian and British blood, of "the class of Coloured Englishmen," as he described himself.[7] Their children were, therefore, what many British referred to as Eurasian, and it is certain that the family felt the sting of discriminatory policies. One of the children of her niece's mixed marriage was Anna's great-nephew William, known to us under his stage name of Boris Karloff.

We cannot responsibly speculate that Anna Leonowens rewrote some of her own history to hide the evidence of her mixed blood, since we simply have no evidence that she was of mixed blood. We can responsibly speculate that she rewrote her history to hide her class. As Bristowe claims, the changes in her autobiography allowed her to present herself, not as a lower-class working girl, but "as a young gentlewoman whom ill-fate had forced to work for a living."[8] Leonowens effectively took three years off her age, revised her father and husband into gentlemen of good family, and had herself born in Britain of good family as well. She changed names and places to hide the working-class origins of her family and her husband. In a world where good blood and good breeding mattered, Leonowens rearranged the facts to have both.

Was Anna Leonowens a liar? It seems so. Even if she'd been told as a child that she was born in Wales, that her father's name was Crawford, and that her birth date was 1834, by the time she married she was old enough to know her husband's real name, class, and army rank (if any). There is no question that we must hold Anna Leonowens responsible for a deliberate revision of her autobiography.

And then there is Mr. Badger. Perhaps it was an educational tour. Nonetheless, as a young girl about fifteen years old Anna Edwards did go to the Middle East with an unmarried man of about thirty or thirty-one (the difference in age seems irrelevant when we recall that her sister at fifteen had married a man of thirty-eight) and remain with him for an undetermined amount of time, between several months and two years. Whatever the degree of innocence this relationship may (or may not) have had in reality, its appearance is disreputable. What was Anna Edwards doing from age fourteen, when she arrived back in India, to age eighteen, when she married Tom Owens? If her relationship with Mr. Badger was as disreputable as it appears, some of her later lies may have been not so much a matter of social climbing as of escaping from that early loss of reputation. Her lies not only elevated her class, they gave her what might well have been a much-needed respectability. Anna Crawford, widow of Major Leonowens, could not be that sinful Anna Edwards who went off to Egypt with Mr. Badger, then returned to India and married Tom Owens.

Whatever her motives, Anna Leonowens lied. Each reader must decide for herself or himself what her opinion of Anna Leonowens's character will be, and what effect this knowledge of Leonowens's character will have on evaluating her as a narrator. My own outrage on the subject of Leonowens's lies is minimal. Disliking the cultural ideologies that would evaluate and treat people according to their family, breeding, class, and sexual experience more than I dislike lies that individuals tell to protect themselves from being victimized by those cultural evaluations and treatments, I think Leonowens's response could well be practical, sensible, possibly even courageous.

Finally, I do not think knowing that Leonowens lied about her past is much help in determining her true character. What has Bristowe exposed after all? Was Leonowens an iconoclast or a social climber, a daring individualist who rejected the socially and professionally limiting facts of her birth or a sordid hustler with delusions of grandeur? I don't think we will ever know. Moreover, the more we insist that Leonowens "really" was lower class, the less we can explain her high level of articulateness—and the more impressive it becomes. Nineteenth-century lower-class British women, in England or in India, seldom completed grade school, let alone studied at the upper levels or attended college. Families of upper-class women sent their daughters to good boarding schools and/or hired private tutors for educating them at home. It is unlikely that either of these possibilities was open to Leonowens. One of many fascinating mysteries about her is where she got the education that enabled her to express herself so well.

Certainly, that Leonowens told lies about her own life reinforces the suspicion that she told lies about life in the royal harem of Siam. It is impossible for any reader to read *The Romance of the Harem* as a factual history. But that need not mean that we discount *The Romance of the Harem* as not being history at all. Perhaps what it does mean is that we should understand the book to be fictionalized history or historical fiction. Leonowens, after all, quite explicitly entitled it, not history, but "Romance." Her title seems appropriate to the strange mix of fact and fancy that characterizes this work in a way that later titles, particularly twentieth-century reprints suggesting that it is a factual exposé, do not. Whatever the label, and in spite of the fact that its author was a liar, *The Romance of the Harem* has its own truths to tell.

The first, and probably the most important, reason for attending to *The Romance of the Harem* is that, whoever Anna Leonowens was, something amazing, something truly unusual and truly fascinating, did happen to her. That much no one can deny. Leonowens was, at least historically speaking, incredibly lucky. Without, apparently, being particularly adventurous or heroic or exceptional in her talents and skills—apart from an impressive ability for self-invention—Leonowens found herself to be the right person in the right place at the right time. Having been doing some teaching in Singapore after her husband died, Leonowens was offered the position of English tutor to the royal children of Siam. She spent five and a third years, from March 1862 to July 1867, with a unique and almost unlimited access to the royal harem of Siam. Leonowens became fluent in Thai (though Griswold criticizes her translations), got to know well many of the women in that harem, and wrote the only account in existence by a Westerner (and possibly by any Thai) of nineteenth-century life in the Siamese royal harem.

It may be tragic that, given such an amazing opportunity, Leonowens preferred literature to history and chose to present her account of what she saw in the harem more in the language of fiction than of fact. But it may not. Leonowens is a terrible historian, but she is a fine writer. And Leonowens's special situation by itself gives a dimension of historic value to her book that should make it impossible to dismiss. There are, of course, many other reasons as well for valuing this generally excoriated and long-neglected account. But first I want to sketch some of the details of that special situation.

In March 1862, with her son, Louis, about seven years old, Leonowens sailed from Singapore to Bangkok on the steamer *Chao Phya,* a trip that took about five days, to take up her position as English governess to the king's children. Among her royal pupils the most important, and the one most charged to develop a facility in English, was the king's eldest son, Crown Prince Chulalongkorn, then nine years old. Over the years in Bangkok Leonowens would also teach many other princes and princesses, along with any of their mothers and any of the other women in the king's harem who wished to take advantage of this opportunity to study the English language, English knowledge, and English ways.

Leonowens's schoolroom was the marble-floored grand hall of one of the many temples—Wat Khoon Chom Manda Thai, Temple of the Mothers of the Free—within the harem. The name of the royal harem was Nang Harm, which can be translated as Veiled Women. Most Western images of harems are really variants on Hollywood fantasies about the harems of the Middle East. Nang Harm—and possibly any other harem, including those in the Middle East—does not fit this image. What then do we mean by a actual harem, at least when referring to the harem of the king of Siam?

Nang Harm in the 1860s was a walled city. Wide avenues with graceful houses, parks, flower gardens, and small streets crowded with apartments and shops were all enclosed by an inner wall inside the Grand Palace area, with the whole enclosed by an outer wall. Leonowens estimated the population of Nang Harm to be about nine thousand people, all (with the exception of the priests, who visited every morning) women and children, and almost all captive there. Nang Harm functioned in many ways as its own city, with inhabitants in a range of classes, having a range of functions. The highest class consisted of members of the royal family. These women would never leave Nang Harm until, in Leonowens's own phrase, they would "have by age and position attained to a certain degree of freedom" (p. 13). Leonowens's employer, King Mongkut, had a vast number of sisters and aunts, inherited as his responsibility on the death of previous kings. The women under his care included not only the relatives of his father but also those of his immediate predecessor, his elder half brother (not to mention their leftover concubines, and all the ladies' slaves). The royal family also included King Mongkut's wives, his own children (eventually eighty-two of them), and various other relatives.

Apart from the women and children of the royal family, Nang Harm contained a vast number of women who performed the functions needed to maintain the harem. Many of the residents, including children, were slaves. Some of the women were or would be concubines (a title, complete with a decoration, gained by sharing the king's bed at least once) or had been concubines for a night or a week or longer. Some underwent the rigorous training needed to become dancers or performers in the royal theater. A few of the women were or had been the king's "favorite." Even fewer were particularly blessed by being among those lucky enough to have conceived during their time with him, thereby becoming concubine mothers. A fair estimate is that there were several hundred potential concubines, several scores of concubines, three dozen mothers, and several consorts. The rest of the women were all the varied kinds of people it takes to sustain a world. There were endless domestic slaves, cooks and tasters, seamstresses, teachers, soldiers (called the Amazons), even doctors and judges. In short, Nang Harm was an entire society of women and children.

It was an elaborate and absolutely unique world, inaccessible to Westerners and to almost all Siamese as well. Although Anna Leonowens was not literally the first Western woman to have access to the royal harem, she was the first really to do so in terms of being admitted into the confidence and daily affairs of the harem women. In 1851, eleven years before Anna's arrival in Bangkok, King Mongkut had tried for the first time to provide the women of his harem with formal instruction in Western ways by inviting in three wives of Protestant missionaries in American missions in Siam. Mrs. Mattoon, Mrs. Jones, and Mrs. Bradley took turns teaching English to some of the ladies of the harem during two weekday mornings on and off for almost three years until one morning the palace gates were closed to them and the experiment was over. From the king's perspective they must have been abusing their position by using these teaching occasions to distribute religious tracts from their mission and to proselytize for Christianity.

King Mongkut's next effort, probably reflecting his conclusion that he could not usefully recruit from among the pool of Western missionaries living in Bangkok and that other native English speakers in Bangkok would have had no teaching experience, was to bring in an outsider. He hired Anna Leonowens. She was recommended "by his Chinese agent, Tam Kin Ching, in Singapore on the suggestion of John Adamson of the Borneo Company."[9]

This time the plan worked. The king stipulated quite explicitly that the matter for study was to be cultural and intellectual rather than religious. In the king's own words in a letter to Leonowens, "you will do your best endeavour for knowledge of English language, science and literature, and not for conversion to Christianity."[10] For five years and four months Leonowens had virtually daily access to this special female world, though she lived outside its walls. She and her son walked into Nang Harm almost every morning and, just as incredibly, walked out of its gates again at night.

Leonowens's job did not remain solely being the governess to the king's children. During the decade when international business affairs were involving Siam as never before, Leonowens asserts that the king turned to this English teacher to take on the second duty of providing him with secretarial help, at least in the matter of writing his letters in English, often rephrasing them with correct grammar. Leonowens, to the scoffing of her detractors, describes this part of her job as occasionally including as well the task of providing a sounding board for the king's ponderings about how to deal with the Western powers who were competing for trading rights in—and, undoubtedly, for power over—Siam. He would consult her, not on policy matters, but rather on Western customs and attitudes, on possible Western responses to positions he was planning to take. Having some sense of those responses could help him in gauging Western political motives and in choosing his own moves.

What we can be sure of is that this Victorian woman in her early thirties found herself in the amazing and utterly unique position of moving daily between two normally inaccessible spheres: the female world of some of the most powerless people in Siam and the world of the one most powerful person in Siam, who in the 1860s still ruled by divine right. And in certain limited ways she became the confidante, and the advisor, to each.

How did Leonowens view her position, at least as far as we can tell from the evidence of her published writing? She certainly did see her role as romantic. The court of Siam, like any other court, was filled with political intrigue, and dangerous to one not knowing its ways. But more importantly, to Anna Leonowens the world of Nang Harm was one in which numbers of women and children were being crushed, most of them spiritually and many of them physically. She saw it as a world of suffering and despair. Many were born in the harem, or were brought there as young girls, victims of their family's political aspirations or the king's random and roving eye. It was the common practice for locally powerful families all over Thailand to solidify or improve their relations with the king by giving him a young girl from their family in exchange for political favor. Once the girls were in the royal harem, they were usually there forever. But the tragedy of their fates was not simply that they were virtually imprisoned for life. With the exception of those thirty-five who were lucky enough to catch the king's favor and then be able to conceive and bear royal children, these women were doomed to virginity and childlessness, in a society where status for women came through motherhood.

In this grotesquely artificial universe, the presence of Anna Leonowens was certainly exciting, and possibly miraculous. Though a good Christian, at least by the testimony of her writing, and therefore sure her religion was the true one, Leonowens really was a lay person. There is no evidence to suggest that she thought her Christian duty was to try to convert her Buddhist students. She taught them English language and culture, she got to know them, and she felt involved in many of their lives. From her perspective she had been placed, to the extent that she would permit and could bear it, in the position of the go-between. Leonowens presents *The Romance of the Harem* as the story of some of the more memorable incidents from her experiences as friend, defender, and spokesperson for her beloved pupils, the women of Nang Harm.

The Romance of the Harem was first published in late December 1872, with a title page dated 1873, in Boston by James R. Osgood and Company. It was brought out in England in January or early February 1873 by Trubner and Company, probably by arrangement with Osgood during his visit to London in late summer 1872. Already the process of modifying the original Boston title, with the effect of making the book's contents sound more factual and less fictional, had begun. The title Trubner used was *The Romance of Siamese Harem Life*.

The book, with its American title, was also published in Philadelphia sometime during the spring of 1873 by Porter and Coates (but with no date on the title page). The *Atlantic Monthly,* edited by James Fields (previously one of the partners in the publishing house of Tickner and Fields, which became Fields, Osgood, & Co. before it was taken over by James Osgood), had serialized three chapters of *The English Governess at the Siamese Court* in 1870. James Fields was also the book publisher of *The English Governess* in 1870 (though the company was then still Fields, Osgood, & Co.). In 1873, the same publishing house, but evolved into James R. Osgood and Company because Fields had retired, published Leonowens's second book. The *Atlantic Monthly* continued its support of Leonowens's work by publishing a positive review of *The Romance of the Harem.*

By the early 1870s Anna Leonowens had become good friends with Annie Fields, a published poet, well-known hostess, and the wife of James Fields. The two women also shared a mutual friend, Harriet Beecher Stowe. Stowe was one of the most famous of the regular contributors to the *Atlantic Monthly* in the 1860s and 1870s. Her articles, and the sheer association of her name with it, helped to give the magazine its antislavery reputation. A major link between Annie Fields, Harriet Beecher Stowe, and Anna Leonowens was pronounced opinions on the evils of slavery. Leonowens did write more intensely against slavery in her 1873 *The Romance of the Harem* than she had in her 1870 *The English Governess*. Was this difference a way of exploiting the political opinions of her American supporters? Perhaps. Yet I can as plausibly argue that the difference reflects her growing confidence as a writer. In her second book Leonowens had found her true voice and a subject more important to her than a simple travel account of Siam. Her years in Siam coincided with the years of the American Civil War. The issue of slavery was continually under public discussion, even among Westerners so far away as Southeast Asia. There is simply no evidence for doubting the sincerity of Leonowens's declared abhorrence of slavery.

James and Annie Fields and Harriet Beecher Stowe, all important members of the literary establishment in New England, were
certainly fabulous connections for an author to have. *The Romance
of the Harem* received more reviews in the United States than it did
in England. One explanation for the increased attention in America
was the friendship of Stowe and Annie and James Fields. Leonowens, and her work, would have had a visibility for an American
audience that they would not have had for a British.

It is also true that Leonowens was a professional and commercial writer. A large part of why she lectured and wrote about her
experiences in Siam was to make a living. After leaving Siam in
July 1867, Leonowens returned to England from Singapore some
time in the following months. She left Louis at a school in England,
picked up her daughter, Avis, from the school she had been in since
just before Anna and Louis had sailed without her for Siam in 1862,
and moved to America. Leonowens must have arrived in the
United States some time in 1868 or early 1869. She had no income,
no family, and herself and her daughter to support (as well as
needing money to send to England for Louis's support). What
Leonowens did have were her unique experiences in Siam and
talent as a writer.

The Romance of the Harem did not become one of Osgood's
best-sellers. It did not go into a second printing in the nineteenth
century in England or in America. Leonowens moved to Canada
sometime in the 1880s to live with her daughter, who had married a
Canadian. Yet she did continue to have her books published,
though not with Osgood. In 1889 D. Lathrop Company in Boston
published *Our Asiatic Cousins,* a sort of guidebook travelogue with
a title reflecting one of the traditional arguments for the value of
travel writing: that travel shows us our united identity beneath
superficial cultural differences as members of the family of man.
Leonowens' Philadelphia publisher, Henry Coates, published in
1884 a book of memoirs of her experiences before going to Siam
entitled *Life and Travels in India* and reprinted it in 1897. That same
year Coates also reissued her first book, *The English Governess,*
twenty-seven years after it first came out. For this reprinting the

book had a new title, *Siam and the Siamese*. Like the changes made over the years to the title of *The Romance of the Harem,* this change was also a matter of false advertising. The new title implied that the book's contents were more a matter of objective reportage of facts than of personal impressions. After these two reissues at the end of the nineteenth century, Leonowens's books seem to have faded away. They were not to come to life again until 1944.

In 1927 an American woman named Margaret Landon went to live in Siam with her husband, a minister, remaining there for ten years. Around 1929 or 1930 a friend of theirs in Siam lent her copies of *The English Governess at the Siamese Court* and *The Romance of the Harem.* Landon was entranced. She pursued information about Leonowens's life. Almost fifteen years later Landon combined that information (some of it from Leonowens's granddaughter, Avis Fyshe, and also some from people who had known Leonowens in Bangkok) with the biographical information in Leonowens's books into a single semifictionalized biography, *Anna and the King of Siam.* The book was published in 1944 in New York by The John Day Company, then reprinted in New York by Garden City Publishers in 1945 and again in 1947 by John Day. There were several European translations. The book was a huge success. More than thirty years after her death, almost eighty years after she left Siam, Anna Leonowens's amazing adventure was to become famous at last.

The next step in the exploding fame that began with Landon's book was that Hollywood noticed. First came a movie version of Landon's book, starring Rex Harrison and Irene Dunne. Then Broadway noticed, and the movie was followed by a play that would become a classic of American musicals, Rogers and Hammerstein's *The King and I.* It opened on Broadway on March 29, 1951, starring Gertrude Lawrence and Yul Brynner. Finally, Landon's story of Anna Leonowens and the king of Siam reached complete national exposure when *The King and I* was made into a film, starring Deborah Kerr and again Yul Brynner.[11] This movie is now one of the classics of American musical cinema. The adventure of Anna Leonowens has been immortalized, first in black and white and then in living color on a wide screen. Deborah Kerr and Yul Brynner, as the decorous but firm-willed Anna and the despotic but sensitive King Mongkut, formed the unforgettably unlikely couple who continue to dance together in the imaginations of all of us who enjoy the glamorous musicals of the fifties. Without *The King and I,* without Rogers and Hammerstein's fabulous tunes, glittering costumes, and Deborah Kerr's and Yul Brynner's superb acting, this facsimile edition might not exist.[12] Certainly, I would not be writing this introduction.

In response, no doubt, to the popularity of Landon's quasi biography and the first movie and the musical, *The Romance of the Harem* was reprinted at last, eighty years after it first appeared. Arthur Barker published it in London in 1952; then E. P. Dutton brought it out in New York in 1953. These editions sported a new title: *Siamese Harem Life.* A shortened version of the title of the original 1873 London edition, *The Romance of Siamese Harem Life,* this new title abandoned completely the tacit acknowledgment of the book's fictionality implicit in the original American title. The effect of the change is clearly to lay claim to being historical description rather than historical invention.

In spite of these reprintings, and the new title that attempted to give this fantastic book some objective substance by locating its value in its being about "Life" rather than about "Romance," the book has never entered the consciousnesses of American scholars. These fictionalized memoirs have yet to be evaluated for what they can tell us about nineteenth-century British women's lives, about popular culture in the nineteenth century in England and in America and, perhaps most important, about life for at least a few nineteenth-century Thai women.

Scholars' virtually total unfamiliarity with Leonowens's writing, and the complete lack of evaluations of its place within nineteenth-century British and American culture, including Western writings about Eastern places, is in startling contrast to the fame of Leonowens's experiences in twentieth-century American culture. If no one has heard of *The Romance of the Harem,* everyone has heard of *The King and I.* I suspect that those facts are related. It may well be that for twentieth-century academia the fatal flaw in Leonowens's writings—when added to their lack of scholarly knowledge about Siam, their errors in fact, their irrationality, the suspicion that their author isn't all white—is the final crime of their being the subject of not one but two Hollywood movies. The ultimate loss of historical credibility is Leonowens's enshrinement in popular culture.

But movies and plays, for all their glittering power to uphold and transform our cultural myths, are not books. When Prince Chula Chakrabongse, writing about the detrimental effect of *The King and I* on Western ideas about Siam, remarks that "it is almost as fictional as *The Mikado* of Gilbert and Sullivan, but in its case it was advertised as a documentary," his critique is certainly accurate.[13] But *The Romance of the Harem* is not *The King and I*. Neither is it Landon's *Anna and the King of Siam*. Are the portrayals of the Siamese in the two films and the play racist? Absolutely. But is this true of Leonowens's book? Yes again, but neither so simplistically nor so unredemptively. This Victorian woman certainly participated in the white man's biases about both the racial and the cultural inferiority of the Thais. But it matters whether we are referring to Thai men or Thai women. What Leonowens may not have shared is either culture's masculine bias about the inferiority of women.

The first step in evaluating *The Romance of the Harem* and its significance as a nineteenth-century British travel memoir must be to forget its significance as part of the base material used in constructing a major icon of twentieth-century American culture. That icon of our own times should not determine the meaning of Leonowens's book—in her own age or in ours.

The Romance of the Harem has engendered such a checkered publication history in part because of its many weaknesses of scholarship and accuracy and its author's vulnerabilities as an expert on Siam. But part of the energy of the response to *The Romance of the Harem* has also to do with the fact that it takes up in provocative and dangerous ways three of the most incendiary issues in nineteenth-century England and America: relations between the nations of West and East; the hierarchical distribution of rights and privileges in the relations between people within a nation; and, of course, the troubled relations between individual men and women. Exploitation of other countries, of other classes within one country, of people of the opposite sex—these are the big nineteenth-century issues of imperialism, slavery, and women's rights.

In *The Romance of the Harem* all three of these major issues have been cavalierly united in one populist book, written by an author with no claims through birth or breeding or education or any officially sanctioned forms of experience to have any authority on such problematic subjects. Moreover, on every one of these issues the author comes down, sometimes only implicitly, sometimes waveringly, and sometimes quite dramatically, on the side I might call liberal or reformist. *The Romance of the Harem,* though in its own fantastical and culturally chauvinistic way, does challenge some of the most beloved ideologies of nineteenth-century British and American culture.

Western imperialist attitudes to the small kingdom of Siam in Southeast Asia were a different matter from imperialist attitudes to other parts of the East, particularly to the Middle East and the Far East. One simple reason, too often overlooked by twentieth-century intellectuals, is that the East is no more monolithic than the West is. Different Western attitudes to Siam had to do, in the first place, with the fact that different countries, and therefore different cultures, were involved. The United States was simply not interested in Siam the way it was in, say, China or Japan. Although the United States had an appointed consul in Bangkok by the middle of the nineteenth century, the position was unpaid. No money was approved by Congress for a consular salary until 1864.[14] The major U.S. presence in Bangkok throughout most of the century was religious, in the form of the various Protestant missions.

Britain's major imperialist energies were expended in trying to maintain India. Though both Western nations might well have been willing to scoop up Siam if given an opening, they showed no special eagerness to do so. They did not have any pressing political or economic reasons to decide that the effort could justify (morally as well as financially) the cost. And the lack of those pressing reasons was a result both of Siam's strategic diplomacy, carefully choreographed by King Mongkut, and of the economic success of the various forms of Western involvement in Siam.

A major reason that the British did not feel pressed to use their superior force to take Siam is that in 1855 the British had successfully negotiated a treaty that gave them most of what they wanted anyway. Sir John Bowring, the British governor of Hong Kong, negotiated an agreement that resulted in opening up Siam to "large-scale foreign commerce."[15] The Bowring Treaty allowed Britain to trade freely in Siam with minimal taxes or duty, allowed British subjects to reside in and own land in Siam, and provided British consular jurisdiction over British nationals. Effectively, the British could now live in and do business in Siam, and their host country could not say much about how they went about it (though Siam's revenues did double as a result of the increase in trade).

After signing the Bowring Treaty with Britain, the Thais signed similar agreements with several other countries, including the United States. By the time Anna Leonowens arrived in Siam seven years later, Bangkok was, in commercial terms, an international city. Leonowens's appointment reflected the established policy of King Mongkut of ensuring that his country would be as well prepared as possible in the dangerous business of successfully evading "the direct colonial control of the Western powers" and also providing for the "survival of an independent Siam."[16]

King Mongkut and his son and heir, King Chulalongkorn, were successful in the difficult task of directing Siam to a strong independence. Thailand is the only country in Southeast Asia that has never been colonized or occupied. Western imperialism, with its implicit theoretical concern about the very definition of human nature and, at the same time, its practical concern about who would or could dominate world markets by controlling not only the means of production but also the raw materials, operated in a special way in the relations between Britain and Siam. The attack was not a matter of literal force but of economic invasion.

A substantial factor in Siam's successful defense of its independence was the royal harem. The harem was stocked (and that may be the most appropriate word) with girls and women given to the king by their noble and powerful families all over Siam. The royal harem helped to keep Siam independent because it helped in part to keep Siam united. Unlike India when faced with the British threat, Siam did not present itself as an uneasy grouping of disparate regions ruled by competing and quarrelsome princes, none of whom qualified as the head of state. The harem, with its group of royal mothers coming from families all over Siam, had a key political function as a unifying force, existing in relation to one central paternal figure with the power to make state decisions for all the territories of Siam. Through the harem, almost everyone with any power in the country was a relative of the king. If we consider just King Mongkut and his eighty-two children, his relatives from those children constituted a staggering family group. The combination of monarch and harem helped to limit the internal disputes that could make civil decision making a struggle and thus could weaken Siam's resistance to foreign takeover.

Siam's strategy also included becoming familiar with foreign ways, to the point of having the members of the royal harem trained by an Englishwoman. Given her own cultural context, that Englishwoman could not but disapprove of the very existence of the harem. Leonowens, certainly, did not see it as an empowering social institution that strengthened Siam's resistance to British imperialism. The idea probably didn't occur to her. Leonowens did want the harem to be abolished. But her distaste, at least as presented in her writings, was hardly based on a canny wish to throw her weight on the side of British ambitions in the region.

Nor does Leonowens's distaste seem to have been a matter of sexual prudishness. One of the common claims of Leonowens's critics is that she could not understand or evaluate properly the life she witnessed in Siam because she was blinded by her religious narrow-mindedness, possibly through being unduly influenced by her association with the American missionary community in Bangkok. The problem with this critique (apart from ignoring that its supposedly ultrapious subject is the very woman who skipped off with Mr. Badger and also rewrote her autobiography) is that it does not fit the textual evidence. *The Romance of the Harem* complains very little on religious grounds about the existence of the royal harem. Leonowens does not energetically object to the harem as polygamous or promiscuous or even as an illicit offense against the principles of Christianity, though she does give token assent to these objections. Whatever her private opinions of Siamese sexuality may have been, what Leonowens explicitly and continually offers as her key objection to the harem arrangement is that, from the perspective of the women living in Nang Harm, their lives are not a matter of free choice.

For Leonowens the political value of an integrating, even a democratizing, social institution that could continually feed the royal bloodlines with new connections from other families in a network of relations large enough to be a significant force in uniting a country did not have the kind of priority it seems to have had for King Mongkut, many other Thais, and many twentieth-century political historians.[17] Perhaps this shows, not her cultural ignorance and narrow-mindedness, but simply different priorities from her detractors. Leonowens objected to the harem, not because she supported British imperialism (though in many ways she did), not because she was a repressed Victorian prude (which I suspect she wasn't), not because she was under the sway of the rigid American Protestant missionaries in Bangkok (a dubious claim), not because she was blinded by her own cultural narrow-mindedness, but because she was opposed to slavery. As she explicitly explained in *The English Governess,* "how I have pitied those ill-fated sisters of mine, imprisoned without a crime!"[18]

Any defense of the social institution of the Siamese harem also involves, however unwittingly, a defense of the social institution of slavery: without slavery the harem could not exist. This interconnection has long been acknowledged by various Thai and Western apologists for the institution of Siamese slavery. An early expression of what would become a familiar Western attitude was Sir John

Bowring's assertion in his 1857 account, *The Kingdom and People of Siam,* that "I saw few examples of harshness in the treatment of slaves, they are generally cheerful, amusing themselves with songs and jokes while engaged in their various toils." Bowring goes on to cite the observations of a presumed authority, a "European gentleman living in Bangkok," who has assured Bowring that "in small families, the slaves are treated like the children of the masters."[19]

Quoting Bowring with some acceptance, and possibly even approval, Griswold articulates what is probably the standard Western attitude in written accounts that do more than simply note the widespread existence of slavery in Siam. Griswold's claim, offered in his admiring book on King Mongkut, is that "slavery in Siam was not the terrible institution it was in some other lands."[20] The particular "other land" of terrible slavery that Bowring's account and Griswold's supportive summary invokes is, of course, the United States. Bowring's account of slavery in Siam is similar to contemporaneous accounts in America describing darkies singing happily on plantations, looked after by their benevolently paternal masters.

Western readers now know enough about the grotesque inhumanity of slavery in nineteenth-century America, and in the British colonies in the eighteenth century, to be skeptical about lenient judgments of slavery, and also of the harem as a particularly benign form of slavery, in nineteenth-century Thailand. Those lenient judgments have emerged in studies of the character and achievement of King Mongkut. Twentieth-century Thai scholars from both the West and Thailand have found much to admire about King Mongkut, a fascinating leader who is credited with taking the first major steps in modernizing Thailand while maintaining its independence from Western control.

What many Thai scholars have found particularly offensive and deceitful about Leonowens's writing is her negative portrait of King Mongkut's rule over the harem. She attributes atrocities that are almost certainly fictional to an actual historic figure, one with real claims to being considered enlightened and progressive. As well as citing the distorting destructiveness of Leonowens's portrait for Mongkut's international reputation, Thai scholars have objected to the sheer ingratitude her writing shows. That February 15, 1873 review in the *Athenaeum* ended by questioning "the propriety of the writer's conduct in spending years in the service of the Siamese King, taking his pay, accepting his kindness, and afterwards publishing" such incidents (no. 2364, p. 207). And in 1961 Griswold quoted the Siamese ambassador to London, who reproached Leonowens for "slandering her employer."[21]

Yet there are many problems with the claim that Leonowens's accounts of incidents in the royal harem are slander. In the first place, there is a lack of supporting evidence on either side. Leonowens's book is, I would guess, heavily fictionalized, maybe even all lies. It is also the only existing eyewitness account accessible to Westerners of the king's treatment of his harem. There is nothing else. On this basis alone, the book's value is immeasurable. Certainly, the royal court records of trials within Nang Harm would provide a superb source for discovering something of what went on in the harem. But they are not available. There is no easy way out of the problem of evaluating the truth of *The Romance of the Harem*.

In the absence of substantial direct evidence, writers who are engaged in what they see as restoring King Mongkut's unjustly slandered reputation point out that Leonowens's harsh critiques are implausible, given what they do know about nineteenth-century Thailand and the particular character of the king. Just two weeks after Prince Mongkut, the rightful heir to the throne, entered the Buddhist priesthood at age twenty to serve for a brief time, as was Siamese custom, his father suddenly died. His elder brother took the throne, and Mongkut remained a monk for the next twenty-seven years until his brother died. He became king in 1851 at age 47. While a monk, Mongkut had become extremely learned, not only in Buddhism but in such areas as the sciences, French, and English. He kept the vows of strict poverty and traveled extensively in his country and among his people. Once crowned, he successfully began the difficult process of modernizing Siam, in part through trying to mitigate some of the injustices suffered by his people.

Rejecting Leonowens's book, with its intense attacks on slavery in the royal harem, and defending King Mongkut as an enlightened head of state rather than an occasional despot who would have his concubines whipped, imprisoned, and tortured have depended on enumerating the special qualities of Mongkut's character and of his life. Mongkut was an intellectual and an ascetic, deeply religious, who for many years lived in a kind of poverty and freedom that acquainted him with his people and their problems in a way most unusual for royalty in any country. No one can deny the extensiveness of slavery in Siam during Mongkut's reign, or the extensiveness of his royal harem. But Mongkut is hardly personally responsible for the institution of slavery in Siam. He was a victim of his historical context, a product of his culture. Moreover, he was more modern than his predecessors. As Griswold and others have pointed out, through some of his edicts King Mongkut specifically addressed the miserable conditions of slaves and worked to improve them.

And yet, after all the qualifications, after all the information that there were four categories of slavery in Siam and that people could buy themselves free, we are left with the fact that in nineteenth-century Thailand some of the people had absolute control over many other people, usually for their entire lives, and often over their children as well. Leonowens's fictional instances of Mongkut's cruelty are unjustified, maybe even slanderous, in attributing to him specific instances of cruelty that I have trouble believing happened quite as she says. On the other hand, it was hardly mere religious narrow-mindedness or cultural blindness for Leonowens to claim that there was a fundamental evil here. Even if we believe that the institution in Thailand was benevolent in relation to its counterpart in the United States, slavery is, by its very nature, violent, abusive, and cruel.

Nineteenth-century Thailand was a deeply hierarchical society, with profound and unmistakable demarcations between classes. Moreover, while nineteenth-century Thai Buddhism was a religion that valued life and peace, it was also one that explicitly ranked women as less human than men. For example, a Buddhist monk would be sullied by the mere touch of a woman's hand. The king, as a deeply religious Buddhist, valued life but did not value women. Moreover, he was historically limited by growing up in a time and place that found customary the evils of slavery. King Mongkut was less despotic a master than his more old-fashioned predecessors. Yet, on the grounds of plausibility, I would argue that King Mongkut did abuse his slaves, including the women in the royal harem.

Did King Mongkut really build a scaffold outside Leonowens's window for Tuptim and her accused lover and there have the tortured and mutilated bodies burned alive? The more extreme specifics of Leonowens's tales are melodramatic and surely false. But the more substantive question is whether the spirit of her stories is to some degree true? Compared to previous kings and to many of his contemporaries, King Mongkut may well have been an enlightened master. But he was also a nineteenth-century man with absolute power who was instructed by both his religion and his culture to view women in terms of their functions rather than their selves.

Did Mongkut, on occasion, capriciously order his slaves, including his women slaves, beaten or whipped or tortured? Was the mere fact of their being slaves, no matter what the particulars, a form of spiritual torture that broke hearts and deadened joy, and for which the king must in part be held accountable? Were these women's own sexual desires, or lack of desires, irrelevant to their sexual usage? Were they ever killed? The religious justification for devaluing women as lesser humans; the mere fact that the women of the harem were kept, usually for life, inside the palace walls, many to be used as sexual pawns; the report in the 1860 *Bangkok Calendar* of an actual incident in 1859 in which a nobleman who had tried to win one of the king's concubines was executed, along with his wife—all suggest that the answer is yes.[22]

From the perspective that slavery in mid-nineteenth-century Siam was a useful and not particularly cruel institution, it is not far to

Griswold's conviction that the women in the royal harem, with a few exceptions, liked it there and were "contented with their lot."[23] Against such convictions, formed from a distance and formed by men, stands the testimony of the only outsider who saw firsthand, saw in depth, and saw from the point of view of being a woman herself. Her opinion is that in every harem the women

> *have the appearance of being slightly blighted. Nobody is too much in earnest, or too much alive, or too happy. The general atmosphere is that of depression. They are bound to have no thought for the world they have quitted, however pleasant it may have been; to ignore all ties and affections; to have no care but for one individual alone, and that the master. But if you become acquainted with some of these very women . . . you might gather glimpses of recollections of the outer world, of earlier life and strong affections, of hearts scarred and disfigured and broken, of suppressed sighs and unuttered sobs. (p. 107)*

These are intense lines, emotional rather than rational, involved rather than detached, perhaps even melodramatic.

Does this style distort or reveal truth? The excessive and melodramatic style of *The Romance of the Harem* is tied to the exaggerated and unbelievable quality of the particular events it narrates. There is a long and honorable tradition in English fiction of insisting that a particular book is actually true. From Aphra Behn's actual letters from a nobleman to his sister, Moll Flanders's true autobiography, and Fanny Burney's authentic exchange of letters between Evelina and her friends and relations, writers of fiction have insisted that they are offering just the facts. *The Romance of the Harem* does seem a long way from the "realism" of Victorian fiction, particularly of George Eliot's kind of mid-nineteenth-century realism. Yet its language often recalls the tone of high sympathy sometimes used by Eliot's narrators. And in many of its qualities *The Romance of the Harem* is similar to the work of other Victorian novelists. With its bizarre characters, its eerie atmosphere, its tales of social injustice, its villains and pure heroines, its pervasive focus on the sufferings of innocent children, and above all its sentimental language that would move us to tears, Leonowens's book evokes the work of Charles Dickens.

But Dickens did not cast real public figures in English in the roles of his villains. Why did Leonowens? Why give us the fabulous yet use actual historical people and label the whole combination real? The question, I think, leads back to another. To whom in Siam did Leonowens really owe her gratitude? In other words, for what in her experiences as the governess in Nang Harm did Leonowens most deeply feel grateful? The explicit claim of her writing is that Leonowens is most grateful for the friendship and the example of the Siamese women she got to know inside the palace.

In spite of the opinion of many of its detractors, *The Romance of the Harem* is a tribute to Thailand. But it pays tribute to Siamese women as opposed to Siamese men. Moreover, that the women were opposed to the men is not an emotional but a structural truth, a given of their situation. This opposition is inherent in the very institution of the harem; and it is created not by the women but by the men. The book, then, pays tribute to the women of Nang Harm through displaying the power of their characters as they respond to their state of oppression. For the oppression of its women is the truth of Nang Harm.[24]

The Romance of the Harem, in all its excess, uncovers that consistently hidden, politically inconvenient truth. It also offers another, that the women in Nang Harm are not mere victims, any more than they are less fully human than men or that their lives and personal suffering are less important than the greater good of a unified Thailand. *The Romance of the Harem* presents these foreign women as great heroines. It does not do so through an objective or sociological account of the facts, any more than Dickens presented mid-century London through detached eyes. The book would have us honor the women of Nang Harm even as we cry for them. The tales constitute a fantastic gesture, in which the evils and the heroism are both painted larger than life. Against the cruel and all-powerful masters are pitted the courage and purity of these outwardly powerless women; of Tuptim, the innocent sixteen-year-old bricklayer who defies torture and death; of L'ore, the Mohammedan slave and daughter of a slave who bore years of misery for the right to be free; of May Peâh, the stalwart Laotian whose loyalty to her friend outwits the forces of the whole Siamese penal and legal system; of Boon, whose generous love is stronger than the weakness of women and the fickleness of men.[25]

The tales in *The Romance of the Harem* are all preposterous. But they speak for the women of the harem as no other writing about Nang Harm has. Their excess is their gift. The book will not allow us to conclude that these women were "contented with their lot." The irreducible factual basis of these stories is one woman looking at other women's lives, seeing how they are blighted, and being horrified. It insists on responsibility by actually naming the times, the place, and the man in charge of this blight. Yet the emphasis of the book falls, not on the situation, but on how these women deal with it. Finally, *The Romance of the Harem* is about the greatness of their response. As the Dedication says, the book is written for "the noble and devoted women whom I learned to know, to esteem, and to love in the city of Nang Harm."

Acknowledgments

I am grateful to many people and institutions for making this new edition possible: to Vassar College for first supporting my research on Victorian women's travel writings; to the Huntington Library and the Echols Collection at Cornell University for the use of crucial original materials; to Martin Ridge at the Huntington Library, for his continuing encouragement and willingness to share his knowledge of editing issues; to Karen Langlois for her clarity in explaining to me nineteenth-century American publishing practices; to all my dear friends at the Huntington for providing a warm as well as an exciting intellectual context; to Jerome McGann, whose energy in appreciating this project helped to make it real; to David Wyatt, whose unlimited generosity in sharing what he knows accounts for most of what is accurate in my description of nineteenth-century Thailand; and to my acquisitions editor, Nancy Essig, for having that perfect combination of experience, patience, and enthusiasm.

Mecklenburg, N.Y.
1990

Notes

1. Trubner responded by a notice in the March 15, 1873, issue of the *Athenaeum* that the publishing company had received the two photographers' permission to reproduce their work as the illustrations.
2. As David Wyatt pointed out to me in conversation, the ruins were hardly "lost." The Thais and Cambodians knew all about them. But Westerners had not heard of them.
3. Reported in the *New York Times*, August 8, 1970, p. 25.
4. A. B. Griswold, *King Mongkut of Siam* (New York: Asia Society, 1961), p. 3.
5. W. S. Bristowe, *Louis and the King of Siam* (New York: Thai-American Publishers, 1976), p. 27.
6. Bristowe, "Anna Unveiled," *Louis and the King of Siam*, pp. 23–31.
7. This is from a letter to the India Office, protesting their discriminatory policies. It is quoted by Bristowe in *Louis and the King of Siam*, p. 29.
8. Ibid., p. 30.
9. Ibid., p. 22.
10. Ibid., p. 22.
11. Jill Castleman points out that Yul Brynner even went on to recreate the role of King Mongkut in a short-lived television series, *Anna and the King,* in 1972, as well as recreating the role at least once more on Broadway. "For most people, Yul Brynner *is* the King of Siam." "The Making of a Myth: Anna Leonowens and Thailand," undergraduate paper, Cornell University, 1985, p. 5.
12. The costumes for the movie were of Thai silk using authentic nineteenth-century designs. All were provided from the expert designs of Jim Thompson, one of the other famous Europeans in Thailand. Thompson had "vanished" inexplicably in 1938, but was credited with almost single-handedly reviving the silk industry in Thailand.
13. Chula Chakrabongse, Prince of Thailand, *Lords of Life: The Paternal Monarchy of Bangkok, 1872–1932* (London: Alvin Redman Ltd., 1960), p. 209.
14. *Records of the United States Consul in Bangkok, 1856–65* (Washington: National Archives and Records Service, 1960).
15. David Wyatt, *Thailand: A Short History* (New Haven: Yale University Press, 1982), p. 185. I owe an extensive debt throughout this discussion to this now classic study, pp. 100–242.
16. Ibid., p. 181.
17. And who is to say to what extent the social institution of groups of girls at the service of one man has really benefitted Thailand? I suspect that the nineteenth-century customs of slavery and the harem have their twentieth-century incarnation in the widespread prostitution in

Thailand, complete with child prostitution, poor families selling their daughters, and slave markets where you can buy young girls.

18. Anna Leonowens, *The English Governess at the Siamese Court: Being Recollections of Six Years at the Royal Palace in Bangkok* (Boston, 1870; rpt., Singapore: Oxford University Press, 1988), p. 103.

19. Griswold, quoted in *King Mongkut of Siam*, p. 35.

20. Griswold, *King Mongkut of Siam*, p. 35.

21. Ibid., p. 49.

22. The report in the *Calendar*, cryptic and tantalizing, was that on June 29 "a young Siamese Nobleman was executed for the crime of seeking to win one of the 1st King's Concubines for a wife. The wife of the man was also executed for having abetted him in his designs." (*Bangkok Calendar* [Bangkok: American Missionary Association, 1860], p. 50.)

23. Griswold, *King Mongkut of Siam*, p. 45.

24. It is one of the oddities of history that Louis Leonowens, when he returned to Thailand as a grown man, kept a small harem there before he married.

25. The tale of Boon was surely inspired by the incident recorded in the 1860 *Bangkok Calendar*. Like much of the rest of the book, it is probably grounded in actual events—but doesn't stay on the ground.

Anna Leonowens

Note on the Text

The text of this edition is that of the first edition, printed in Boston by James R. Osgood and Company. The first edition is dated 1873, but actually appeared in late December 1872.

THE IDOL OF BUDDHA.

THE

ROMANCE OF THE HAREM.

BY

MRS. ANNA H. LEONOWENS,

AUTHOR OF "THE ENGLISH GOVERNESS AT THE SIAMESE COURT."

Illustrated.

THE EMERALD IDOL.

BOSTON:

JAMES R. OSGOOD AND COMPANY,

LATE TICKNOR & FIELDS, AND FIELDS, OSGOOD, & Co.

1873.

PREFACE.

———

"TRUTH is often stranger than fiction," but so strange will some of the occurrences related in the following pages appear to Western readers, that I deem it necessary to state that they are also true. Most of the stories, incidents, and characters are known to me personally to be real, while of such narratives as I received from others I can say that "I tell the tale as it was told to me," and written down by me at the time. In some cases I have substituted fictitious for real names, in order to shield from what might be undesired publicity persons still living.

I gladly acknowledge my indebtedness to Mr. Francis George Shaw for valuable advice and aid in the preparation of this work for the press, and to Miss Sarah Bradley, daughter of the Rev. Dr. Bradley of Bangkok, for her kindness in providing me with photographs, otherwise unattainable, for some of the illustrations.

NEW BRIGHTON, STATEN ISLAND,
    September 13, 1872.

DEDICATION.

To the noble and devoted women whom I learned to know, to esteem, and to love in the city of the Nang Harm, I dedicate the following pages, containing a record of some of the events connected with their lives and sufferings.

LIST OF ILLUSTRATIONS.

CONTENTS.

———◆———

CONTENTS.

ROMANCE OF THE HAREM.

CHAPTER I.

"MUANG THAI," OR THE KINGDOM OF THE FREE.

SIAM is called by its people "Muang Thai" (the king-dom of the free). The appellation which we employ is derived from a Malay word *sayâm* (the brown race), and is never used by the natives themselves ; nor is the country ever so named in the ancient or modern annals of the kingdom.

In the opinion of Pickering, the Siamese are of Malay origin. A majority of intelligent Europeans, however, regard the population as mainly Mongolian. [1] But there is much more probability that they belong to that power-ful Indo-European race to which Europe owes its civiliza-tion, and whose chief branches are the Hindoos, Persians, Greeks, Latins, Kelts, and the Teutonic and Sclavonic tribes. The original site of this race was in Bactria, and the earliest division of the people could not have been later than three or four thousand years before the Chris-tian era. [2] Comparative philology alone enables us to trace the origin of nations of great antiquity. According to the researches of the late king, who was a very studious and learned man, of twelve thousand eight hundred Siamese words, more than five thousand are found to be Sanskrit, or to have their roots in that language, and the rest in the Indo-European tongues ; to which have been superadded a

great number of Chinese and Cambodian terms. He says:
" The names of temples, cities, and villages in the kingdom of Siam are derived from three sources, namely, Sanskrit, Siamese, and Cambodian.   The names which the
common people generally use are spoken according to the
idiom of the Siamese language, are short and easily pronounced ; but the names used in the Court language and
in the government documents, which receive the government seals, are almost all of Sanskrit derivation, apt to be
long ; and even though the Sanskrit names are given at
full length, the people are prone to speak them incor-
rectly.   Some of our cities and temples have two and even
three names, being the ancient and modern names, as they
have been used in the Court language or that of the people."

As the words common to the Siamese and the Sanskrit
languages must have been in use by both peoples before
their final separation, we have here a clew to the origin
and degree of civilization attained by the former before
they emigrated from the parent stock.

Besides the true Siamese, a great variety of races inhabit the Siamese territories.   The Siamese themselves
trace their genealogy up to the first disciples of the Buddha, and commence their records at least five centuries
before the Christian era.   First, a long succession of dynas-
ties, with varying seats of government, figure in their
ancient books, in which narrations of the miracles of the
Buddhas, and of the intervention of supernatural beings, are
frequently introduced.   Then come accounts of matrimo-
nial alliances between the princes of Siam and the Imperial family of China ; of embassies to, and wars with, the
neighboring countries, interspersed with such relations of
prodigies and such marvellous legends as to surpass all
possible conception of our less fertile Western imaginations.
It is only after the establishment of Ayudia as the capital
of Siam, A. D. 1350, that history assumes its rightful

functions, and the course of events, with the regular succession of sovereigns, is registered with tolerable accuracy.

The name of Siam was first heard in Europe — that is,
in Portugal — in the year 1511, nine years after Alfonso
d'Albuquerque, the great Viceroy of the Indies, had
landed on the coast of Malabar with his soldiers, and
conquered Goa, which he made the seat of the Portugo-
Indian government, and the centre of its Asiatic opera-
tions. After establishing his power in Goa, D'Albuquerque
subdued the whole of the Malabar, the island of Ceylon,
the Sunda Isles, the peninsula of Malacca, and the beautiful island of Ormuz, at the entrance to the Persian Gulf.

It was here that D'Albuquerque is said to have received
the ambassadors of the Emperor of Persia, sent to collect
the tribute formerly paid to him by the sovereigns of the
island, and, instead of the customary gold and silver, to
have laid before them iron bullets and a sword, with:
"This is the coin in which Portugal pays those who demand tribute from her." Whether this incident really
occurred or not, it is certain that D'Albuquerque made
the name of Portugal so feared and respected in the East,
that many of the potentates in that region, and among
them the kings of Siam and Pegu, sent embassies to him,
and sought his alliance and protection. The profitable relations anticipated from this opening were interrupted, however, by the long and bitter war which shortly broke out
between Siam and Birmah, and the intercourse between the
Siamese and Portuguese was not renewed for a long time.
As early as the fifteenth century the celebrated German
traveller, Mandelslohe, visited Ayudia, the capital of Siam,
and called it the Venice of the East, — a title equally appli-
cable to the modern capital, Bangkok.[3] The Portuguese
explorer, Mendez Pinto, who was in Siam in the sixteenth
century, gives a very favorable account of the country,
and, in my opinion, deserves more credit for the truth of

his statements than was accorded to him by his contemporaries. In 1632 an English vessel is said to have reached Ayudia, and to have found it in ruins, the country having been laid waste by successive incursions of the Birmese.

The great river Mèinam is the Nile of Siam. Rising among the southern slopes of the snow-covered mountains of Yunan, it traverses the whole length of the valley, receiving in its course the waters of many other streams, the most important being the Mèikhong, which in its length of nearly one thousand miles drains the eastern provinces of 'Laos and Cambodia. Ancient annals relate that in the fifteenth and as late as the seventeenth century, Chinese junks ascended the river as far as Sangkalok, nearly one hundred and twenty leagues from its mouth ; now, owing to the increasing alluvial deposit, it is not navigable more than fifteen leagues at most.

In the month of June, the mountain snows begin to melt, the deluging rains of the wet season set in, the strong southerly winds dam up the waters of the Mèinam, and it begins to rise, — an event most eagerly looked for by the people, and hailed by them as a blessing from Heaven. In August the inundation is at its height, and the whole vast valley is like one immense sea, in which towns and villages look like islands, connected by drawbridges, and interspersed with groves and orchards, the tops of which only are seen, while boats pass to and fro without injury to the rice and other crops starting beneath them. The whole valley is intersected by canals, some of great size and extent, in order to distribute as far as possible the benefits of this grand operation of nature ; but the lands situated about the middle of the great plain derive the greatest advantage therefrom.

When the inundation is supposed to have reached its

height, a deputation of Talapoins, or priests, sent by the
king, descend the river in magnificent state barges, and
with chants and incantations and movements of magical
wands command the waters to retire. Sometimes, however, the calculations prove to have been incorrect, the
river continues to rise, and it is they who are compelled
to retire, filled with chagrin and disappointment.

The popular river festival, which takes place after the
waters begin to subside, both in origin and character belongs to the Hindoos, rather than to the Buddhists.[4] It is
an annual festival held at night, and the scene which is
exhibited during its celebration is exceedingly beautiful.
The banks of the Mèinam are brilliantly lighted up;
accompanied and announced by numerous flights of rockets, a number of floating palaces, built on rafts, come sailing down the stream, preceded by thousands of lamps
and lanterns wreathed with chaplets of flowers, which
cover with their gay brilliancy the entire surface of the
flashing water. The rafts, which are formed of young
plantain-trees fastened together, are often of considerable
extent, and the structures which they bear are such as
Titania herself might delight to inhabit. Towers, gates,
arches, and pagodas rise in fantastic array, bright with a
thousand colors, and shining in the light of numberless
cressets, — so the fairy-like spectacle moves on, while admiring crowds of men, women, and children throng the
'oanks of the river, not only to join the brilliant pageant,
ut to watch their own frail little bark, freighted, per-
hance, with a single lamp, yet full of life's brightest
nopes, as it floats unextinguished down the rapid stream,
glimmering on with ruddy flame amidst the shadows of
night.

The products of Siam, as may be supposed from its
range of latitude, its tropical heats, its variety of climate,
and the fertility of the valley, annually renewed by the

inundation, are very diversified, and almost unlimited in quantity. Its rice, of which there are forty varieties, is excellent, and its sugar is esteemed the best in the world. Among the other exports are cotton, tobacco, hemp, cutch, dried fish and fruits, cocoanut-oil, beeswax, precious gums, spices, dye and other woods, especially teak, ivory, and many articles too numerous to mention. The mineral riches of the country are still almost entirely in an undeveloped state.

The search for sparkling gems has in all ages been eagerly engaged in; diamonds and other precious stones are frequently offered for sale, but the precise locality in which they are found is kept secret by the natives. The thousand-fold more valuable seams of coal and iron have remained unsought and most imperfectly worked as yet. A beginning has at last been made by the present king, and the last and best, though poetically maligned, age of iron is about to spread its blessings over the Siamese Empire.

The population of Siam cannot be ascertained with correctness, owing to the custom of enumerating only the men. When I was in Bangkok, the native registers gave the number of them as four million Siamese, one million Laotians, one million Malays and Indians, one million five hundred thousand Chinese, three hundred and fifty thousand Cambodians, fifty thousand Peguans, and the same number of mountain tribes; in all, nearly eight millions. If these figures are even approximately correct, and the women and children bear the same proportion to the men as in other countries, the total population of Siam far exceeds the numbers which have hitherto been assigned to it.

No people in the world exhibit so many exceptional developments of human nature as the different races occupying the eastern peninsula of India. The most impressible of races, ideas and views of life take root among them such as would find no acceptance elsewhere. Supple and pliant in their bodily frames, they are equally so in their mental and moral constitution; and upon no other race has the force of circumstance and the contagion of example so potent an influence in determining them towards good or evil. Royalty, therefore, to them, is not a mere name. It has taken such hold on their affections that it usurps the place of a religious sentiment. The person of the king is sacred. He is not only enthroned, he is enshrined. His rule may be called despotic, but it is tempered by law and by not less revered custom. He may name his successor by Will, but the Royal or Secret Council will determine whether that Will shall be carried into effect. A second king, selected, like the first or supreme king, from the royal family, is also appointed by the Secret Council. Whatever may have originally been the functions of this second king, his exercise of them appears, from incidents of the late reign, to be dependent upon the disposition of the supreme king, and his desire or disinclination to concentrate in his own person all the powers of the throne.

The whole empire is divided into forty-nine provinces, with their respective Phayas, or governors; and these again are subdivided into districts under inferior officers, respecting whose administration but little that is good can be said.

Every subject, even the most humble, has by law the right to complain to the king in person against any official, however exalted; and the king sits in public at the eastern gate of the palace to receive the petitions of his people.

Two or three centuries after Brahminism and caste had been authoritatively established in the Hindoo code, there arose a new religion which totally ignored the old one, and almost immediately supplanted it as the state religion

of India. This was Buddhism, founded by Gotama, otherwise called Sakya Muni, a Kshatrya Prince of Oude. A
high-priest of the Abstract, and believing that the only
possible revelation from the Supreme is that which comes
from within, Gotama educed a new faith from the
luminous depths of his own soul. His object was not
only a religious but a social revolution. A good deal of
what was venerated as religion he found to be merely
social usage, for which a Divine sanction was feigned.
Gotama, without hesitation, rejected all this, by denying
the inspiration of the Vedas, the existence of the popular
gods, and the spiritual supremacy of the Brahmins. His
greatest blow to the old religion, however, was in his explicit repudiation of caste. He offered his religion to all
men alike, Brahmin and Sudra, high and low, bond and
free; whereas, for a Sudra even to look on the Vedas, or
to be taught their contents, was strictly forbidden by the
Brahminical system. Buddha boldly expounded to the
people that, according to their own books, all men were
equal; that Brahma himself, when asked to whom all the
prayers of the different nations and races of the earth were
addressed, replied : "I bear the burden of all those who
labor in prayer. I, even I, am he who prayeth for them
through their own lips ; and they, even they, who involun-
tarily worship other gods believingly, worship even me." *

He also did away with the endless formalism of the old
faith, and enjoined only a simple observance of the fundamental points of morality ; and it was only after he had
aided in removing the social and spiritual shackles that
oppressed the people, that he directed their attention to
the simple and weightier matters of religion.

Hence the popularity it attained, spreading among the
low caste as well as among the rich and great, until it has
become the dominant faith from the Himalayas to Ceylon,

---

* See the Siamese work, " Phra thi Sang."

and thence to Siam, China, Japan, and the neighboring isles.

Buddhism, therefore, the religion of the Eastern world, as Christianity is that of the Western, is the state religion of Siam and that of most of its inhabitants, but all religions are tolerated and absolutely free from interference. All the pagan sects who inhabit this part of India agree excellently, and each frequently takes part in the festivals of the other; and I also observed that not a few Buddhists, his late Majesty included, wear on their foreheads the sectarial mark of Vishnu and Siva united.

The doctrine of Buddha inculcates a belief in one God, Adi Buddha.* This I infer, not only from the universally avowed conviction of the Buddhists with whom I have conversed, but from Buddha's own words, where he says: "Without ceasing shall I run through a course of many births, looking for the *maker* of this tabernacle,† who is not represented by any outward symbol, but in a series of Buddhas, who have been sent with divine powers to teach the human race and lead it to salvation." These are represented by images, often of colossal size and great beauty, and to them the prayers of worshippers are addressed. It inculcates, also, a belief in the law of retribution or compensation, and of many births or stages of probations, through which the human soul may finally attain beatitude. Buddhism has its priests and nuns, separated from the world, and vowed to poverty, celibacy, and the study of the Divine law. Unlike the silent and long-forsaken temples of Egypt, Greece, and Italy, the architectural grandeur of the Buddhist pagodas and temples is enhanced by the presence of thousands of enthusiastic worshippers. The sound of a bell, or gong, or

* Supreme Intelligence.
† See Siamese work, " Phra thi Sang," and Lecture on Buddhist Nihilism, by F. Max Müller.

1*

of the sacred shell, indicates the hours of the priests'
attendance at the temples. At such times the priests are
to be seen officiating at the shrines, where, amid the noise
of many instruments playing in concert, the smoke of
fragrant incense, and the perfumes of fresh flowers, they
are uttering sacred invocations or incantations, and presenting the offerings of the worshippers. In the sermons
preached daily in these immense temples, thronged with
men and women, the chief themes are humanity, endurance, patience, submission. Among the practical precepts
are these: " Love your enemies. Sacrifice your life for
truth. Be gentle and tender. Abstain from war, even in
self-defence. Govern yourselves in thought, word, and
deed. Avoid everything that may lead to vice. Be
obedient to your parents and superiors. Reverence old
age. Provide food and shelter for the poor, the aged, and
the oppressed. Despise no man's religion. Persecute no
man."

But alas ! in Siam, as in all the rest of the world, the
practice falls far short of the precept.

Nevertheless, I have found among the Siamese, also,
men and women who observe faithfully the precepts of
their religion, whose lives are devoted to charity and good
works ; and there were some—not one alone, but many—
who during the years I lived in Bangkok sacrificed their
lives for truth, and even under the torture and in death
showed a self-sacrificing devotion and a courage not to
be excelled by the most saintly of the Christian martyrs.

Polygamy — or, properly speaking, concubinage — and
slavery are the curses of the country. But one wife is
allowed by law ; the king only may have two, a right and
a left hand wife, as these dual queens are called, whose
offspring alone are legitimate. The number of concubines
is limited only by the means of the man. As the king
is the source of all wealth and influence, dependent

kings, princes, and nobles, and all who would seek the royal favor, vie with each other in bringing their most beautiful and accomplished daughters to the royal harem.

Here it is that the courage, intrepidity, and heroism of these poor, doomed women are gradually developed. I have known more than one among them who accepted her fate with a repose of manner and a sweet resignation that told how dead must be the heart under that still exterior; and it is here, too, that I have witnessed a fortitude under suffering of which history furnishes no parallel. And I have wondered at the sight. Though the common people have but one wife, the fatal facility of divorce, effected by the husband's simply taking the priestly vows, which can be revoked at will, is often the cause of great suffering to the women. The husband and father have unlimited power, even of life and death, over the wife and children, but murders are extremely rare. Woman is the slave of man; but when she becomes a mother her position is changed, and she commands respect and reverence. As a mother with grown children she has often more influence than her husband. Hence maternity is the supreme good of the woman of Siam; to be childless, the greatest of all misfortunes.

As was ancient Ayudia, so is Bangkok, the present capital of Siam, the Venice of the East.[5] Imagine a city with a large network of water-roads in the place of streets, and intersected with bridges so light and fanciful that one might almost fancy them to have been blown together by the breath of fairies. A large proportion of its inhabitants live in floating houses, which line both banks of the Mèinam, and, tier upon tier, extend for miles above and below the walls. The city itself is surrounded by a battlemented and turreted wall, fifteen feet high and twelve feet broad, which was erected in the early part of the reign of Phaya Tak, about 1670. The grand palaces

and royal harem are situated on the right hand as you
ascend the river, on a circular plot of ground formed by
a sudden bend of the river, enclosing it on the west;
while the eastern side is bounded by a large, deep canal.
This plot of ground is encompassed by two walls running
parallel to each other.   Within the outer of these walls
are the magazines, the royal exchange, the mint, the supreme courts of justice, the prisons, temples, and fantastic
pleasure-grounds, dotted with a multitude of elegant
edifices, theatres, and aviaries, some of which are richly
gilt and ornamented.   In the centre of a very handsome
square rise the majestic buildings of the Maha Phra Sâât,
the roof of which is covered with tiles, beautifully var-
nished, and surmounted by gilded spires, while the walls
are studded with sculptures, and the terraces decorated
with large incense vases of bronze, the dark color and
graceful forms of which stand in beautiful relief against
the white marble background of the palace.

Not far from this is another semicircular space surrounded by a high wall, which defends all entrance to the
part enclosed by the inner of the two parallel walls before
mentioned; and here stands the city of the Nang Harm,
or Veiled Women.   In this city live none but women and
children.   Here the houses of the royal princesses, the
wives, concubines, and relatives of the king, with their
numerous slaves and personal attendants, form regular
streets and avenues, with small parks, artificial lakes, and
groups of fine trees scattered over miniature lawns and
beautiful flower-gardens.   These are the residences of the
princesses of Siam.   On the east, high above the trees,
may be seen the many-towered and gilded roofs of the
grand royal palace, brilliant as sapphire in the sunlight,
and next to this is the old palace, to both of which is a
private covered entrance for the women; at the end of
each of these passages is a bas-relief representing the head

of an enormous sphinx, with a sword through the mouth, and this inscription: "Better that a sword be thrust through thy mouth than that thou utter a word against him who ruleth on high." Not far from this are the barracks of the Amazons, the women's hall of justice, and the dungeons (where, as in the days of old, female judges daily administer justice to the inhabitants of this woman's city), the beautiful temple, with its long, dim gallery and antique style of architecture, in which I taught the royal children, the gymnasium, and the theatre, where the princesses and great ladies assemble every afternoon to gossip, play games, or watch the exercises of the dancing-girls.

In the southern part of this strange city, which is the most populous, the mechanical slaves of the wives, concubines, and princesses live, and ply their trades for the profit of their mistresses. This woman's city is as self-supporting as any other in the world: it has its own laws, its judges, police, guards, prisons, and executioners, its markets, merchants, brokers, teachers, and mechanics of every kind and degree; and every function of every nature is exercised by women, and by them only. Into this inmost city no man is permitted to enter, except only the king, and the priests, who are admitted every morning under guard, in order that the inmates may perform the sacred duty of giving alms. The slave women are allowed to go out to visit their husbands, or on business of their mistresses; but the mistresses themselves never leave it except by the covered passages to the palaces, temples, and gardens, until they have by age and position attained to a certain degree of freedom. The permanent population of this city is estimated at nine thousand.[6] Of the life passed therein, volumes would not give an exact description; but what I am about to relate in the pages that follow will give the general reader, perhaps, some idea of many of the stirring incidents of that life.

CHAPTER II.

TUPTIM: A TRAGEDY OF THE HAREM.

THOSE of my readers who may recur to my late work, "The English Governess at the Siamese Court," will find on the 265th page mention of "a young girl of fresh and striking beauty, and delightful piquancy of ways and expression, who, with a clumsy club, was pounding fragments of pottery — urns, vases, and goblets — for the foundation of the Watt (or Temple) Rajah Bah ditt Sang. Very artless and happy she seemed, and as free as she was lovely; but the instant she perceived that she had attracted the notice of the king, — who presided at the laying of the foundation of the temple, and flung gold and silver coins among the workwomen, — she sank down and hid her face in the earth, forgetting or disregarding the falling vessels that threatened to crush her; but the king merely diverted himself with inquiring her name and parentage, and some one answering for her, he turned away." This is all that is there said of her.

A week later I saw the girl again, as I was passing through the long enclosed corridor within the palace on my way to my school-room in the temple. She was lying prostrate on the marble pavement among the offerings which were placed there for the king's acceptance, and which he would inspect in his leisurely progress towards his breakfast-hall.

I never went that way without seeing something lying there, — bales of silk on silver trays, boxes of tea, calicoes, velvets, fans, priests' robes, precious spices, silver, gold, and curiosities of all kinds, in fact, almost anything and everything that money could purchase, or the most abject sycophancy could imagine as likely to gratify the despot. Every noble, prince, and merchant sought to obtain the royal favor by gifts thus presented, it being fully understood between the giver and receiver that whoever gave the most costly presents should receive the largest share of royal patronage and support. But the most precious things ever laid upon that pavement were the young hearts of women and children.

Two women were crouching on either side of the young girl, waiting for the entrance of the king, in order to present her to him. I was hardly surprised to see her there. I had grown accustomed to such sights. But I was surprised at the unusual interest she appeared to excite in the other women present, who were all whispering and talking together about her, and expressing their admiration of her beauty in the most extravagant language.

She was certainly very beautiful by nature, and those who sent her there had exhausted all the resources of art to complete, according to their notions, what nature had begun, and to render her a fitter offering for the king. Her lips were dyed a deep crimson by the use of betel ; her dark eyebrows were continued in indigo until they met on her brow ; her eyelashes were stained with kohl ; the tips of her fingers and her nails were made pink with henna ; while enormous gold chains and rings bedizened her person. Already too much saddened by the frequency of such sights, I merely cast a passing glance upon her and went my way ; but now, as I see in memory that tiny figure lying there, and the almost glorified form in which I beheld it for the last time, I cannot keep the tears from my eyes, nor still the aching of my heart.

About three months or so later we met again in the same place. I was passing through to the school-room, when I saw her joyously exhibiting to her companions a pomegranate which she held in her hand. It seemed to be the largest and finest fruit of the kind I had ever seen, and I stopped to get a closer view both of the girl and of the fruit, each perfect in its kind. I found, however, that the fruit was not real, only an imitation. It was a casket of pure gold, the lids of which were inlaid with rubies, which looked exactly like the seeds of the pomegranate when ripe. It was made to open and shut at the touch of a small spring, and was most exquisitely moulded into the shape and enamelled with the tints of the pomegranate. It was her betel-box. [7]

" Where did you get this box ? " I inquired.

She turned to me with a child's smile upon her face, pointed to the lofty chamber of the king, and said, " My name, you know, is Tuptim" (Pomegranate). I understood the gift.

Afterwards I saw her frequently. On one occasion she was crying bitterly, while the head wife, Thieng, was reproving her with unusual warmth for some fault. [8] I interrupted Thieng to ask for some paper and ink for the school-room, but she paid no attention to my demands. Instead of complying with them at once, as usual, she inquired of me, " What shall I do with this Tuptim ? She is very disobedient. Shall I whip her, or starve her till she minds ? "

" Forgive her, and be good to her," I whispered in Thieng's ear.

" What ! " said the offended lady in an angry tone, " when she does wrong all the time, and is so naughty and wilful ? Why, when she is ordered to remain up stairs, she runs away, and hides herself in Maprang's or Simlah's rooms, and we are taken to task by his Majesty, who accuses us of jealousy and unkind treatment towards her. Then we have to search all the houses of the Choms (concubines) until we find her, either in hiding or asleep, and bring her to him. The moment she comes into his presence she goes down upon her knees, appearing so very bashful and innocent that he is enraptured at the sight, and declares that she is the most perfect, the most fascinating of women. But as soon as she can get away, she does the same thing again, only finding some new hiding-place, and so she makes an infinity of trouble. Now, she says she is ill, and cannot wait upon the king, while the physicians declare that there is nothing whatever the matter with her. I really don't know what to do or what to say, for I don't dare to tell the truth to the king, and I'm in constant fear that she will come to a bad end, if she doesn't follow my advice and make up her mind to bear her life here more patiently."

I pitied the poor girl, who really looked either sick or unhappy. Child as she was, there was a great deal of quiet dignity about her, as, with eyes filled with tears, she protested that she was utterly sick at heart, and could not go up stairs any more. I was sure that Thieng's sweeping reproof did not indicate any malice or real anger towards the girl, and, putting my arms around the elder lady, I succeeded in soothing her indignation, and at length obtained permission for Tuptim to be absent from duty for a few days. A grateful smile lit up the girl's tearful face as she crept away.

"That girl is too artless," said kind-hearted Thieng to me, as soon as the child was out of sight; "and she will not even try to like her life here. I pity her from my very heart, mam dear, but it would not do to show it. She would take advantage of my kindness, and keep away from the king altogether, as Marchand does; and in all such cases we head wives have to bear the brunt of the king's displeasure, and are thought to be jealous and intriguing, when the holy Buddh in heaven knows that there is only kindness in our hearts."

B

Not long after the above conversation, Tuptim began to come to school. She wanted to learn to write her name in English, she said, and she came to me once or twice a week until she had acquired that accomplishment, which seemed to give her immense satisfaction. After she had done this, she asked me if I would write the name "Khoon Phra Balât" for her in English. I wrote it for her at once, without asking her why she wanted it or whose name it was. I did not even know if it was the name of a man or a woman, as the Siamese have no masculine and feminine terminations to their names and titles. She immediately began to trace the letters for herself, and I could see a world of tenderness in her large dreamy eyes as she copied and recopied the name in its English characters. I cannot rightly remember how often or how long she came to the school, for she was but one among many; but, whenever she found me engaged with the princes and princesses, she would sit for hours on the marble floor, and listen to our simple exercises of translating English into Siamese or Siamese into English, with increasing interest and delight expressed in her pure, guileless face. I do remember that she was never alone, but always accompanied by two or three young companions of about her own age, who were as listless and idle as she was absorbed and interested.

Perhaps this was the reason — with her extreme youth, for she was still but a child, and seemed even younger than she really was — why I never attempted to enter into conversation with her, or to learn anything about her history and her feelings. If I had done this, I might have succeeded in winning her confidence, and perhaps have been the means of reconciling her to her life in the palace. That I did not, will ever be a source of poignant regret to me.

One afternoon, as I was about leaving the palace after

school, she came running up to me, took a scrap of paper from under her vest, and held it silently before my eyes, while I read what was written upon it. It was the name "Khoon P'hra Bâlât," carefully written in English characters, and she seemed delighted with the praise I bestowed on the writing.

"Whose name is it, Tuptim?" I asked.

She cast down her eyes and hesitated for a moment; then, raising them to mine, she replied: "It is the name of the favorite disciple of the high-priest, Chow Khoon Sah; he lives at the temple of Rajah Bah ditt Sang, and sometimes preaches to us in the palace."

The expression of deep reverence that animated her face as she spoke revealed to me a new phase in her character, and I felt strongly attracted towards her. I nevertheless left the palace without further conversation, but, on my way home, formed a vague resolution that I would endeavor to become better acquainted with her, and attempt to win her confidence.

My half-formed resolve was without result, however, since, for some reason unknown to me, she never came to the school-room again; and, as I did not chance to meet her on my visits to the palace, she soon passed from my thoughts, and I forgot all about her.

Some nine months, or perhaps a year, after my last encounter with Tuptim, I became conscious of a change in the demeanor of my elder pupils; they were abstracted, and appeared desirous to get away from their studies as soon as possible. It seemed as if there were some secret they had been ordered to conceal from my boy and me. My imagination immediately took the alarm, and I became possessed with the idea that some grave calamity was impending.

One day, when breaking up school for the afternoon, I heard one of the princes say to the others in Siamese: "Come, let's go and hunt for Tuptim."

"Why! where has she gone?"

As soon as I asked the question, Princess Ying Yonwa-lacks angrily seized him by the arm and hurried him away.[9] I had no wish to inquire further. What I had heard was enough to excite my imagination afresh, and I hurried home full of anxiety about poor little Tuptim, thus suddenly brought back to my remembrance.

On the following evening, it being Sunday, one of my servants informed me that a slave-girl from the palace wished to speak with me in private. When she came in, her face seemed familiar, but I could not remember where I had seen her or whose slave she was. She crawled up close to my chair, and told me in a low voice that her mistress, Khoon Chow Tuptim, had sent her to me. "You know," she added, "that my mistress has been found."

" Found!" I exclaimed; "what do you mean?"

She repeated my question, and in great astonishment asked: "Why! did you not know that my mistress had disappeared from the palace; that his Majesty had offered a reward of twenty caties (about fifteen hundred dollars) to any one who would bring any information about her; and that no trace of her could be discovered, though everybody had been searching for her far and near?"

"No, I have never heard a word about it. But how could she have got out of the palace, through the three rows of gates that are always bolted, and not be seen by the Amazons on guard?"

"Alas! my lady, she did get out," replied the girl, who looked very wan and weary, whose eyes seemed to have been shedding tears for a long time, and who was on the point of breaking down again. She then went on to tell me that two priests had that morning discovered her mistress in the monastery attached to the temple of Rajah Bah ditt Sang, and had brought the information to the king, by whose order she had been arrested and imprisoned in one of the palace dungeons.

"But what good can I do, Phim?" I asked, sorrowfully.

"O mam dear, if you don't help her, she's lost, she'll be killed!" cried the girl, bursting into a passion of tears. "Oh! do, do go to the king, and ask him to forgive her. He'll grant her life to you. I'm sure he will. Oh! oh! what shall I do! I've nobody to go to but you, and there's nobody but you can help her!" And her tears and sobs were truly heart-rending.

I tried to soothe her. "Tell me, Phim," I said, "why did your mistress leave the palace, and who helped her to get away?"

The girl would not answer my question, but kept repeating, "Oh! do come and see her yourself! Do come and see her yourself! You can go to the palace after dark, and the gate-keepers will let you in. Nobody need know that you are going to see my dear mistress."

As there was no other method of quieting the poor girl, I finally made the promise, though I did not see what good my going could do, and was fully convinced that Phim had abetted Tuptim in her wrong-doing, whatever that might have been.

After the slave-girl had left me, I sat by my window and watched the stars as they came out, one by one, and shone with unusual splendor in the cloudless sky. It was a lovely night, and I felt the soothing influence of the Christian Sabbath even in that pagan land; but the one idea that took possession of my mind was: "Poor little Tuptim, in that dreadful dungeon underground." Still, and notwithstanding my promise, I felt a strong reluctance to respond to the cry which had reached me from her, and wished that I had never heard it. I was tired of the palace, tired of witnessing wrongs I could not remedy, and

half afraid, too, to enter that weird, mysterious prison-
world after nightfall. So I sat still in dreamy uncertainty,
till a warm hand was laid upon mine, and I turned my
eyes from the stars above to the poor slave-girl's sad, tear-
stained face at my feet.

" The gates are open for the prime-minister, mam dear,"
said she, in a low, pleading voice, " and you can get in now
without any difficulty."

I rose at once, resolutely cast my cowardly fears behind me, told my boy where and why I was going, put
twenty ticals in my purse, wrapped my black cloak about
me, and hurried towards the palace gate. Phim had run
back at once, for fear of being shut out for the night. The
women at the gates, who were all friendly to me, admitted
me without question, and, as I passed, I dropped two
ticals into the hand of the chief of the Amazons on
guard, saying that I had been called into the palace on
important business, and begging her to keep the inner
gates open for my return.

"You must be sure and come back before it strikes
eleven," said she, and I passed on. As soon as I entered
the main street within the walls, the slave-girl joined me,
and led the way, crouching and running along in the deep
shadow of the houses, until we reached the gate of the
prison in which Tuptim was immured, when she immediately disappeared.

The hall I entered was immense, with innumerable
pillars, and a floor which seemed to be entirely made up
of huge trap-doors, double barred and locked, while the
lanterns by which it was dimly lighted were hung so high
that they looked like distant stars. There were about a
dozen Amazons on guard, some of whom were already
stretched in sleep on their mats and leather pillows, their
weapons lying within reach. The eyes of all the wakeful
custodians of the prison were fixed upon me as I entered.

A courteous return was made to my polite salutation, and Ma Ying Taphan — Great Mother of War — addressed me kindly, inquiring what was my object in coming there at that time of night. I told her that I had just heard of Tuptim's having got into trouble and being imprisoned, and had come to ascertain if I could be of any assistance to her.

"The child is in trouble, indeed," replied Ma Ying Taphan; "and has not only got herself into prison, but her two young friends, Maprang and Simlah, who are confined with her."

"Can I not help them in any way?" I asked.

"No," said the Amazon, gently, "I fear you cannot. Her guilt is too great, and she must take the consequences."

"What has she been doing?"

To this question I could get no answer; and after vainly attempting to persuade Ma Ying Taphan to tell me, I tried to induce her to let me go down and visit poor Tuptim. "Myde" (impossible), was the reply, "without an express order from the king. When you bring us that, we will let you in, but without it we cannot." And "myde" was the only answer I could get to my repeated and urgent entreaties. I sat there, hopelessly looking at the Amazons, who, in the dim light of the distant lanterns overhead, seemed to me to be changed from tender-hearted women, as they were, into fierce, vindictive executioners, and at the huge trap-door at our feet, beneath which the three children, as the Amazon had rightly called them, were imprisoned, but from which no sound, no cry, no indication of life escaped, until, tired and despairing, I rose and left the place.

As soon as I was out of the building I saw Phim, the slave-girl, crouching in the shadows on the opposite side of the street, and keeping pace with me as I went towards

the palace gate. When I turned into another street she
joined me, and I found that she had been hidden under
the portico of the prison, and had heard all my conversation with the Amazons. Prostrating herself till her forehead touched my feet, she implored me, in the name of
the P'hra Chow in heaven, not to forsake her dear mistress. "She is to be brought before the court in the
outside hall of justice to-morrow," she said. " Oh! do
come early. Perhaps you can persuade Koon Thow App
to be merciful to her." And, with a sickening sense of
my utter powerlessness, I promised to be present at the
trial.

CHAPTER III.

TUPTIM'S TRIAL.

A BOUT seven o'clock on the following morning I was in the Sala or San Shuang, which is within the second enclosure of the palace, but outside of the third or inner wall, which is that of the harem. This building is of one story only, and totally unlike that occupied for similar purposes in the interior of the grand palace. The main entrance was through a long, low corridor, on both sides of which opened apartments of different dimensions, so dilapidated as to be scarcely habitable, looking out upon the barracks, the magazine, and the fantastic grounds of the palace gardens. On entering the hall one was at once struck by the incongruities that met the eye; the windows were large and lofty, and might have served for the casements of a royal residence, while the doors were very narrow and mean, and the floor merely a collection of worm-eaten boards roughly nailed down. One interesting and picturesque peculiarity was the monstrous size of the spiders, who must have had undisturbed possession of the walls and ceiling for at least a century. Altogether, it was very dark, dull, and dreary, even depressing and sepulchral, when not illumined by the direct rays of the sun.

Several of the men and women judges were already there, interchanging greetings and offerings of the contents of their betel-boxes. P'hayaprome Baree Rak, the chief of the men, and Khoon Thow App, chief of the women judges, sat apart, the latter with her head bowed in an attitude of reflection and sadness. Before them were low tables, on which lay dark rolls of laws, Siamese

2

paper, pens, and ink. Some lower officials and clerks crouched around. They all eyed me with curiosity as I entered and took a seat at the end of the hall, near the two priests who were present as witnesses; but no one made any objection to my stay.

I had not been there long when a file of Amazons appeared, bringing in Tuptim and the two other girls under guard. These were Maprang and Simlah, Tuptim's most intimate friends, whom I had always seen with her when she came to the school-room.

But was that Tuptim? I sat stupefied at the transformation that had been wrought in the Tuptim I had known. Her hair was cut close to her head, and her eyebrows had been shaved off. Her cheeks were hollow and sunken. Her eyes were cast down. Her hands were manacled, and her bare little feet could hardly drag along the heavy chains that were fastened to her ankles. Her scarf was tied tightly over her bosom, and under it her close-fitting vest was buttoned up to the throat. Her whole form was still childlike, but she held herself erect, and her manner was self-possessed. When she spoke, her voice was clear and vibrating, her accent firm and unflinching.

The Amazons laid before the judges some priests' garments and a small amulet attached to a piece of yellow cord. The vestments, such as are worn by a nain (young priest), were those in which Tuptim had been arrested, and in which she had probably escaped from the palace; the amulet, in appearance like those worn by all the natives of the country, had been taken from her neck. On opening the yellow silk which formed the envelope of the latter, a piece of paper was found stitched inside, with English letters written thereon. Khoon Thow App was sufficiently versed in English to spell out and read aloud the name of " Khoon P'hra Bâlât."

Tuptim was then ordered to come forward. She dragged herself along as well as she could, and took her place in the centre of the hall. She made no obeisance, no humble, appealing prostration, but neither was there any want of modesty in her demeanor. She sat down with the air of one who suffered, but who was too proud to complain. I caught a glance of her eyes; they were clear and bright, and an almost imperceptible melancholy smile flitted across her face as she returned my greeting. I was more astonished than before; the simple child was transfigured into a proud, heroic woman, and, as she sat there, she seemed so calm and pure, that one might think she had already crystallized into a lovely statue.

Simlah and Maprang were examined first, and, without apparent reluctance, confessed all that poor Tuptim had ever confided to them, and a great many other irrelevant matters. But when Simlah spoke of her friend's escape from the palace as connected with Khoon P'hra Bâlât's coming in for alms,* Tuptim interrupted her, telling her to stop, and saying: "That's not true. You are wrong, Simlah, you know nothing about it. You know you don't. And it was not at that time." Then, as if recollecting herself, she added, proudly: "No matter. Go on. Never mind me. Say all that you want to say"; and resumed her former position.

"Well!" said P'hayaprome Baree Rak, the chief man judge; "if your companions know nothing about it, perhaps you will tell us exactly how it was."

"If I tell you the whole truth, will you believe me and judge me righteously?" asked the girl.

"You shall have the bastinado applied to your bare back if you do not confess all your guilt at once," replied the judge.

Tuptim did not speak immediately; but by the expres-

* "The English Governess at the Siamese Court," p. 95.

sion of her eyes and the alternate flushing and paling of her face it was evident that she was debating in her own mind whether she should make a full confession or not. Finally, with an air of fixed determination she turned towards Khoon Thow App, and, addressing her exclusively, said : " Khoon P'hra Bâlât has not sinned, my lady, nor is he in any way guilty. All the guilt is mine. In the stillness of the nights, when I prostrated myself in prayer before Somdetch P'hra Buddh, the Chow, thoughts of escaping from the palace often and often would distract me from my devotions and take possession of my thoughts. It seemed to me as if it were the voice of the Lord, and that there was nothing for me to do but to obey. So I dressed myself as a priest, shaved off my hair and my eyebrows —"

" Now," interrupted P'hayaprome Baree Rak, "that 's just what we want to hear. Tell us who it was got the priest's dress for you, and shaved off your hair and your eyebrows. Speak up louder."

" My lord, I am telling what I did myself, and not what any one else did. Hear me, and I will speak the truth, so far as it relates to myself; beyond that I cannot go," replied Tuptim, a sudden flush covering her face, and making her look lovelier than ever.

" Go on," said the dreadful man, with a scornful smile at the childish form before him; " we shall find a way to make you speak."

" Dèck nak " (she is very young), said Khoon Thow App, gently.

Tuptim was silent for some moments. The sunlight, streaming across the hall, fell just behind her, revealing the exquisite transparency of her olive-colored skin, as, with a look more thoughtful and an expression more serenely simple still, she continued : —

" At five o'clock in the morning, when the priests were

admitted into the palace, I crawled out of my room and joined the procession as it passed on to receive the royal alms. No one saw me but Simlah, and even she, as she has told me herself, did not recognize me, but wondered why a priest came so near to my door."

"That is true!" broke in Simlah; "I never even knew that Tuptim had run away until Khoon Yai (one of the chief ladies of the harem) sent to inquire why she was absent from duty so long, and then I began to think that the young priest I had seen had something to do with it. But I was afraid to say anything of this to the women who searched the houses, lest· we should be accused of having helped her to escape."

When Simlah had done speaking, Tuptim continued : —

"I know not why, but, when I found myself outside of the palace walls, I went straight to the temple of Rajah Bah ditt Sang, and sat down at the gate. Towards evening the good priest, Chow Khoon Sah, came out, and, on seeing me, asked me why I sat there. I did not know what else to say, and so I begged him to let me be his disciple and live in his monastery. 'Whose disciple art thou, my child?' he asked. At which I began to cry, for I did not wish to deceive the holy man. Seeing my distress, he turned to P'hra Bâlât, who was following him with other priests, and bade him take me under his charge and instruct me faithfully in all the doctrines of Buddha. Then P'hra Bâlât took me to his cell; but he did not recognize in the young priest I seemed to be the Tuptim he had known in his boyhood, and who had once been his betrothed wife."

At this part of Tuptim's recital, the women held up their hands in profound astonishment, and the men judges grinned maliciously, displaying their hateful gums, red with the juice of the betel-nut.

The poor girl's pale lips quivered, and her whole face testified to the immensity of her woe, as with simple, truthful earnestness she asseverated : " P'hra Bâlât, whom you have condemned to torture and to death, has not sinned. He is innocent. The sin is mine, and mine only. I knew that I was a woman, but he did not. If I had known all that he has taught me since I became his disciple, I could not have committed the great sin of which I am accused. I would have tried, indeed and truly, I would have tried to endure my life in the palace, and would not have run away. O lady dear! believe that I am speaking the truth. I grew quiet and happy because I was near him, and he taught me every day, and I can say the whole of the Nava d'harma (Divine Law) by heart. You can ask his other disciples who were with me, and they will tell you that I was always modest and humble, and we all lay at his feet by night. Indeed, dear lady, I did not so much want to be his wife after he became a p'hra (priest), but only to be near him. On Sunday morning, those men," pointing to the two priests who sat apart, " came to the cell to see P'hra Bâlât, and it so happened that I had overslept myself. I had just got up and was arranging my dress, thinking that I was alone in the cell, when I heard a low chuckling laugh. In an instant I turned and faced them, and felt that I was degraded forever.

" Believe me, dear lady," continued Tuptim, growing more and more eloquent as she became still more earnest in her recital. " I was guilty, it is true, when I fled from my gracious master, the king, but I never even contemplated the sin of which I am accused by those men. I knew that I was innocent, and I begged them to let me leave the temple, and hide myself anywhere, telling them that P'hra Bâlât did not know who I was, or that I was a woman; but they only laughed and jeered at me. I fell on my knees at their feet, and implored them, entreated them in the name of all that is holy and sacred, to keep my secret and let me go; but they only laughed and jeered at me the more; they would not be merciful," — here the poor girl gasped as if for breath, while two large tears coursed down her cheeks, — "and then I defied them, and I still defy them," she added, shaking her manacled hands at them.

The two priests looked at the girl unmoved, chewing their betel all the while; the judges listened in silence, with an air of amused incredulity, as to a fairy-tale. She continued: —

"Just then P'hra Bâlât and his other disciples returned from their morning ablutions. I crawled to his feet, and told him that I was Tuptim. He started back and recoiled to the end of the cell, as if the very earth had quaked beneath him, leaving me prostrate and overwhelmed with horror at what I had done. In a moment afterwards he came back to me, and, while weeping bitterly himself, begged me that I would cry no more. But the sight of his tears, and the grief in my heart, made me feel as if I were being swallowed up in a great black abyss, and I could not help crying more and more. Then he tried to soothe me, and said, 'Alas! Tuptim, thou hast committed a great sin. But fear not. We are innocent; and for the sake of the great love thou hast shown to me, I am ready to suffer even unto death for thee.' This is the whole truth. Indeed, indeed, it is!"

"Well, well!" said P'hayaprome Baree Rak, "you have told your story beautifully, but nobody believes you. Now will you tell us who shaved off your hair and your eyebrows, and brought you that priest's dress you had on yesterday?"

The simple grandeur of that fragile child, as she folded her chained hands across her bosom, as if to still its tumultuous heaving, and replied, "I will not!" defies all description.

I had drawn quite near to Tuptim when she began her
simple narrative, and was so much absorbed in attention
to what she said, and in admiration of the fearlessness as
well as of the beauty and majesty of that little figure,
that I had remained rooted to the spot, standing there
mechanically, and hardly noting what was going on
around me. But the effect of that reply was startling;
it brought me suddenly to my senses and to a full appreciation of the scene before me.

There was a child of barely sixteen years hurling defiance, at her own risk and peril, at the judges who appeared
as giants beside her. To make such a reply to those ex-
ecutors of Siam's cruel laws was not only to accept death,
but all the agonies of merciless torture. As her refusal
fell like a thunderbolt upon my startled ears, she seemed
a very Titan among the giants.

"Strip her, and give her thirty blows," shouted the in-
furiated Phayaprome Baree Rak, in a voice hoarse with
passion; and Khoon Thow App looked calmly on.

Presently the crowd opened, and a litter borne by two
men was brought into the hall. On it lay the mutilated
form of the priest Bâlât, who had just undergone the torture, in order to make him confess his guilt and that of
his accomplice, Tuptim; but as the minutes of the ecclesiastical court stated, "it had not been possible to elicit
from him even an indication that he had anything to confess." His priestly robes had been taken from him, and
he was dressed like any ordinary layman, except that his
hair and eyebrows were closely shaven. They laid him
down beside Tuptim, hoping that the sight of her under
torture would induce him to confess.

The next moment Tuptim was stripped of her vest and
bound to a stake, and the executioners proceeded to obey
the orders of the judge. When the first blow descended
on the girl's bare and delicate shoulders, I felt as if bound

A SIAMESE SLAVE-GIRL.

and lacerated myself, and losing all control over my actions, forgetting that I was a stranger and a foreigner there, and as powerless as the weakest of the oppressed around me, I sprang forward, and heard my voice commanding the executioners to desist, as they valued their lives.

The Amazons at once dropped their uplifted bamboos, and "Why so?" asked the judge. "At least till I can plead for Tuptim before his Majesty," I replied. "So be it," said the wretch; "go your way; we will wait your return." * Tuptim was unbound, and the moment she was released she crouched down and concealed herself under the folds of the canvas litter in which the priest lay motionless and silent.

I forced my way through the curious crowd, who stood on tiptoe and with necks outstretched, trying to get a sight of the guilty pair. On leaving the hall, I met the slave-girl Phim, who followed me into the palace, wringing her hands and sobbing bitterly. The king was in his breakfast-hall, and the smell of food made me feel sick and dizzy as I climbed the lofty staircase, for I had eaten nothing that day. Nevertheless, I walked as rapidly as possible up to the chair in which the king was seated, fearing that I might lose my courage if I deliberated a moment. "Your Majesty," I began to say, in a voice that seemed quite strange to me, "I beg, I entreat your pity on poor Tuptim. I assure you that she is innocent. If you had known from the beginning that she was betrothed to another man, you would never have taken her to be your wife. She is not guilty; and the priest, too, is innocent. Oh! do be gracious to them and forgive

* I cannot account for the regard paid to my words on this and other occasions by the officers of the court, except from the fact of the general belief that I had great influence with the king, and the supposition entertained by many that I was a member of the Secret Council, which is, in reality, the supreme power in Siam.

them both! I pray your Majesty to give me a scrap of writing to say that she is forgiven, and that the priest, too, is pardoned, through your goodness; only let me — " My voice failed me, and I sank upon the floor by the king's chair. "I beg your Majesty's pardon — " "You are mad," said the monarch; and, fixing a cold stare upon me, he burst out laughing in my face. I started to my feet as if I had received a blow. Staggering to a pillar, and leaning against it, I stood looking at him. I saw that there was something indescribably revolting about him, something fiendish in his character which had never struck me before, and I was seized with an inexpressible horror of the man. Stupefied and amazed quite as much at finding myself there as at the new development I witnessed, thought and speech alike failed me, and I turned to go away.

"Madam," said that man to me, "come back. I have granted your petition, and the woman will be condemned to work in the rice-mill. You need not return to the court-house. You had better go to the school now."

I could not thank him; the revulsion of feeling was too great. I understood him perfectly, but I had no power to speak. I went away without a word, and at the head of the stairs met one of the women judges bringing some papers in her hand to the king. Instead of going to the school I went home, utterly sick and prostrated.

CHAPTER IV.

THE KING CHANGES HIS MIND.

A BOUT two o'clock that very afternoon I was startled to see two scaffolds set up on the great common in front of my windows, opposite the palace. A vast crowd of men, women, and children had already collected from every quarter, in order to see the spectacle, whatever it might happen to be. A number of workmen were driving stakes and bringing up strange machines, under the hurried instructions of several high Siamese officials. There was an appearance of great and general excitement among the crowd on the green, and I became sufficiently aroused to inquire of my maid what was the reason of all this preparation and commotion. She informed me that a Bâdachit (guilty priest) and a Nangharm (royal concubine) were to be exposed and tortured for the improvement of the public morals that afternoon. It was afternoon already.

As I afterwards learned, I had no sooner left the king than the woman judge I had met at the head of the staircase laid before him the proceedings of both the trials, of Bâlât and Tuptim. On reading them he repented of his promised mercy, flew into a violent rage against Tuptim and me, and, not knowing how to punish me except by showing me his absolute power of life and death over his subjects, ordered the scaffolds to be set up before my windows, and swore vengeance against any person who should again dare to oppose his royal will and pleasure. To do justice to the king, I must here add that, having been educated a priest, he had been taught to re-

gard the crime of which Tuptim and Bâlât were accused
as the most deadly sin that could be committed by man.

The scaffolds or pillories on which the priest and
Tuptim were to be exposed were made of poles, and about
five feet high; and to each were attached two long levers,
which were fastened to the neck of the victim, and prevented his falling off, while they were so arranged as to
strangle him in case this was the sentence.

All the windows of the long antechamber that filled
the eastern front of the palace were thrown open, and I
could see the hurried preparations making for the king,
the princes and princesses, and all the great ladies of the
court, who from there were to witness the exquisite torture that awaited the hapless Tuptim.

Paralyzed by the knowledge that the only person who
could have done anything to mitigate the barbarous
cruelty that was about to be perpetrated — her Britannic
Majesty's Consul, T. G. Knox, now Consul-General — was
then absent from Bangkok, I looked in helpless despair
at what was going on before me.[10] I longed to escape
into the forest, or to take refuge with the missionaries,
who lived several miles down the river; but so dense
was the crowd and so horrible the idea of deserting poor
Tuptim and leaving her to suffer alone, that I felt obliged
to stay and sympathize with her and pray for her, at the
least. I thus compelled myself to endure what was one
of the severest trials of my life.

A little before three o'clock the instruments of torture
were brought, and placed beside the scaffolds. Soon a
long, loud flourish of trumpets announced the arrival of
the royal party, and the king and all his court were visible
at the open windows; the Amazons, dressed in scarlet and
gold, took their post in the turrets to guard the favored
fair ones who were doomed to be present and to witness
the sufferings of their former companion.

Suddenly the throng sent up a thrilling cry, whether of joy or sorrow I could not comprehend, and, the moment after, the priest was hoisted upon the scaffold to the right, while Tuptim tranquilly ascended that to the left, nearest my windows. I thought I could see that the poor priest turned his eyes, full of love and grief, towards her.

I need not attempt to depict the feelings with which I saw the little lady, with her hands, which were no longer chained, folded upon her bosom, look calmly down upon the heartless and abandoned rabble who, as usual, flocked around the scaffold to gloat upon the spectacle, and who usually greet with ferocious howls the agonies of the poor tortured victims. But, on this occasion, the rabble were awed into silence; while some simple hearts, here and there, firm believers in Tuptim's innocence, were so impressed by her calm self-possession, that they even prostrated themselves in worship of that childish form.

My windows were closed upon the scene; but that tiny figure, with her scarlet scarf fluttering in the breeze, had so strong a fascination for me, that I could not withdraw, but leaned against the shutters, an unwilling witness of what took place, with feelings of pain, indignation, pity, and conscious helplessness which can be imagined.

Two trumpeters, one on the right and one on the left, blared forth the nature of the crime of which the helpless pair were accused. Ten thousand eyes were fixed upon them, but no sound, no cry, was heard. Every one held his breath, and remained mute in fixed attention, in order not to lose a single word of the sentence that was to follow. Again the trumpets sounded, and the conviction of the accused, with the judgment that had been passed upon them, was announced. Then the spell was broken, and some of the throng, as if desirous to propitiate the royal spectator at the window, made the air ring with their shouts; while others, going still further, showered all manner of abuse upon the poor girl, as she stood calmly awaiting her fate upon those shaking wooden posts.

Nothing could surpass the dignity of demeanor with which the little lady sustained the storm of calumny from the more mercenary of the rabble around her; but the rapidity with which the color came and went in her cheeks, which were now of glowing crimson and now deadly pale, and the astonishment and indignation which flashed from her eyes, showed the agitation within.

The shrill native trumpets sounded for the third time. The multitude was again hushed into a profound silence, and the executioners mounted a raised platform to apply the torture to Tuptim. For one moment it seemed as if the intense agony exceeded her power of endurance. She half turned her back upon the royal spectator at the window, her form became convulsed, and she tried to hide her face in her hands. But she immediately raised herself up as by a supreme effort, and her voice rang out, like a clear, deep-toned silver bell: "Chân my di phit; Khoon P'hra Bâlât ko my me phit; P'hra Buddh the Chow sap möt." She had hardly done speaking when she uttered an agonized cry, wild and piercing. It was peculiarly touching; the cry was that of a child, an infant falling from its mother's arms, and she fell forward insensible upon the two poles placed there to support her.

The attendant physicians soon restored her to consciousness, and, after a short interval, the torture was again applied. Once more her voice rang out more musical still, for its quivering vibrations were full of the tenderest devotion, the most sublime heroism: "I have not sinned, nor has the priest my lord Bâlât sinned. The sacred Buddh * in heaven knows all." Every torture that

---

* The Siamese in their prayers and invocations abbreviate the titles of the Buddha; the more educated using the word "Buddh," and the common people "P'huth."

would agonize, but not kill, was employed to wring a confession of guilt from the suffering Tuptim; but every torture, every pang, every agony, failed, utterly and completely failed, to bring forth anything but the childlike innocence of that incomparable pagan woman. The honor of the priest Bâlât seemed inexpressibly more precious to her than her own life, for the last words I heard from her were: " All the guilt was mine. I knew that I was a woman, but he did not."

After this I neither heard nor saw anything more. I was completely exhausted and worn out, and had no strength left to endure further sight of this monstrous, this inhuman tragedy. Kind nature came to my relief, and I fainted.

When I again looked from my window the scaffolds were removed, the crowd had departed, the sun had set. I strained my eyes, trying if I could distinguish anything on the great common before the house. There was a thick mist loaded with sepulchral vapors, a terrifying silence, an absolute quiet that made me shudder, as if I were entombed alive. At last I saw one solitary person coming towards my house through the gather.ng darkness. It was the slave-girl, Phim, whose life had been saved by the resolute bravery of her mistress; for it was she who had bought the priest's dress and aided her mistress to escape from the palace. She came to me in secret to tell me that the most merciful and yet the most dreadful doom, death by fire, — which is the punishment assigned by the laws of Siam to the crime of which they were accused, — had been pronounced upon the priest and Tuptim by that most irresponsible of human beings, the King of Siam; that they had suffered publicly outside of the moat and wall which enclose the cemetery Watt Sah Katè; and that some of the common people had been terribly affected by the sight of the priest's invincible courage and of Tuptim's heroic fortitude. With her low,

massive brow, her wild, glistening eyes, and her whole
soul in her face, she spoke as if she still beheld that fragile form in its last struggle with the flaming fire that
wrapped it round about, and still heard her beloved mistress's voice, as she confronted the populace, holding up
her mutilated hands, and saying: "I am pure, and the
priest, my lord Bâlât, is pure also. See, these fingers
have not made my lips to lie. The sacred Buddh in
heaven judge between me and my accusers!"

The slave-girl's grief was as deep and lasting as her
gratitude. Every seventh day she offered fresh flowers
and odoriferous tapers upon the spot where her mistress
and the priest had suffered, firmly believing that their
disembodied souls still hovered about the place at twilight, bewailing their cruel fate. She assured me that she
often heard voices moaning plaintively through the mellow
evening air, growing deeper and gathering strength as she
listened, and seeming to draw her very soul away with
them; now tenderly weeping, now fervently exulting,
until they became indistinct, and finally died away in the
regions of the blessed and the pure.

I afterwards learned that the fickle populace, convinced
of the innocence of Bâlât and Tuptim, would have taken
speedy vengeance on the two priests, their accusers, had
they not escaped from Bangkok to a monastery at Pak-
nâm; and that the twenty caties offered for the capture
of Tuptim had been expended in the purchase of yellow
robes, earthen pots, pillows, and mats for the use of the
bonzes at Watt Rajah Bah ditt Sang, no priest being
allowed to touch silver or gold.

The name Bâlât, which signifies "wonderful," had been
given to the priest by the high-priest, Chow Khoon Sah,
because of his deep piety and his intuitive perception of
divine and holy truths. The name which his mother bestowed upon him, and by which Tuptim had known him

in her earlier years, was Dang, because of his complexion, which was a golden yellow. On being bereft of Tuptim, to whom he was tenderly attached, he entered the monastery, and became a priest, in order that, by austere devotion and the study of the Divine Law, he might wean his heart from her and distract his mind from the contemplation of his irreparable loss.

For more than a month after Tuptim's sad death I did not see the king. At last he summoned me to his presence, and never did I feel so cold, so hard, and so unforgiving, as when I once more entered his breakfast-hall. He took no notice of my manner, but, as soon as he saw me, began with what was uppermost in his mind. "I have much sorrow for Tuptim," he said ; "I shall now believe she is innocent. I have had a dream, and I had clear observation in my vision of Tuptim and Bâlât floating together in a great wide space, and she has bent down and touched me on the shoulder, and said to me, 'We are guiltless. We were ever pure and guiltless on earth, and look, we are happy now.' After discoursing thus, she has mounted on high and vanished from my further observation. I have much sorrow, mam, much sorrow, and respect for your judgment; but our laws are severe for such the crime. But now I shall cause monument to be erected to the memory of Bâlât and Tuptim."

Any one who may now pass by Watt Sah Katè will see two tall and slender P'hra Chadees, or obelisks, erected by order of the king on the spot where those lovely Buddhists suffered, each bearing this inscription : 'Suns may set and rise again, but the pure and brave Bâlât and Tuptim will never more return to this earth."

CHAPTER V.

SLAVERY IN THE GRAND ROYAL PALACE OF THE "INVINCIBLE AND BEAUTIFUL ARCHANGEL." *

ONE morning in the early part of May, 1863, I went at the usual hour to my temple school-room, and found that all my pupils had gone to the Maha P'hra Sâât to attend a religious ceremony, at which I also was requested to be present.

Following the directions of one of the flower-girls, I turned into a long, dark alley, through which I hurried, passing into another, and keeping, as I thought, in the right direction. These alleys brought me at last into one of those gloomy walled streets, into which no sunlight ever penetrated, and which are to be found only in Bangkok, the farther end of which seemed lost in mist and darkness.

Stone benches, black with moss and fungi, lined it at intervals, and a sort of pale night-grass covered the pathway. There was not a soul to be seen throughout its whole length, which appeared very natural, for it did not seem as if the street were made for any one to walk in, but as if it were intended to be kept secluded from public use. I walked on, however, looking for some opening out of it, and hoping every moment to find an exit. But I suddenly came to the end. It was a *cul-de-sac*, and a high brick wall barred my further progress.

In the middle of this wall was set a door of polished brass. The shadow of a tall and grotesque façade rested upon the wall and on the narrow deserted street, like an

* This is the official title of the royal palace at Bangkok.

immense black pall. The solitude of the place was
strangely calm. With that frightful din and roar of the
palace life so near, the silence seemed almost supernatural. It cast a shadow of distrust over me. I almost felt
as if that wall, that roof with its towering front, were
built of the deaf stones spoken of in Scripture. All at
once the wind rattled the dry grass on the top of the
wall, making a low, soft, mournful noise. I started from
my revery, hardly able to account for the feeling of dread
that crept over me. Half ashamed of my idle fears, I
pushed at the door with all my might. Slowly, noiselessly, the huge door swung back, and I stepped into a
paved court-yard, with a garden on one side and a building
suggestive of nocturnal mystery and gloom on the other.

The façade of this building was still more gloomy than
that on the outside of the wall. All the windows were
closed. On the upper story the shutters were like those
used in prisons. No other house could be seen. The
high wall ran all round and enclosed the garden. The
walks were bordered with diminutive Chinese trees, planted in straight rows ; grass covered half of them, and
moss the rest.

Nothing could be imagined more wild and more deserted than this house and this garden. But the object
that attracted my immediate attention was a woman,
the only animate being then visible to me in the apparent
solitude. She was seated beside a small pond of water,
and I soon discovered that she was not alone, but was
nursing a naked child about four years old.

The moment the woman became conscious of my presence, she raised her head with a quick, impetuous movement, clasped her bare arms around the nude form at her
breast, and stared at me with fixed and defiant eyes. Her
aspect was almost terrifying. She seemed as if hewn out
of stone and set there to intimidate intruders. She was

large, well made, and swarthy; her features were gaunt
and fierce, but looked as if her face might once have been
attractive.   I relaxed my hold of the door; it swung
back with a dull, ominous thud, and I stood half trembling beside the dark, defiant woman, whose eyes only
gave any indication of vitality, hoping to prevail upon
her to show me my way out of that dismal solitude.

The moment I approached her, however, I was seized
with inexpressible dismay; pity and astonishment, min-
gling with a sense of supreme indignation, held me speech-
less for a time.   She was naked to the waist, and chained,
— chained like a wild beast by one leg to a post driven
into the ground, and without the least shelter under that
burning sky.

The chain was of cast-iron, and heavy, consisting of
seven long double-links, attached to a ring, and fitted close
to the right leg just above the ankle; it was secured to
the post by a rivet.   Under her lay a tattered fragment
of matting, farther on a block of wood for a pillow, and
on the other side were several broken Chinese umbrellas.

Growing more and more bewildered, I sat down and
looked at the woman in a sort of helpless despair.   The
whole scene was startlingly impressive; the apathy, the
deadness, and the barbarous cruelty of the palace life, were
never more strikingly brought before me face to face.
Here there was no doubting, no denying, no questioning
the fact that this unhappy creature was suffering under
some cruel wrong, which no one cared to redress.   Naked
to the waist, her long filthy hair bound in dense masses
around her brow, she sat calmly, uncomplainingly, under
a burning tropical sun, such as we children of a more
temperate clime can hardly imagine, fierce, lurid, and
scorching, nursing at her breast a child full of health and
begrimed with dirt, with a tenderness that would have
graced the most high-born gentlewoman.

I remained long and indignantly silent, before I could find voice for the questions that rose to my lips. But at length I inquired her name. "Pye-sia" (begone), was her fierce reply.

"Why art thou thus chained? Wilt thou not tell me?" I pleaded.

"Pye" (go), said the woman, snatching her breast impatiently from the sucking child, and at the same time turning her back upon me.

The child set up a tremendous scream, which was re-echoed through the strange place. The woman turned and took him into her arms; and as if there were an indwelling persuasiveness about them, he was quieted in an instant.

Rocking him to and fro, with her face resting against his unwashed cheek, she was no longer repulsive, but glorious, clothed in the beauty and strength of a noble human love. I rose respectfully from the low wall of the pond, where I had seated myself, and took my place on the heated pavement beside the woman and her child; then as gently and as kindly as I could I asked his name and age.

"He is four years old," she replied, curtly.

"And his name?"

"His name is Thook" (Sorrow), said the woman, turning away her face.

"And why hast thou given him such a name?"

"What is that to thee, woman?" was the sharp rejoinder.

After this she relapsed into a grim silence, seeming to gaze intently into the empty air. But at length there came a sob, and she passed her bare arms slowly across her eyes. This served as a signal for the little fellow to begin to scream again, which he did most lustily; the woman, after quieting him, turned to me, and to my great surprise began to talk of her own accord, with but few questions on my part.

"Hast thou come here to seek me, lady? Has the Naikodah, my husband, sent thee? Tell me, is he well? Hast thou come to buy me? Ah! lady! will thou not buy me? Will thou not help me to get my pardon?"

"Tell me why thou art chained. What is thy crime?"

This seemed a terrible question for the poor woman. In vain she attempted to speak; her lips moved, but uttered no sound, her features quivered, and with one convulsive movement she threw up her arms and burst into an agony of tears. She sobbed passionately for some time, then, passing into a quieter mood, turned to me and said, bitterly: "Do you want to know of what crime I am accused? It is the crime of loving my husband and seeking to be with him."

"But what induced you to become a slave?"

"I was born a slave, lady. It was the will of Allah."

"You are a Mohammedan then?"

"My parents were Mohammedans, slaves to the father of my mistress, Chow Chom Manda Ung. When we were yet young, my brother and I were sent as slaves to her daughter, the Princess P'hra Ong Brittry."

"If you can prove that your parents were Mohammedans, I can help you, I think; because all the Mohammedans here are under British protection, and no subject of Britain can be a slave." [11]

"But, lady, my parents sold themselves to my mistress's grandfather."

"That was your father's debt, which your mother and father have paid over and over again by a life of faithful servitude. You can insist upon your mistress accepting your purchase-money."

"Insist," said the woman, her large, dark eyes glowing

with the tears still glistening in them. "You do not know what you say. You do not know that my mistress, Chow Chom Manda Ung, is mother-in-law to the king, and that her daughter, Princess P'hra Ong Brittry, is his favorite half-sister and queen.[12] My only hope lies in a special pardon from my mistress herself."

"And your friends," said I, "do they know nothing of your cruel captivity?"

"Nothing, indeed. I have no opportunity to speak even to the slave-woman whose duty it is to feed us daily. And her lot is too sad already for her to be willing to run any great risk for me. The secrecy and mystery of my sudden disappearance have been preserved so long because I am chained here. No one comes here but my mistress, and she only visits this place occasionally, with the most tried and trusted of her slave-women."

Eleven o'clock boomed like a death-knell through the solitude. The woman laid herself down beside her sleeping boy to rest, apparently worn out with a sense of her misery. I placed my small umbrella over them; and this simple act of kindness so touched the poor thing, that she started up suddenly, and, before I could prevent her, passionately kissed my soiled and dusty shoes.

I was so sorry for the unhappy creature that tears filled my eyes. "My sister," said I, "tell me your whole story, and I will lay it before the king."

The woman started up and adjusted the umbrella over the sleeping child. Her eyes beamed with a fire as if from above, while with wonderful power, combined with sweetness and delicacy, she repeated her sad tale.

"There is sorrow in my heart, lady, where once there was nothing but passive endurance. In my soul I now hear whisperings of things that are between heaven and earth, yea, and beyond the heaven of heavens, where once there was nothing but blind obedience. Unconscious of the beauty of life, my heart was as if frozen and inert until I met the Naikodah, my husband. Lady, as I told you, I and my brother were born slaves; and so faithful were we, that my brother obtained, as proof of the trust my lady reposed in him, the charge of a rice plantation at Ayudia, while I was promoted to be the chief attendant of the Princess P'hra Ong Brittry.

"One day my mistress intrusted to my care a bag of money, to purchase some Bombay silk of the Naikodah Ibrahim. As it was the first time for many years that I had been permitted to quit the gates of the gloomy palace, I felt on that day as if I had come into the world anew, as if my previous life had been nothing but a dream; and my recollections of that day are always present to my mind, and saying to me, 'Remember how happy you were once, be patient now.'

"Oh! On that day the Mèinam splashed and rippled more enchantingly, seemed broader and more beautiful, than ever! The green leaves and buds seemed to have burst forth all of a sudden. How beautifully green the grass was, and how clearly and joyously the birds on the bushes and in the trees poured forth their song, as if purposely for me, while from the distant plain across the river floated the aromatic breath of new-blown flowers, filling me with inexpressible delight! I was silent with a feeling of supreme happiness. On that day a new light had risen in the east, a light which was to enlighten and to darken all my coming life.

"We moored our boat by the bank of the river, and made our way to the shop of the Naikodah, which my companions entered, while I sat outside on the steps until the bargain should be completed. My companions and the merchant could come to no terms. I entered with the bag of money, hoping by the sight of the silver to induce him to sell the silk for the price offered; but on

A SIAMESE FLOWER-GIRL.

entering I seemed to be dazzled by something, I know not what. The merchant's eyes flashed upon me, as it were, with a look of recollection, and by their expression reminded me of some face I had seen in my infancy, or, perhaps, in my dreams. I drew my faded, tattered scarf more tightly around my chest, and sat down silent and wondering, not daring to ask myself where I had seen that face before, or why it produced such an effect upon me.

"After a great deal of talking and bargaining about the silk, we came away without it, but the next day went again to the merchant and purchased it at his own price. I was surprised, however, to find that, when I paid him the money, he left five ticals in my hands. 'That is our kumrie' (perquisite), said the women, snatching the ticals out of my hand and pocketing them. Time after time we repeated our visits to the merchant, who was constantly kind and respectful in his manner towards me. He always left five ticals for us. My companions took the money, but I persistently refused to share in this pitiful kind of profit.

"The merchant began to observe me more closely, and, as I thought, to take an interest in me, and one day, after we had purchased some boxes of fragrant candles and wax-tapers, and I had paid him the full price for his goods, he left twenty ticals on the floor beside me. My companions called my attention to the money; when the merchant, observing my unwillingness to receive it, took up fifteen ticals, leaving the usual kumrie of five upon the floor, which my companions picked up and appropriated.

"We returned, as was our custom, by the river, slowly paddling our little canoe down the broad and beautiful stream, and enjoying every moment of our permitted freedom. I was sorely unwilling to return to the palace;

3   D

I was even tempted to plunge into the water and make good my escape; but the responsibility of the money intrusted to my care made me hesitate, and the tranquil surface of the Mèinam, broken only by its circling ripples, helped to dissipate my wicked thoughts. Still I indulged, though almost unconsciously, the hope of obtaining my freedom some day, without even forming a thought as to how it could ever be accomplished. How or why I began to think of getting free I know not. I seemed to inhale a longing for freedom with the fragrance of flowers wafted to me on the fresh, invigorating air; every tree in blossom, every wild flower clothed in its splendor of red and orange, made me dream as naturally of liberty as it did of love; and I prayed for freedom for the first time in my life, even as for the first time I felt the strength of a supreme emotion overpowering me."

Here the woman paused for a few moments, and I was surprised to find that she expressed herself so well, until I remembered that the princesses of Siam make it a special point to educate the slaves born in their household, so that in most Oriental accomplishments they generally surpass the common people who may have become slaves by purchase. There was something very simple and attractive in the way she spoke of herself, and throughout our whole interview she manifested such gentleness and resignation that she completely won my affection and pity.

After a while she smiled sadly, and said softly: "Ah, lady! we all love God, and we are all loved by him; yet he has seen fit to make some masters and others slaves. Strange as the delusion may appear to you, who are free and perfectly happy, while the slave is not happy, the more impossible seemed the realization of my hope of freedom, the more I thought of it and longed for it.

"One day a slave-woman came to my mistress with

some new goods from the Naikodah, and on seeing me she begged for a drink of water and some cere (betel-leaf). As I handed her the water, she said to me in a low tone: 'Thou art a Moslem; free thyself from this bondage to an unbelieving race. Take from my master the price of thy freedom; come out of this Naiwang (palace) and be restored to the true people of God.'

"I listened in amazement, fearing to break the enchanting spell of her words, and hardly believing that I had heard aright. She quitted me suddenly, fearful of exciting suspicion, and left me in such a disturbed state of mind as I had never before experienced. My thoughts flew hither and thither like birds overtaken by a sudden storm, flapping their silent and despairing wings against the closed and barred gates of my prison. I found comfort only in trusting to the *Great Heart* above, and with the instinct of all sufferers I turned at once to him.

"When I saw the woman a second time I embraced the opportunity to say to her, 'Sister, tell me, how shall I obtain my purchase-money? Will not thy master hold me as his slave?'

"'He will give thee the money, and will never repent having freed a Moslem and the daughter of a believer from slavery.'

"'O thou angel of life!' said I, clasping her to my throbbing heart, 'I am already his slave.'

"She released my arms from around her neck, and, taking some silver from her scarf, tied it firmly into mine without another word; and I, fearing lest I should be discovered with so much money in my possession, came here by night and hid it under this very pavement on which we are seated.

"Some weeks after we were sent again to the Naikodah to buy some sandal-wood tapers and flowers for the cremation of the young Princess P'hra Ong O'Dong. I never was so conscious of the shabbiness of my dress as when I entered the presence of the good merchant. We made our purchase, paid the money, and as I rose to depart, my friend D'hamni, the slave-woman who had been employed by the Naikodah to speak to me, beckoned me to come into an inner chamber. I was followed by her master, who addressed himself to me, and said,—I remember the words so well, — 'L'ore! thou art of form so beauteous, and of spirit so guileless, thou hast awakened all my love and pity. See, here is the money thou hast just paid me; double the price of thy freedom, and forget not thy deliverer.'

" ' May Allah prosper thee ! ' said D'hamni.

" I was overwhelmed; my astonishment and my gratitude at his goodness knew no bounds. I tried to speak; my tongue clave to the roof of my mouth as if held back by an evil genius; I could not give utterance to a single word in expression of my feelings. My heart heaved, my eyes glowed, my cheeks burned, my blushes came and went, showing the depth of my emotion, and I burst into tears. I returned to the palace, hid the money, and waited my opportunity.

" Thus I lived in bondage within and bondage without. Freedom within my grasp and slavery in my heart. ' I am more a slave than ever,' said I to myself; ' alas! the servitude of the heart, the sweet, feverish servitude of love, who will ransom me from these ? Who can buy me freedom from these ? Henceforth and forever I am the good merchant's slave.'

" I waited my time like a lover lying in wait for his mistress, like a mother watching the return of an only child, and I waited long and anxiously, praying to God, calling him Allah! calling him Buddha! Father! Goodness! Compassion! praying for liberty only, praying only for freedom.

"One day my mistress, Chow Chom Manda Ung, was so kind and pleasant to me that I believed my opportunity had come. I seized it, threw myself at her feet, and said, 'Lady dear, be pitiful to thy child, hear but her prayer. It is the only desire of her heart, the dream of thy slave's life. As the thirsty traveller beholds afar off the everlasting springs of water, as the dying man has foretastes of immortality, even so thy slave L'ore has, through thy goodness, tasted of freedom, and would more fully drink of the cup, if thou in thy bountiful goodness would but let her go free. Here is the price of my freedom, dear lady; be pitiful, and set me free.'

"'Thou wert born my slave,' said my lady, 'I will take no money for thee.'

"'Take double, lady dear, but O, let me go!'

"'If thou wishest to be married,' said my mistress, 'I will find thee a good and able husband, and thou shalt bear me children, even as thy mother did before thee; but I will not let thee go free.'

"In my despair I prayed, I entreated, with tears blinding my eyes. I promised that my children yet unborn should be her slaves, if she would only let me go.

"It was all in vain. I gathered up my silver and returned to my slave's life, hopelessly defeated. I soon recovered from my disappointment, however, because I was strengthened by the determination to escape at the first opportunity that offered itself to me. This enabled me to bear my captivity bravely. My mistress distrusted me for a long time; my companions, seeing that I had fallen into disgrace, pitied me, but I did my best to show myself willing, obedient, and cheerful, until, when nearly two whole years had passed away, my mistress gradually took me again into her confidence, and at last arranged a marriage for me with Nai Tim, one of her favorite men-slaves. To all her plans I offered not a word of objection.

I pretended that I was really pleased at the prospect of being free to spend six months of every year with my husband.

"The day before my marriage I was sent to see Nai Tim's mother, with a small present from my mistress. Two strong women accompanied me. Hidden in my p'ha nung (under-skirt) was my purchase-money. As soon as we entered my future mother-in-law's house, I requested permission to speak with her alone. Supposing that I had some private communication to make to her from my mistress, she took me into the back part of the house, and I seated myself on the edge of the bamboo raft, which kept her little hut afloat on the Mèinam, rushing by so strong and swift. Without giving her time to think, I told her my whole story from beginning to end, put the money into her hands, and before the startled woman could refuse or remonstrate I plunged with one sudden bound into the bosom of the broad river. I heard a shriek above me as I disappeared under the waters that received me into their cool, refreshing depths.

"How desperately I swam through the strong currents, coming up to the surface from time to time to draw a long breath, then diving back into its protecting shelter again! Finding my strength failing me, I made for the opposite bank, climbed its steep sides, and dried my clothes in the soft, delicious breezes that came upon me as if just let free from the highest heavens. Filled with the inspiration of freedom and of love, I had accomplished that which had been the beginning and the ending of all my thoughts for so long a time. For one moment it seemed to me an impossibility, but on the next my joy was so excessive that I stooped down and kissed the earth, and then laughed outright.

"From day to day my soul had been slowly withering away, now it blossomed forth afresh as if it had never known a moment of sorrow. My glad laughter came back to me, and in very truth, lady, I shall never again rejoice and sing in the desert places of my heart, or in the solitary places of my native land, as I did on that day. In my extreme emotion I forgot that night was a possibility. I could do nothing but rejoice. Suddenly the sun set. The night descended. Darkness covered the earth as with a mantle ; the wind began to blow in gusts ; I heard strange sounds, — sounds which seemed to come, not from the earth, but from some frightful realm beyond. But I knew there were angels who heard the cries of human distress. I prayed to them to come and hover near me, and as I prayed a deep sleep came upon me.

"When I woke the stars were in the sky, but the strange noises disturbed me so that I fell on my knees and cried, 'O God ! where art thou ? O, bring the day ! come with thy swift chariot and bring the light ! come and help thy unworthy handmaiden !' 'To believe,' says the prophet, 'is to have the world renewed every day.' So in answer to my prayer came the angel Gibhrayeel and snatched away the dark mantle of P'hra Khām (the god of night), and swift came P'hra Athiet (the god of day), scattering the shadowy monsters of the world of night, and making his glory fill my heart with praise, even as it filled my glad eyes with light.

"I had been dazzled with the idea of liberty, I had thought only of getting free. But now came the questions, Where shall I go ? Who will employ me ? And the answer was clear to me. There was no one in all this vast city to whom I could turn but the merchant and his slave-woman D'hamni, and to them I went. It was evening when I entered the hut of the slave D'hamni, footsore, hungry, and weary. D'hamni was overjoyed to see me ; she gave me food and shelter and her best robe.

"Some days after the good merchant came to visit me.

I felt dimly that the hardness of my heart would be complete if I resisted his kindness. To his celestial tenderness I opposed no word of doubt, yet I could not believe that the rich merchant would marry an outcast slave like me.

"One morning I found robes of pure white in my humble shed, in which D'hamni proceeded to array me. After which she brought me into the presence of the Moolah (Mohammedan priest), the merchant, and a few trusty friends.

"The Moolah quietly put down his hookah (pipe), stood up, and, putting his hands before his face, uttered a short prayer. After this he took the end of my saree (scarf) and bound it securely to the end of the merchant's angrakah (coat), gave us water in which had been dipped the myrtle and jessamine flower, placed a ring of gold on my finger, blessed us, and departed. That was our marriage ceremony.

"During all the days that followed I moved about as one drunk with strong wine; I enjoyed every moment; I thanked God for the sun, the beautiful summer days, the radiant yellow sky, the fresh dawn, and the dewy eve. Light, pure light, shone upon me, and filled my soul with intense delight, and it blossomed out into the perfect flower of happiness.

"One day, about three or four months after my marriage, as I was seated on the steps of my home, I thought I heard a voice whisper in my ear. I had hardly time to turn when I was seized, gagged, bound hand and foot, and brought back to this place. As soon as I was taken into her presence, my mistress had me chained to this post, but caused me to be released when my time of delivery approached. A month after his birth," pointing to the sleeping boy, "I was chained here again, and my child was brought to me to nurse; this was done until he could come to me alone. But they are not unkind; when it is very wet the slave-woman takes him to sleep under the shelter of her little shed.

"I could free myself from these chains if I would promise never to quit the palace. That I will never do." She said this in a feeble and almost inarticulate voice. It was her last effort to speak. Her head drooped upon her breast as if an invisible power overwhelmed her at a blow; she fell exhausted upon the stones, her hands clasped, her face buried in the dust.

It was a strange sight, and possible only in Siam. Certainly great misfortunes as well as great affections develop the intelligence, else how had this slave-woman reached the elevation to which she had evidently attained?

But excess of sorrow had made her almost visionary. When I tried to comfort her, she turned her haggard face with its worn-out, weary look upon me, and asked if she had been dreaming. Her brain seemed to be in such an abnormal yet frightfully calm condition, that she half be- lieved she was in a dream, and that her life was not a frightful reality. It was out of my power to comfort her, but I left her with a hope that grew brighter as I retraced my steps out of that weird place.

After some tiresome wanderings I found my way out of the place at last. When I reached the school-room it was twelve o'clock, and my pupils were waiting.

In the afternoon of the same day I went to the house of the Naikodah Ibrahim, and told him that I had seen his wife and child. He was much affected when he heard they were still alive, and was moved to tears when I told him of their sad condition.

That night a deputation of Mohammedans, headed by the Moolah Hâdjee Bâbâ, waited upon me; we drew up a petition to the king, after which I retired, thankful that I was not a Siamese subject.

3 *

CHAPTER VI.

KHOON THOW APP, THE CHIEF OF THE FEMALE JUDGES.

NEXT morning, as if some invisible power were working to aid my plans, I was summoned early to the
palace. I carried my petition and a small book entitled
"Curiosities of Science" with me.

The king was very gracious, and so pleased with the
book that I took the opportunity of handing in my
petition. He read it carefully, and then gave it back
to me, saying, "Inquiry shall be made by me into this
case."

On the day after I received the following little note
from the king : —

LADY LEONOWENS : — I have liberty to do an inquiry
for the matter complained, to hear from the Princess P'hra
Ong Brittry, the daughter of the Chow Chom Manda Ung,
who is now absent from hence. The princess said that
she knows nothing about the wife of Naikodah, but that
certain children were sent her from her grandfather maternal, that they are offspring of his maid-servant, and
that these children shall be in her employment. So I
ought to see the Chow Chom Manda Ung, and inquire
from herself.

                               S. P. P. MAHA MONGKUT, RX.

His Majesty was as good as his word, and when the
Chow Chom Manda Ung returned, he ordered the chief
of the female judges of the palace, her ladyship, Khoon
Thow App, to investigate the matter.

Khoon Thow App was a tall, stout, dark woman, with

soft eyes, but rather a heavy face, her only beauty being in her hands and arms, which were remarkably well formed. She was religious and scrupulously just, had a serious and concentrated bearing. Everything she said or did was studied, not for effect, but from discretion. A certain air of preoccupation was natural to her. She knew everything that took place in the harem, and concealed everything within her own breast. By dint of attention and penetration she had attained to her high office, and she retained it by virtue of her supreme but unassuming fitness for the position. She was like a deaf person whose sight is quickened, and like one blind whose sense of hearing is intensified. That hideous symbolical Sphinx, with a sword drawn through her mouth, babbled all her secrets and sorrows in her ear. She inspired confidence, and she never decided a case in private. She lived alone, in a small house at the end of the street, with only four faithful female slaves. The rest she had freed. It was before this woman that, by order of the king, I brought my complaint in behalf of L'ore; she raised her eyes from her book, or rather roll, and said, " Ah! it is you, mam. I wish to speak to you."

" And for my part," said I, with a boldness at which I was myself astonished, " I have something to say to your ladyship."

" O, I know that you have a communication to make, which has already been laid before his Majesty. Your petition is granted."

" How! " said I, " is L'ore really free to leave the palace ? "

" O no; but his Majesty's letter is of such a character that we have the power to proceed in this matter against the Chow Chom Manda Ung. Though we are said to have the right to compel any woman in the palace to come before us, these great ladies will not appear personally, but send all manner of frivolous excuses, unless summoned by a royal mandate such as this."

She then turned to one of the female sheriffs, and despatched her for the Chow Chom Manda Ung, P'hra Ong Brittry, and the slave-woman L'ore.

After a delay of nearly two hours, Chow Chom Manda Ung and her daughter, the Princess P'hra Ong Brittry, made their appearance, accompanied by an immense retinue of female slaves, bearing a host of luxurious appendages for their royal mistresses' comfort during the trial, with the sheriff bending low, and following this grand procession at a respectful distance.

The great ladies took their places on the velvet cushions placed for them by their slaves, with an air of authority and rebellion combined, as if to say, " Who is there here to constrain us ? "

The chief judge adjusted her spectacles, and as she looked fixedly at the great ladies she asked, " Where is the slave-woman L'ore ? "

The old dowager cast a malicious glance at the judge ; but there was still the same silence, the same air of defiance of all authority.

All round the open sala, or hall, was collected a ragged rabble of slave women and children, crouching in all sorts of attitudes and all sorts of costumes, but with eyes fixed on the chief judge in startled astonishment and wonder at her calm, unmovable countenance.   Superciliousness and apparent contempt prevailed everywhere, yet in the midst of all the consciousness of an austere and august presence was evident ; for not one of those slave-women, lowly, untaught, and half clad as they were, but felt that in the heart of that dark, stern woman before them there was as great a respect for the rights of the meanest among them as for those of the queen dowager herself.

The chief judge then read aloud in a clear voice the

letter she had received from the king, and, when it was finished, the dowager and her daughter saluted the letter by prostrating themselves three times before it.

Then the judge inquired if the august ladies had aught to say why the slave-woman L'ore should not have been emancipated when she offered to pay the full price of her freedom.

The attention of all was excited to the highest degree; every eye concentrated itself on the queen dowager.

She spoke with difficulty, and answered with some embarrassment, but from head to foot her whole person defied the judge.

"And what if every slave in my service should bring me the price of her freedom?"

All eyes turned again to the judge, seated so calmly there on her little strip of matting; every ear was strained to catch her reply.

"Then, lady, thou wouldst be bound to free every one of them."

"And serve myself?"

"Even so, my august mistress," said the judge, bowing low.

The dowager turned very pale and trembled slightly as the judge declared that L'ore was no longer the slave of the Chow Chom Manda Ung, but the property of the Crue Yai (royal teacher).

"Let her purchase-money be paid down," said the dowager, angrily, "and she is freed forever from my service."

The judge then turned to me, and said, "You are now the mistress of L'ore. I will have the papers made out. Bring hither the money, forty ticals, and all shall be settled."

I thanked the judge, bowed to the great ladies, who simply ignored my existence, and returned perfectly happy for once in my life to my home in Bangkok. Next day, after school, I presented myself at the court-house.

Only three of the female judges were present, with some of the p'ha khooms (sheriffs). Khoon Thow App handed me the dekah, or free paper, and bade one of the p'ha khooms go with me to see the money paid and L'ore liberated.

Never did my feet move so swiftly as when I threaded once more the narrow alley, and my heart beat quickly as I pushed open the ponderous brass door.

There was L'ore, chained as before. In the piazza sat the Princess P'hra Ong Brittry and her mother, surrounded by their sympathizing women.

The p'ha khoom was so timid and hesitating, that I advanced and laid the money before the great ladies.

The queen dowager dashed the money away and sent it rolling hither and thither on the pavement, but gave orders at the same time to release L'ore and let her go.

This was done by a female blacksmith, a dark, heavy, ponderous-looking woman, who filed the rivet asunder.

In the mean time a crowd had collected in this solitary place, chiefly ladies of the harem, with some few slaves.

So L'ore was free at last; but what was my amazement to find that she refused to move; she persistently folded her hands and remained prostrate before her royal persecutors as if rooted to the spot. I was troubled. I turned to consult the p'ha khoom, but she did not dare to advise me, when one of the ladies — a mother, with a babe in her arms — whispered in my ear, "They have taken away the child."

Alas! I had forgotten the child.

The faces of the crowd were marked with sympathy and sadness; they exchanged glances, and the same woman whispered to me, " Go back, go back, and demand to buy the child." I turned away sorrowfully, hastened to Khoon Thow App, and stated my case. She opened a box, drew out a dark roll, and set out with me.

The scene was just as I had left it. There sat the august ladies, holding small jewelled hand-mirrors, and creaming their lips with the most sublime air of indifference. L'ore still lay prostrate before them, her face hidden on the pavement. The crowd of women pressed anxiously in, and all eyes were strained towards the judge. She bowed before the ladies, opened the dark roll, and read the law: "If any woman have children during her bondage, they shall be slaves also, and she is bound to pay for their freedom as well as her own. The price of an infant in arms is one tical, and for every year of his or her life shall be paid one tical." This declaration in terms so precise appeared to produce a strong impression on the crowd, and none whatever on the royal ladies. Ever so many betel-boxes were opened, and the price of the child pressed upon me.

I took four ticals and laid them down before the ladies. The judge, seeing that nothing was done to bring the child to the prostrate mother, despatched one of the p'ha khooms for the boy. In half an hour he was in his mother's arms. She did not start with surprise or joy, but turned up to heaven a face that was joy itself. Both mother and child bowed before the great ladies. Then L'ore made strenuous efforts to stand up and walk, and, failing, began to laugh at her own awkwardness, as she limped and hobbled along, borne away by the exulting crowd, headed by the judge. Even this did not diminish her happiness. With her face pressed close to her boy's, she continued to talk to herself and to him, "How happy we shall be! We, too, have a little garden in thy father's house. My Thook will play in the garden; he will chase the butterflies in the grass, and I will watch him all the day long," etc.

The keepers of the gates handed flowers to the boy, saying, "P'hoodh thŏ, dee chai nak nah, dee chai nak nah" (pitiful Buddha! we are very glad at heart, very, very glad).

The news had spread, and, before we reached the river, hosts of Malays, Mohammedans, and Siamese, with some few Chinese, had loosened their cumberbunds (scarfs) and converted them into flags.

Thus, with the many-colored flags flying, the men, women, and children running and shouting along the banks of the Mèinam, spectators crowding into the fronts of their floating houses, L'ore and her boy sailed down the river and reached their home.

The next day her husband, Naikodah Ibrahim, refunded the money paid for his wife and child, whose name was changed from Thook (Sorrow) to Urbanâ (the Free).

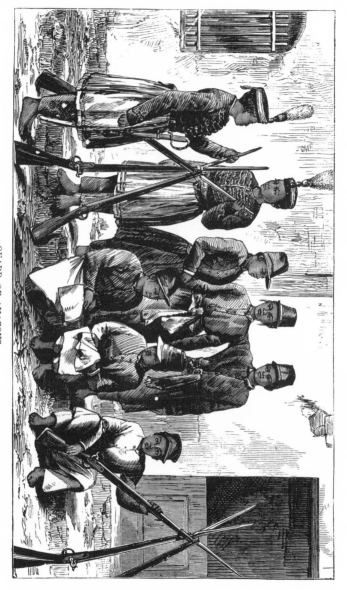

GUARD OF AMAZONS.

CHAPTER VII.

THE RAJPOOT AND HIS DAUGHTER.

BANGKOK is full of people. Every day crowds of men and boys are pouring into the great metropolis from all parts of the country to have their names enrolled on the books of the lords and dukes to whom they belong.

There are no railroads, no steamboats, so the vast companies of serfs travel together, — the rich by means of their boats and gondolas, and the poor on foot, following the course of the great river Mèinam.

Sometimes caravans of whole tribes may be seen encamped during the intense noonday heat by the banks of the stream, under the shade of some neighboring trees. These weary marches are always commenced at sunset, and continued till noon of the next day, when the overpowering heat forces man and beast under shelter.

There existed in Siam under the late king a mixed system of slavery, in part resembling the old system of English feudal service, in part the former serfdom of Russia, and again in part the peonage of Mexico.

In the enrolment, called Sâk, an institution peculiar to the country, every man is obliged to receive an indelible mark on his arm or side, denoting the chief to whom he belongs.

The process is exactly like tattooing. The name of the chief is pricked into the skin with a long slender steel having a lancet-shaped point, just deep enough to draw a little blood ; after which the bile of peacock mixed with Chinese ink is rubbed over the scarification.

This leaves an indelible mark.

E

All the male children of those so marked are obliged at the age of fourteen to appear in person to have their names enrolled on their master's books, and themselves branded on their arms.

The king's men, that is, those who have to attend on royalty as soldiers, guards, or in any other capacity, are marked on the side, a little below the armpit, to distinguish them from the other serfs of the princes, dukes, or lords of the realm.

Among the vast crowds who were pouring through the many gates and avenues into the city in July, 1862, was seen a stately old Rajpoot, weary and travel-stained, leading a low-sized, shaggy pony on which was seated a closely veiled figure of a young woman.[13] A stranger could not but observe the proud, forbidding look of the old man as he urged and stimulated his weary beast through the crowd.

Behind the veiled figure were two leathern bags which contained some wearing apparel and a supply of provisions to serve them during their stay in the capital.

There are no such places as inns or caravansaries to lodge the multitude who are thus forced into Bangkok every year. Those who have boats live in them on the river and its numerous canals, others take refuge in the Buddhist monasteries, while the poorer classes have the bare earth, dry or wet as the weather may be, for their couch.

It was not until they were quite exhausted, and could no longer maintain the pace at which they had been making their way through the crowded city, that the old man began to look around him for some spot where they could encamp. The place at which they had arrived was the southern gate of the citadel, called Patoo Song Khai (Gate of Commerce). Here they came upon the haunts of commerce and traffic, — market and trades-women were hurrying to and from the inner city. All around was noise and confusion, and here, beneath the shadow of a projecting porch and wall, the old man suddenly halted, and, lifting the girl lightly to the ground, said in a low, deep, and not unmusical voice, " Let us abide here, my child ; and though we can call nothing our own, we shall live like the bright gods, feeding on happiness."

There was something tender in the way he said this, but the girl did not appear to heed him. Looking about her with a startled and bewildered gaze, she seemed to be haunted by apprehensions of being led captive to some gloomy place, where she would be chained and scourged, and, worse than all, where she would never see her father but through iron gratings and bars. Her terrors at length became so real that she wrapped her faded " saree " more closely around her, and burst into tears.

"Art thou afraid ?" inquired the old man. " Why, thou hast less to fear here by my side than if I had left thee behind in the mountains of Prabat."

He then proceeded to unpack his beast, while the girl timidly made ready to cook their evening meal of boiled rice and fish.

There was a certain sense of safety in the shadow of the grand royal palace that seemed to restore the girl to a state of moderate tranquillity, and the Amazons who loitered round the gate watched the travellers with some degree of interest, which arose partly from curiosity and partly from want of something better to do. The old man seemed a sombre sort of being to them ; but the girl was an object of wonder and delight, as, though she replied to her father in a language foreign to the listeners, she frequently intermingled her remarks with the Siamese word " cha " (dear), which pleased the stout-hearted guardians of the gate so much that they made no objections to the travellers' resting there.

In such a spot as this there was, indeed, more of danger than of safety both for father and child, if they could but have known it; but the poorer class of strangers clung to the name of the great king Maha Mongkut as a babe clings to its mother's arms, and the old man felt as safe as if lodged in an impregnable castle, surrounded by a million of guardian angels; while the girl, gathering courage from the satisfaction that settled on her father's face, began to take note of what was passing around her, and her fears soon gave place to a variety of happy thoughts.

The freshness of the evening air, the song of the merry birds, the beauty of the wild flowers that grew among the tangled bushes on the banks of the river, and, above all, the constant stream of richly gilded boats and gondolas that glided past on the limpid waters, now glittering in the roseate hues of the setting sun, soothed and gladdened, as with tender, loving words, the heart of the lonely mountain girl.

At sunset the Amazons shut the gates and disappeared. The old man unrolled a small carpet, covered himself with a worn-out old cloth, and, taking his daughter under his stalwart arm, he laid himself down to rest beneath the canopy of the wide sky. The girl, from her place near the corner made by the gate and the wall, could only see one star overhead, and the shadow in which she slept seemed so dark that her heart sunk within her, as she silently prayed to the angel of the sky not to desert them. But, tired and weary, she soon slept as soundly as her father.

Meanwhile the city of the "Invincible and Beautiful Archangel" slumbered, and "the great stars globed themselves in heaven," and seemed to bridge the gulf that separates the infinite from the finite with their tender, loving light. Who can say but that the fond spirit of a dead wife and mother beamed in love and pity over the father and child sleeping thus alone in the heart of a great city? for the girl dreamed a dream which seemed a warning to her. Suddenly she started in her sleep, and saw in the distance a company of men armed with swords and spears, carrying lanterns in their hands, marching slowly towards the spot where they lay.

These were the night-guards patrolling outside the walls of the inner city.

While she looked they seemed to expand. They were now colossal, — monsters that filled the earth, air, and sky. Full of dismay, she clung closer to the side of her father. Their heavy tramp came nearer, and she could hear them stop. How desperately her heart beat under the covering! What if they should find her out! The captain of the guards approached, passed his lantern slowly over the face of the old man, and perceiving that he was one of the many strangers called into the city at this time of the year, he and his company went on their rounds.

No sooner had the glimmer of their lanterns vanished in the distance, than the girl sprang up, and, casting a cautious glance all round, drew out in the darkness a small brass image of Indra, which she wore within her vest, and placed it at her father's head; then, loosening a silk cord from her neck, to which was attached a silver ring inscribed with the mystic triform used by the Hindoo women, she proceeded to implore the protection of the gods, and to describe several weird circles and waves over herself and her father.

This done she slept sweetly, feeling in the presence of that brass image a sense of security that many a Christian might have envied.

Just at this moment, one of the guards in passing on the other side of the city remarked that they ought to

have aroused the old khaik (foreigner) and exacted a toll
from him for taking up his quarters so near the walls of
the royal palace.

"That very thought has just crossed my mind," said
the captain, "and mine, and mine," echoed a number of
voices. "It is hardly midnight yet; let us turn back
and see what we can squeeze out of the old fellow."

No sooner said than done. The chief led the way, and
the whole company rapidly retraced their steps to where
the travellers slept.

It would be difficult to reproduce the picture that must
have presented itself to the captain of the night-guards,
who, after having stationed his men at a little distance,
advanced noiselessly, approached the old man, and drew
off lightly the covering that wrapped the sleeper, in order
to make some guess from his dress and appearance as to
the amount of money they might demand from him.

The eye turns instinctively to the faintest glimmer of
light. So the light reflected from the calm face of the
mysteriously beautiful dreamer as she lay beside her
father, her head resting on his arm, and her face turned
mutely up to the dark sky, staggered the captain, who
started back as if he had received a sudden blow, or as if
some unexpected event had forced him into the presence
of a supernatural being, while the brazen image of Indra
gleamed with a lurid brightness that reddened the pale
atmosphere around, as if in the vicinity of some confla-
gration.

Buddhist as he was, he had a sort of ancestral reverence for the gods of the Hindoos. He also believed in
the ancient tradition that no one could injure the innocent. The shadow of the shade grew darker, and he
thought the eyes of the god were fixed intently upon
him. All his unrighteous desires quelled, he stood trans-
fixed reverently to the spot. A serious smile, almost

stern in its expression, passed over the girl's face, as he stood contemplating her. That seemingly slumbering statue was conscious of an intruder, and she quietly opened her eyes on him.

The captain's lantern lighted up his face, and, stout-hearted, fearless man that he was, he trembled as he met that calm, inquiring look. But before he could retire or bring himself to speak, the girl uttered a sudden cry of terror, so pathetic and terrible that the old man sprang to his feet, and the guards, who heard it in the distance, felt their blood run cold with horror and dismay.

There was a moment of hesitation as the old Rajpoot confronted the guardsman face to face. The next instant the lantern was dashed from his trembling hand, and he lay prostrate on the ground, while his enemy grappled at his throat with the fury of a wild beast. The remainder of the guards rushed to the scene of conflict, but even they stood confounded for a second or two at the sight of the strange, terrified girl. They soon recovered from their astonishment, however, and proceeded to capture the old man, when Smâyâtee sprang to her feet at once, like some spectre rising from the ground, and, pushing back the soldiers with all her might, clasped her father round the neck. Thus clinging to him, she turned a face of defiance on the guardsmen of the king. The aspect of the girl, who thought to restrain by an electric glance an armed force, excited such derision in the breasts of the soldiers, that they rudely tore her from her father, bound her with the silken bridle-reins that had served for her pony, and carried them both off to separate cells, while a party of them remained behind to restore their fallen chief.

CHAPTER VIII.

AMONG THE HILLS OF ORISSA.

BEFORE proceeding further, it will not be amiss to give the reader some account of this Rajpoot and his daughter. And that he may better understand the personal anecdotes of bravery, honest zeal, and devotedness that distinguished him in life, I must turn to the still broader and deeper historical incidents which are the marked characteristics of the race to which he belonged. I do not undertake to treat of this portion of India at large, but only to look at the small corner of it in which Rama the Rajpoot was born.

In the district of Orissa stands on a cluster of hills, in the midst of an arid and undulating plateau, the city of Megara, composed for the most part of houses of mean aspect, with only a few handsome mansions and stately edifices to relieve their monotonous insignificance, possessing few fine trees large enough to afford shade, with the exception of the sacred groves dedicated to the earth-goddess Dâvee and the sun-god Dhupyâ; and with water barely sufficient to quench the excessive thirst of its parched inhabitants, alternately swept by piercing blasts and scorched by intense heats, Megara would certainly present but few attractions to the traveller but for the mysterious reverence which has rested ever since the time of Alexander over the illimitable plains of Hindostan. Tragic and terrible are the memories that poetry has woven about this land of undefined distances and nearly fabulous magnificence, where men adopt, from father to son, the professions of murderers, highwaymen, robbers, soldiers, warriors, and priests, where each man lives as if surrounded by internal and external enemies, and expects from every circling point of the horizon a foeman instead of a friend.

From the remotest times there has been a ceaseless march of tribes into this vast peninsula, from which there is no outlet. Pouring across the Indus or straggling down through the passes of the Himalaya, each wave of immigration pushed its predecessors farther into the country. Thus the Aryan nations followed in their turn, at the same time reacting powerfully on the creeds and usages of the primitive people. But various remains of the earlier and rude aboriginal tribes are still found here among the hilly regions and woody fastnesses of the peninsula. Many of them are quite distinct from one another, evidently belonging to different eras of an indefinitely remote and abysmal past.

The Rajpoots are the most remarkable of these aboriginal tribes, and they are described as a noble race, tall and athletic, with symmetric features, half-way between the Roman and Jewish types, large eyed, and with fine long hair falling in natural locks upon their shoulders; high-bred, though with the decline of their country under British rule the decline of their character has kept pace. Revolutions have done their work upon them, if, indeed, the word "revolution" may be applied to the insurrections and mutinies that have kept this portion of India in a state of petty warfare for the last three hundred years.

The comparatively treeless character of the hills where they dwell appears to indicate that, in former times, large spaces had been laid under cultivation, whereas at present they lead a savage life as freebooters and robbers.

Around these desolate hills and valleys cluster a variety of tribes and races, of diverse tongues and customs, creeds and religions, — worshippers of Mohammed and of the

4

Buddha, followers of Brahma and of Indra, of Vishnu and Siva, of the many-breasted and teeming Dâvee, and the triple-headed and triple-bodied Dhupyâ. Over all these different peoples the Rajpoot, or warrior caste, has held for centuries an undisputed sway. Among all these tribes the " Meriâh " sacrifice prevails, as the only means of propitiating the earth-goddess.

The victims for these yearly sacrifices are furnished by a regular class of procurers, who either supply them to order or raise them on speculation. They are bought from their parents in hard famine times, or they are kidnapped on the plains. Devoted often in their childhood to the earth-goddess Dâvee, they are suffered to grow up as consecrated privileged beings, to marry, to hold lands and flocks and herds and other worldly goods, and are cherished and beloved by the community for whom they are willing to be offered up to serve as mediator and friend in the shadowy world beyond the grave for the short space of one year, when the insatiable earth-goddess is said to demand a fresh victim.

I ought not to omit to say here, as a faithful recorder of the facts that have reached me, that in spite of the tremendous doom that overshadows the victims consecrated to Dâvee's altar, they lead resigned and even joyous lives up to the last moment of their existence ; and the saying is, that the soul of a god enters the martyr, and transfigures him into a divine, ineffable being, incapable of feeling any pain or regret at the moment of death.

For unnumbered centuries the vast hilly province of Orissa verging on Gondwana, and comprising all the eastern portion of the Vindhya chain, has been the scene of this revolting and inhuman custom ; and from time immemorial thousands of men whom we in our enlightenment call " savage hordes " have offered themselves up for the good of their fellow-men. Surely an effluence from the

Divine Soul must have passed over these strange mystic mediators, as they stood trembling upon Dâvee's altar, clutching the sharp knife in their uplifted hand, their faces turned towards the darkening earth, singing the supreme song, and uttering the supreme cry, " O Dâvee! do all thy acts to me. Spend all thy fury upon me. Spare my race from the hungry grave (earth). Drink of my blood, and be appeased." And as the echoes of this cry of triumph and of despair die away in the distance, the self-sacrificing victim plunges the bright steel into his own warm heart, bends forward to sprinkle with his life's blood the insatiable earth, repeating his song in whispers that grow fainter and fainter as he slowly draws out the fatal steel and falls dead upon her bare bosom.

The Rajpoots are still the chiefs. They levy a tax on the various tribes who inhabit these hilly regions, and who are, in great measure, dependent upon them, trained warriors from their childhood, for their protection. They are not distinct from their neighbors, so far as the ceremonials of religion are concerned. The number of marriages among them is, however, contracted by the exclusion of all but their own peculiar clan or caste. Marriage itself is an expensive thing, from the costly usages with which it is attended among them, while at the same time celibacy is disgraceful. An unmarried daughter is a reproach to her parents and to herself; therefore it has been an established custom with the Rajpoot to preserve the chastity of his daughter and the honor of his house by doing away with his female children a few hours after their birth. When a messenger from the Zennânâ announces to him the birth of a daughter, the Rajpoot will coolly roll up between his fingers a tiny ball of opium, to be conveyed to the mother, who thereupon, with many a bitter tear, rubs on her nipple the sleep-giving poison, and the babe drinks in death with its mother's milk.

Here again we find a striking anomaly in the Hindoo character. The parental instinct is as strong in the people of India as in any people of the world; and even where no parental tie exists, the tenderness with which strong, bearded men devote themselves to the care of young children is as touching as it is remarkable. A childless woman, too, is a miserable creature, a hissing and a reproach among men, and barrenness is only accounted for as a punishment for some grievous sin committed against the gods in a pre-existent state. Nevertheless, among the high-caste Rajpoot tribes female infanticide is universally practised; so that, in the district in which Rama was born, owing to its decline from the prosperity of former years, a high-born girl was rarely if ever heard of.

On a high and projecting rock, whose scarped and rugged outlines bid defiance to the pedestrian, stood the stately mansion of Dhotee Bhad, the chieftain of Megara, and the father of Rama, recognizable by its grand appearance, its balconies of fretted stone, and its long windows, which commanded for miles the surrounding country. It is a wild and solitary spot, and out of the direct road to any place; but it had two advantages, — it was almost inaccessible, and it overlooked valleys which were as luxuriant with verdure as the hills around were sterile and barren. Two miles from this spot rises the Ghât Meriâh, crowned with a grove of stately trees, whose profound brown shadows and lurid gloom is said to be caused by the spirits of the victims offered up yearly there, and whose grand proportions are dimly visible at points here and there as you approach the grove. At the foot of this Ghât, in a thick and all but impenetrable forest, are several magnificent ponds from which the inhabitants draw their water.

Such was the home and the birthplace of our hero Rama.

CHAPTER IX.

THE REBEL DUKE P'HAYA SI P'HIFOOR.

IN the year 1831 a revolutionary war broke out in the northern provinces of Siam. The ringleader of this disaffected part of the country was the Duke P'haya Si P'hifoor, a man who, from his high position, great warlike talents, and immense wealth, possessed an unbounded influence over the inhabitants of the northern provinces. It is said that even from his infancy the demon Ambition had taken such possession of him that he used to imagine himself a king, and that, from that time to the fatal termination of his life, he dreamt of nothing but the sceptre and the supreme sway.

It was one of his first efforts, therefore, to gather from distant lands all the disaffected and ambitious spirits he could muster together, — men who would be brave and skilful enough to take the helm in the storm that must follow his inexorable bidding.

In 1821 he sent secret agents by an Indian merchant ship to Calcutta to enlist for him a troop of hardy warriors of the Rajpoot tribe. Among this troop hired in Calcutta and transshipped to Siam was our prisoner, Rama Singalee, — Rama the lion. He, with the rest of his party, had been implicated in some incipient rebellion against the British government, and had fled for concealment to the densely populated city of Calcutta, where, after several years of hard struggling to obtain some means of livelihood not derogatory to their high caste, they were induced to sell their services to the agent of the Duke P'haya Si P'hifoor. This band of hired mercenaries landed secretly in the Gulf of Martaban, at the mouth of the Irrawady, whence by night travel they arrived at P'hra Batt. Here portions of land in the tenure of the duke were allotted to them, and they were dispersed until a fitting opportunity should offer for striking the final blow which was to place their master on the throne of Siam, and themselves in offices of trust in the kingdom.

So things went on for several years, when Rama fell in love with a Loatian girl of singular beauty, but could not collect money enough to satisfy the demands of her parents.[14]

It was the custom of the Duke P'haya Si P'hifoor to make an annual visit to P'hra Batt, ostensibly with varied offerings to the footprint of Buddha, from which the whole mountainous district is named, but in reality to muster his retainers, give them presents, and exact fresh promises of service, or to traverse the entire country gaining fresh adherents to his cause.

On one occasion a dreadful fever ravaged his party; many of them had to be left at the different monasteries to be cared for, while Rama and a few followers only accompanied him. Just as the sun was setting behind the mountains, Rama, who acted as pioneer, heard the sound of some animal in the thick underwood. He crept quickly back, motioned his companions to halt, and advanced alone. A few yards from him he saw a tiger, immovable, yet stealthily watching his opportunity to make a spring. Night was fast approaching, and so was death; but Rama drew near, his eyes fixed steadily and unfalteringly on those of the beast. At last he took his position, and for a moment or two they glared one upon the other. Then in the distance the rest of the party, breathless, their hearts beating quickly, heard the dismal roar of a goaded and infuriate animal, and the heavy blows of a battle-axe. Their terror was only equalled by their joy when they

saw the huge creature extended before them in death.
The duke came up, and instantly rewarded the brave warrior with a hundred pieces of gold.

Gold enough to buy Malee, the beautiful Loatian girl!

Next morning he prostrated himself before the duke,
and requested permission to return at once to P'hra Batt,
which was granted him. Thus did the Rajpoot obtain to
wife the woman he loved.

Meanwhile the duke, still cherishing his darling ambition, consulted all the astrologers in the country, who
drew auguries from ants, spiders, and bees, and predicted
for him a brilliant career. This so worked upon the
already inflamed imagination of P'haya Si P'hifoor, that
he was led, in an unguarded moment, to throw down the
gauntlet and declare open war against the king of Siam,
whom he branded with the titles of fox and usurper.

Through his secret emissaries he caused edicts to be
proclaimed everywhere, nominating himself in the name
of the people and of heaven as the lawful successor to the
throne.

The entire army of the priesthood and the people were
on his side. Hosts of men from all parts of the country
flocked to his standard. The duke, mounted on a white
elephant, headed the rabble crowd. Before him, on horseback, rode the hired Rajpoot band of warriors.

Tidings of this alarming insurrection soon reached the
enraged monarch at Bangkok, who instantly summoned a
council of war, and sent trumpeters all over the land to
blast forth a direful malediction, in the name of all the
hosts of heaven, upon the rebel duke and his followers.

The rebel duke and his frenzied legions made rapid
progress, however. They could be seen covering the
entire face of the country, rushing on with shouts and
cries and furious bounding of elephants and horses, with
flourish of trumpets and of banners, — a terrible, undisci-

plined, myriad-faced monster, being neither burnt up with
the scorching rays of Suriya, nor scattered by the thunder-
bolts of Indra. The king, who had stormed so loud and
so lustily from behind the purdah-curtain of his throne,
now trembled and cowered in the midst of his fifteen
hundred wives, and let the duke ride triumphantly, almost
to the very gates of his palace at Ayudia.

In this emergency the prime minister, Somdetch Ong
Yai, the father of the present premier, assumed the command of the army, transshipped all the guns he could
muster into small crafts, — the river at Ayudia being too
shallow for ships of great tonnage, — taking with them an
ample supply of ammunition, and with hardly twelve
thousand men sailed up the river, amid the shouts and
prayers of the terrified inhabitants.

On their arrival at Ayudia the guns were conveyed on
trucks to the point whence the attack was expected.
Here Somdetch Ong Yai hastily erected several batteries,
and awaited the attack.

Scarcely four hours had elapsed after the completion of
these preparations, when the whole neighborhood was
aroused by the war-cry of the rebel army, which appeared
in sight, headed by the duke. The Rajpoot cavalry,
armed with long rifle-guns, bows and arrows, and poisoned
lances, prepared to storm the batteries. There was a moment of fearful silence, followed by a flash and the
thundering roar of the artillery from the other side. The
monster army of the rebel duke reeled, scattered, and gave
way, all but the Rajpoot cavalry, almost every one of
whom lay dead or dying on the field. The prime minister, Somdetch Ong Yai, rushed forward and captured the
rebel duke, wounding, in the attempt, one gigantic, desperate soldier, who fought with a recklessness of daring
in behalf of his misguided leader that won the admiration of friend and foe.

PALM-TREES NEAR THE NEW ROAD, BANGKOK.

Where was the monster army now ?

Of the dead and dying there were a thousand or more, of living captives only two, — the Duke P'haya Si P'hifoor, and one faithful soldier, Rama Singalee. The rest had, at the first sound of the cannon, fled far beyond its range. Like a wave of the ocean it had swept out of sight. P'haya Si P'hifoor was carried to Bangkok, tried, and sentenced to death. A general amnesty was proclaimed, and the generous premier, Somdetch Ong Yai, took Rama into his own household, had him cared for and promoted to a place of trust. As for the wretched duke, on his arrival at Bangkok he was condemned first to have his eyes put out, and then to be placed in an iron cage, which was suspended from a scaffolding in the middle of the river, so that the unfortunate captive could manage just barely to touch with the tips of his fingers the waters as they rippled under it.

Here he was left by that most inhuman of the kings of Siam, P'hendin Klang, without food or raiment, exposed to the burning heat of the noonday sun, to suffer from the acutest agonies of thirst, within hearing and touch of the waters that flowed in perpetual eddies beneath his feet.

How ardently must that poor, unhappy man have prayed for death; and that dark angel, at all times too ready to come unbidden to the good and happy, stood aloof, and seemed to mock at his misery for many and many a weary day and night, until at length it began to be whispered among the people — many of whom would gladly have brought him food and drink, but for the dreadful punishment threatened on all such as should attempt in any way to mitigate his tortures — that the angels, pitying his sufferings, brought him nightly portions of the " amreeta," on which they feed so plentifully in heaven.

But the truth was, that Rama Singalee was the stout-hearted angel who battled nightly with the strong currents of the Mèinam, and brought, at the risk and peril of his life, some boiled rice and water in the hollow of a bamboo cane, which, as he floated beneath the iron cage, he held up to his late master's mouth, who sucked therefrom the scanty portion of food it contained.

The last night of the unfortunate prisoner's life, Rama set out as usual, ignoring the pain of his wounds, and, swimming manfully against the strong tide that threatened to bear him away with it, he reached the spot about three o'clock in the morning, stealthily approached the cage, keeping his head under water, but his heart above the clouds, with those heroic souls who follow in the path of the Son of Heaven. He swam right under the cage, and looking up in the darkness towards it, saw no shadow there. He held up the long bamboo, and rested it against the iron bars, but no eager, trembling hand grasped it, as it was wont to do. He called out in hoarse whispers, "P'hakha, p'hakha, soway tho" (master, master, pray eat). No sound, no movement, reached his anxious ears.

Ah, happy man! the loving voice of his devoted follower reached his ears, and penetrated far into his sinking heart, as he lay in his last agonies, coiled up on the floor of his cage, and in the double darkness of night and sightlessness, he saw the brave, strong face of this one great soul that loved him in spite of all his sin and misery; and, even as he caught the vision, a smile such as would have irradiated the throne of God, passed over that blind, distorted face, and the soul flitted away rejoicing, leaving behind it an expression of serenity and peace, as if that proud, turbulent, and ambitious spirit had at last been taught the meaning of a higher love, and through it had breasted the waters, and gained the shore "Where the wicked cease from troubling, and the weary are at rest."

After some years of service in the army, the premier,

Somdetch Ong Yai, being dead, Rama, having been regu-
larly branded as the vassal of his eldest son, Chow P'haya
Mândtree, obtained permission to return home to his wife.
Just eight years after these events, and the very year after
his return home, there was born to this brave man a
daughter, who, as it sometimes happens, by some singular
freak of nature, or, perhaps, by some higher law of development, was so wondrously beautiful, that when Rama,
faithful to the custom of his ancestors, handed to his wife,
a few hours after her delivery, a ball of opium to be
rubbed on her breasts, she turned up to him a scared and
wondering look, muttering, " She is, — she is the smile of
God," the deadly ball dropped from her pulseless hands,
and her spirit passed away ; and he, broken hearted and
baffled, rightly interpreted the significance of her dying
words, not only spared the child's life, but named her
Devo Smâyátee (the God smiles).   Thus a new life stole
into the heart and the arms of the old warrior of Orissa.

CHAPTER X.

THE GRANDSON OF SOMDETCH ONG YAI, AND HIS TUTOR P'HRA CHOW SADUMAN.

WHEN Rama and his daughter were carried off to prison, poor Smâyâtee hardly realized what was going to happen. But when a couple of Amazons forced her away from her father, and she understood the full meaning of what had befallen them, she began to shout and scream aloud for help. But none came.

A child of the mountains and hills, she had as yet developed none but the natural instincts of what civilization would call a savage. Combined with her fine organization, she inherited a passionate nature, and an intense love for the mountains and woods, the earth and sky, which were to her so many beautiful gods. To some she had been accustomed to offer flowers, to others fruit, oil, wine, honey, water. She always set apart a portion of every meal for her favorite god Dâvee, the earth-goddess. To such a nature only to live was worship. To see, to hear, to gather thoughts and pictures, to feel the throbbing pulses; to fill the eye with images of beauty, the heart with impulses of love and joy; to place the mind face to face with the unwritten mysteries which nature unfolds to it, — is, indeed, the highest sphere of contemplation and worship, as well for the savage as the child of civilization.

The Amazons who guarded the cell chatted together in a low tone, while Smâyâtee, exhausted by her cries and screams for help, had sunk into a deep sleep. They remarked on the beauty of her skin, the roundness of her limbs, the softness of her cheeks, and the superb lashes that rested so lightly upon them, and wondered who she could be; for though her dress bespoke her of the peasant class of the Loatians, her form and face betokened high birth.

"He must have stolen her," said one of the women; "she cannot be his daughter, though she calls him father."

"He has brought her here for sale, of course," added another; "else why should he have chosen such a place as this, so near the royal palace, for encampment."

"Ah, well! whatever be her lot, poor child, let us not add to her sufferings; she will have enough of them in this life," rejoined the kind-hearted chief officer.

The bell above the prison gate, with its brazen tongue, tolled out twelve (i. e., five in the morning); the girl, aroused as it were by the voice of an angel, started, rubbed her eyes, and looking around seemed to recall the events of the last night. She then made several profound salutations and invocations to a gleam of sunlight that came straggling into her cell, wrapped her saree over her head and face, and placed herself near the door, so as to be able to pass out the moment it should be opened.

"Take something to eat, child," said the chief of the Amazons on guard, who was partaking of a breakfast of cold rice and fish, "and wait till the sun is higher in the heavens, and I will go with you; it is not fit that one so young and beautiful should go out alone and unprotected."

She was too kind-hearted to tell her that she was a prisoner, and no longer free to go in and out.

Smâyâtee had hardly swallowed a few mouthfuls of rice, when the guardsman of the previous night appeared, with orders to the Amazons to take her to the Sala of the Grand Duke, Chow P'haya Mândtree; as they, on discovering from the mark on the old man's arm that he was a vassal of that nobleman, had resigned him to the custody of his officers.

The Amazons led the way, and Smâyâtee followed with faltering steps. Nobody noticed her. Everybody seemed excited and eager. Every one hurried towards the same spot.

In her uncertainty the girl could see nothing in the world but the river running strong, yet running calmly on. After a little while she began to trace the opposite bank; a little way to the left something hanging midway in the sky, as she supposed, or rather in mid-distance; there being as yet no sky, no heaven, no earth; nothing but the river. This was a bridge; they cross the bridge. Where does it lead to? Whither flows this mysterious stream, of which the coming and the going are equally full of wonder and dread to her? What mysterious, enchanted palaces and temples are those looming out yonder on the other side? To her ignorance they are but infinitude and the unknown. Now they near the duke's palace; the odors of orange-flowers and spice-groves reach them, like airs that breathe from paradise.

Having come to the great hall, the Amazons take their places on one of the lowest steps, Smâyâtee seated between them; they are contented to chew their betel and to wait.

The hall is full of men. The work of branding and enrolling goes briskly on under the orders of a young nobleman, called Nai Dhamaphat, the grandson of Somdetch Ong Yai. Every now and then some persons are brought forward to be admonished, fined, or whipped. Sometimes from among this crowd a boy is dragged out forcibly, and branded.

Through the masses of men, lighted up now by the full blaze of sunlight, Smâyâtee sought one form and one figure only, and he was nowhere to be seen.

Suddenly the Grand Duke was announced; he entered the hall with conscious swagger, followed by a long train of attendants and slaves.

No words could express what there was in the face and figure of this man, as he rolled rather than walked into the centre of the hall.

Work instantly ceased; all around crouched and hid their faces. This did not rouse his huge, drowsy nature into even a look of recognition; he growled rather than spoke the orders for the workers to continue, and turned to his son and said, "Dhamaphat, what is this about Rama Singalee having attacked the captain of the royal guards?"

"My Lord," replied the latter, "the captain, as far as I can learn, is as much to blame as the old soldier, who says he only struck him in defence of his daughter."

"A daughter, eh! I did not know the old fellow had a daughter."

At this point in the conversation Smâyâtee, who had been listening with deep attention, leaned forward, and fearlessly addressed the duke, said, "Do you want that I should tell you how it happened, my lord?"

"Well, speak out!" said the duke, turning savagely upon the girl for having dared to interrupt him unbidden.

He checked himself, however, as his eye fell upon the graceful, veiled figure, and said rather more gently, "Go on, how was it?"

Smâyâtee threw back her covering, sat up, and repeated the story of her long journey, her father's fears to leave her alone at home, their encampment near the royal palace, her fearful alarm, and how it was to save her that her father struck the captain of the king's guard.

The girl never looked so beautiful, so fearless; there was in her look the innocence and the ignorance of a babe. It was not the words she uttered, but the face she presented, the look so sad and yet so full of trust, which served to rouse the drowsy nature of the duke, and to change his repulsiveness into something more hideous still.

Dhamaphat listened, too, with intense interest; it

seemed as if his whole soul were concentrated into his eyes and ears.

The duke was puzzled what to say. He turned to exchange a few words, in an undertone, with his son, and then dismissed the Amazons, charging them, on the peril of their lives, not to lose sight of the girl, and promising the latter to have the matter investigated on the following day.

In Siamese life the lights and shadows are equally strong. At once-brilliant and gloomy, smiling and sombre, lighted as by the radiance of dawn, and at the same time enveloped in the darkness of night.

The branding and enrolling for the day was over. The crowds dispersed to their various homes.

When the young man, Nai Dhamaphat, went out, he had but one thought; it was to follow that girl, and try, if possible, to see her face and hear her voice again.

There was something in that face that had changed the whole current of his being, and had set him, charged with a new force, in the midst of a little world all by itself, the horizon of which was bounded by her possible smile.

He turned his steps towards the grand palace, and gazed upon the place where she was imprisoned; he was almost at the gate. He wavered in his mind; custom and his natural reserve forbade him to speak to a strange woman; with a bewildered air he retraced his steps and went home.

That part of Bangkok in which Chow P'haya Mând-tree lived was laid out in small squares, each walled in by low ramparts, enclosing the residence and harem of some great noble; but the duke's palaces were surrounded by a wall only on three sides, from which ran, parallel to the river-front, several streets, and among them the gold and silver streets, so designated from their being inhabited by artists skilled in the working of those metals.

The sun had set when Dhamaphat reached his home, but it was already night. Here there is no twilight, — that soft messenger that lingers, unwilling, as it were, to usher in the darkness of night.

Moonlight, with its silvery touches, rested on the palace roofs and made even ugliness and decay beautiful. The tall cocoa and betel palms, moved by the wood-nymphs, fluttered and waved their branches to and fro, beckoning him nearer and nearer, and presenting a spectacle, strange, yet lovely in the extreme.

The bright moon was soon lost to view, except where it penetrated the thick, overhanging foliage. On the gateway the pendent branches of the bergamot gave forth a rich perfume. The shrill chirping of myriads of grasshoppers, which seem never to sleep, with the sounds of distant music, fell upon his ear, as his father's temples and palaces burst upon his view, a mingled scene of fairy beauty, artificial elegance, and savage grandeur, — domes, turrets, enormous trees, and flowers such as are met with nowhere else beneath the sun. The oldest temples in Siam stood here, containing strange and wonderful objects, with stranger and more wonderful recollections attached to them. That one on the right was once, in the reign of the usurper, P'haya Tak, the principal stronghold of his ancestors, and where, even after long years, they were still wont to repair, at a particular moon in every year, to pray beside the golden pagoda that enshrined the charred bones of his forefathers. That gray palace had witnessed many a gay assemblage, held by the old duke, Somdetch Ong Yai, his grandfather.

He entered the temple, beneath the portal of which were some deeply graven rhymes from the Vedas, to him equally dark as the dark image of Buddha that had slumbered for centuries at the base of the glittering altar. Yet, wonderful as were the objects that met the eye of the young man, he simply prostrated himself before the altar, and turned to his father's palace.

A low, open verandah faced the entrance. Choice birds were singing in their cages, and soft lights of cocoanut-oil were gleaming down upon them. A number of noblemen were lounging on cool mats, some playing chess, others engaged in conversation. Slaves were passing round tempting fruits, and refreshing drinks of spiced wines and cocoanut nectar.

Dhamaphat prostrated himself before his father, and took his place on a low seat. He had no sooner done so, than he was startled by the entrance of some armed men, who brought in the old Rajpoot, and stationed him and themselves at the extreme end of the verandah.

There was something particularly interesting about the prisoner. He was a tall, slender, alert-looking man, about sixty, fair, with aquiline features, and expressive and determined countenance. There were lines on his face that told of hardship and suffering, though these seemed in no degree to have depressed his spirits, or to have impaired his youthful vigor and activity. He wore a blue cloak, and an ample turban of blue silk.

The duke at length addressed the prisoner, and said: " Rama, you have committed a crime which, if you had not been my slave, would have handed you over to the criminal's prison for life, or to instant death ; and now, since your daughter has told us with her own lips, that it was in her defence you struck the captain of the royal guards, I am going to pay him a heavy fine, and smother this affair. But only on one condition, however, — "

The duke paused for a reply, or some expression of thankfulness.

None came.

The old soldier turned his head, and looked at him in serious doubt.

After waiting a little while he repeated, "Only on one condition; that thou sell to us, for our service and pleasure, this daughter of thine, and we will take better care of her than thou art able to do."

It was fully half an hour before Rama seemed to comprehend the meaning of his master's words. He had never thought of *his* daughter occupying such a position; he had hardly realized that she was no longer a child. Now his feeling of caste and race rose up within him; his strong nature was moved, as he saw her snatched away from him. All manner of recollections and reveries full of tenderness came whispering at his heart, and the words: "My lord, to this I can never consent," came slowly, brokenly forth, as if out of a heart struggling for mastery over some great emotion.

The duke sprang to his feet, staggered — for he had been drinking heavily — up to the chained prisoner, and, clenching his palsied, trembling hand, he cried in a thundering voice: "You dare to refuse me! By the gods, I will neither eat nor drink until I have seized and given her to my lowest slave! and if you do not quickly repent of your rash refusal, you shall be cast into prison for the rest of your life. Do you forget what my father did for you, you ungrateful dog?" and his dark face became purple with rage and fury.

The old warrior trembled in every limb, not from fear, but from horror. He knew what to expect from the eldest son of his late master. His heart burned with indignation. But what could he do? How could he defend her? He thought bitterly of the weakness that had placed the honor of his house and race at the mercy of a stranger; that little ball of opium would have saved her from all possible insult. He groaned aloud, feeling that this was a just retribution for his innovation upon the ancient custom of his house, and large tears rolled down his rugged face.

The drowning man, overtaken by the supreme agony, lives, in an instant, through all his happy and unhappy past. In a single moment he sees the whole drama of his life reacted before him. Thus it was with Rama; he recalled with anguish the scenes of Smâyâtee's childhood, her youth and growing womanhood, all her early gladness, all her bright hopes and illusions, all her gifts of beauty and affection, which made one picture with her present degradation, and served only to darken the riddle of her life to him.

The courage that had withstood a hungry tiger now gave way before the picture of the deeper degradation that might, because of his refusal, befall his child. He flung himself on the ground, and muttered: "She is yours, my lord."

"Sa-baye" (good), said the duke, clapping his hands; "I knew you would give in; you are no fool, Rama. It is the women whom we find so difficult to manage, when they take an idea into their heads. Take him away to his cell now," said he, addressing the guards, "to-morrow we will make it all right, and when the girl comes to the Sala, we shall apprise her of the high honors in store for her. Here," said he, throwing some money to the jailers, "go you and make merry till morning, and be sure and give the prisoner as much as he can eat and drink."

The guards departed, leading away a fierce, revengeful-looking old man.

When they were gone, the duke, addressing Nai Dhamaphat, said: "What think you of our clemency to our slaves, my son? We would not take possession of this beautiful girl without the old fellow's consent."

He then began to laugh, and added: "Ah, she shall be my cup-bearer, and my good friends here will have an opportunity of admiring her beauty!"

The son simply bowed his head, in seeming acknowl-

edgment of his father's goodness, and after a while retired from the pavilion, passed over the bridge, and out
of the palace gates.

There could not be a greater difference of character
than that which existed between the duke and his eldest
son; the one gross, sensual, cowardly, the other proud and
domineering, yet withal brave, generous, religious, and
impulsive.

Every year found them farther apart in education,
thought, feelings, hopes, and aspirations. The one standing, as it were, with his foot on the first step of a ladder
that was to lead him towards the highest ideal of Christianity, the other sunk beyond all hope in the ignorance
of a savage barbarism.

But now this last scene was too much for the former.
It snapped asunder the fragile cord that still. bound him
to his father, and placed him in the position of an antag-
onist.

Every nation has certain constitutional peculiarities
which give rise to practices and phases of thought very
startling to others, who are, in such points, differently
constituted. The most remarkable peculiarity of this
kind is the reverence with which parents are regarded in
Siam. No matter how unjust, capricious, cruel, and repulsive a parent may be, a child is bound to reverence his
or her slightest wish as a sacred obligation.

For Dhamaphat, therefore, even to question his father's
actions was, he felt, a moral dereliction. He was full of
remorse and regret, and thought with despair of the fate
that awaited him.

He had gained a little wooden bridge, which, thrown
across a canal, led him into a lonely field; here he
motioned back the slaves who attempted to follow him,
and strode rapidly out into the open country, where he
no longer heard the sounds of revelry, feasting, and licen-

tious mirth. Rambling through the many tangled forest-paths, he gradually emerged into a low, wooded expanse. The air was full of delicious fragrance, and alive with strange noises. He saw in the distance the calm, majestic river, all aglow with its myriads of lights and lanterns, yet it failed to call forth a single reflection; he could picture nothing but the face of the strange girl, and that haunted him all the way. He pressed on, tired, feverish, with sad and troubled thoughts; he reached the wall that skirts the city; throwing some silver to the guards, who knew him well, he passed out of the gate, and out of the city of the "Invincible," to the visible archangel of nature.

Here the solitude was startling; no more streets, no more lights, no more houses. Even the quiet river seemed to hush on her white and shining bosom the soft light of the moon, as if it were the face of a beloved child, until she caught a reflection of its beauty, and was transfigured down a hundred feet deep, as far as light could penetrate, into a clear, translucent soul, in its first dreamless sleep.

Moved by some secret purpose, he hurried on through a profusion of flowering plants and trees; he passed un-noticed the slender betel and cocoanut palms, and the numerous species of huge convolvuli "that coiled around their stately stems, and ran e'en to the limit of the land," the long lance-leaves of the wild plantains, the rich foliage of the almonds, the gorgeous oleanders that broke through the green masses in every variety of tint, from the richest crimson to the lightest pink. Presently he dashed aside a huge night-blooming cereus, and stood before a long, low building, a partly ruined monastery, adjoining an ancient and dilapidated Buddhist temple.

The monastery was a sort of long, low corridor or hall, lined on each side with chambers, each about ten feet deep, and lighted by a small aperture in the wall.

It was a gloomy place, old and unhealthy. Poisonous plants, creepers, and flowers reigned jubilant here, with ruin and desolation for companions.

Yet, dismantled, worm-eaten, and ruined as the building appeared, it had been the school of young Dhamaphat for nearly ten years, and it was the home of a solitary old man, who had spent forty years of his lifetime forgetful of friends, affections, food, sleep, and almost of existence in his contemplations of the mystery of things beyond, and that still greater mystery called life; his friends and relations had endeavored by every artifice, the allurements of beauty and every other imaginable gratification, to divert him from the resolution he had adopted. Every attempt to dissuade him had been in vain. And now he had gained a fame as widespread as the most ambitious heart could desire. Among the people he was known under the title of P'hra Chow Sâduman, the sainted priest of heaven. Prodigious stories were afloat about him. Born of noble parents, he had from his early youth practised an asceticism so rigorous and severe that it had prepared him, it was thought, for his supernatural mission. It was not only alleged, but believed, that at the sound of his inspired voice the dead arose and walked, the sick were healed; that diseases vanished at the touch of his hand; sinners were converted by his simple admonition; wild beasts and serpents were obedient to his word; and that in his moments of ecstasy he floated in the air before the eyes of his disciples, passed through stone walls and barred gates, and, in fact, could do whatsoever he willed.

The crumbling old door of the cell was partly open; no light was visible; and, as Dhamaphat stood there hesitating whether he would enter, a low, faint, tremulous sound came out of the darkness within, and floated upward on the silence of night like the voice of some celestial chorister.

It was the Buddhist's evening hymn, or chant, and the
familiar words —

> " Nama Buddsa phakava thouraha,
> Sama Boodhsa thatsa Phutthang
> Purisa thamma sârâthi
> Sangkhang saranang ga cha mi," etc.,

freely translated,

> " O thou, who art thyself the light,
> Boundless in knowledge, beautiful as day,
> Irradiate my heart, my life, my night,
> Nor let me ever from thy presence stray ! "—

touched his better nature and melted his heart. He
stooped forward, and listened to it lovingly as it rose
higher and higher, growing more and more exultant till it
caught his trembling spirit, and bore it away beyond the
confines of this world face to face with a Divine Ineffable Presence full of harmony and beauty.

His anger and his grief were forgotten.

So Dhamaphat turned his face to the sky. One moment
he stood erect in an absolute halo of light, the next he
was combatting darkly with the blind shadows of love
and hate, cause and effect, merit and demerit, the endless evolutions of the " wheel " of an irresistible law into
which all things are cast.

He felt something cold pass over his hand ; he started,
and became aware that the good priest had finished his
devotions. He tapped gently, and was told to enter,
which he did hesitatingly.

In the middle of the cell sat the priest, who seemed,
even in his old age, full of the vigor of manhood ; his legs
were crossed, his arms folded, and his eyes cast down ;
he did not even raise them at the entrance of the young
man ; he was in that semi-stupor commonly called contemplation. In one corner a narrow plank, quite bare, and
a wooden pillow served for his bed ; beside it an old fan,
a pot for water, an earthen vessel for rice, some rude old

instruments and books; beyond these the cell was bare, damp, cold, slimy, and unhealthy. It was without any light, save where the moonlight fell in ghastly lights and shadows through the slits in the wall.

"My father," said the young man, as he reverently prostrated himself before the priest, who half opened his dull eyes, and said: "S'amana phinong" (peace, brother).

"Alas!" replied Dhamaphat; "in this life there is no peace, no rest, no freedom from suffering; the endless revolutions of the wheel only crush out life, to reproduce it again in another form."

"'Take the reins, and ride over it, then,' said the priest, meditatively. "What says the Dharma padam?*

"Stop the chariot valiantly; arrest the horses of desire. When thou hast comprehended that which is made, thou wilt understand that which is not made, — the uncreate. Some do not know that we must all come to an end here; but some do know it, and with them all conflicts cease. He who lives for pleasure only, his passions uncontrolled, immoderate in his enjoyments, idle and weak, him will the tempter overcome, as the wind overcomes a worm-eaten tree.'

"If we could live a thousand years, it would be worth our while to struggle after the pleasures of this world. Death comes too soon. There are many beginnings, but no ending to life. Let us practise the four virtues, my brother; they alone are real, satisfactory, the true illuminators of the mind; without this inward illumination, what is life but darkness, storms, wild, unconscious tumult, the ceaseless tumbling of the fierce tides of passion; and death, but exhaustion?"

"Alas!" cried the young man, in a voice full of emotion; "is life indeed such an empty void? Is there no compensation anywhere?"

* Dharma padam, the "Path of Virtue." — Buddhist Bible.

G

The priest opened wide his half-closed eyes, looked full into Dhamaphat's face, and remarked: "Thou art strangely disturbed to-night, my brother. Is it not well with thee?"

Dhamaphat made no reply.

There was sympathy, and a touch of tender feeling in the voice of the priest, as he bent close to his young pupil, and said: "What is thy suffering? Speak freely to me, and I will aid thee to the utmost of my ability." Saying this, the priest arose, and passed his hand slowly over the clefts in the wall. Instantly the moon withdrew her light.

At this moment the night-owl suddenly gave a harsh and prolonged cry.

"That bird answers to thy thoughts," said the priest.

Dhamaphat shuddered; he believed that in the cry of the bird he heard an echo of his own wild desire to frustrate his father's plans.

Then in a few stirring words he told the priest of his love for the Rajpoot's daughter, of her present situation, and of his desire to help her and her father to escape.

At the words, "Rajpoot's daughter," the old man started, and there passed over his face, unseen, an expression of regret mingled with desire, with which a thirsty man sees afar off, out of his possible reach, a cup of cold water, for which he is dying, but which is not for him. Then, as suddenly, he sat down, and resumed his calm exterior.

A full hour passed in complete silence; the old man and the young man sat in the darkness, with their faces turned to one another, each on his side thinking over the same things, and feeling the same impulses.

"This is very strange," said he, at length; "when I made my annual pilgrimage to P'hra Batt, last year, a lovely girl, Rama the Rajpoot's daughter, who called herself Devo Smâyâtee, brought me food every morning, and washed my feet every evening. She was then hardly a woman, but she filled my heart with a fragrance which is all-abiding. But," added the priest, in an undertone, as if for himself, " death carries off a man who is gathering flowers, as a flood sweeps away a sleeping village. He in whom the desire for the Ineffable (Nirwana) has sprung up, whose thoughts are not bewildered by love, he is the ' Ordhvamsrotas,' borne on the stream of immortality ; he will stand face to face with the Infinite." He spoke slowly and deliberately, repeating each word as if they conveyed some peculiar meaning to his mind and some subtle charm to his senses.

" Nay, father," rejoined the young man, interrupting him, " you do not tell me how I can help her."

The good old priest — for good he was in spite of the strong natural man within him — turned on Dhamaphat a look partly of sorrow and partly of affection. Then, drawing towards him one of his mysterious books, he placed it on his head ; with his hands spread out to heaven, he gradually moved his body to and fro, until his gyrations became rapid and grotesque, uttering strange prayers and incantations. After a short time he began to prophesy, and said, in fitful spasms : " Thy father's days are numbered ; the long night for him is at hand ; fear not, this mountain flower will blossom in spring-time on thy bosom."

For more than an hour a cloud had darkened the sky ; the moment the priest had done prophesying, a ray of moonlight suddenly lighted up his pale face, and was re-flected from his smoothly shaven head like a luminous circle.

After gazing upon it for some ten minutes, Dhamaphat began to tremble, and turned deadly pale ; feeling that he was in the presence of a supernatural being, he once more prostrated himself, and withdrew. Some secret influence from the priest had for the moment benumbed into icy coldness and even indifference his ardent love for Smâyâtee.

It was almost dawn when he sought his couch for rest.

A DREAM OF THE NIGHT.

Meanwhile the prisoner Rama had had a plentiful repast, and was sleeping heavily, with fatigue and despair for a pillow, on the damp floor of his cell.

Towards morning a cold sweat broke out on his brow. He felt creeping over him an indefinable horror, a sort of nightmare, which he struggled in vain to shake off. He groaned, panted, and at length sat up with a tremendous effort.

In a niche in the wall he fancied he saw a pale, blue, misty outline of a human figure, so indistinct that at first he could only distrust his own vision, but gradually it began to take form ; at length it was as clear and palpable as a shape of life. It was the face and figure of the priest P'hra Chow Sâduman, whom he had met a year ago in the mountains of P'hra Batt. He was dressed in a loose robe of cloudy yellow ; his legs were crossed, his arms folded across his breast, his eyes cast down ; he seemed to be praying. The shadow of the shade in the background grew darker, and the form grew lurid, as if surrounded by fire.

Rama stared, rubbed his eyes ; plainer did the figure of the priest appear, until it seemed to rise and swell and fill the whole cell. A dark, heavy mist settled on the prisoner's face, but the apparition grew brighter. He could bear it no longer ; shuddering with horror, he cried : "Speak, whoever thou art, and tell me thy commands ; they shall be obeyed."

Suddenly he felt a violent shaking of the ground on which he was seated ; each moment he expected to be hurled into an abyss below; he clung to the earth, and cried again: "Speak! For by the gods Dâvee and Dhupiyâ I vow to fulfil thy behest, even if it be to offer thee a human sacrifice."

He then perceived a soft cloud filling the cell, and in the centre of the cloud were luminous characters, which he read thus : " Sell not thy daughter to the duke."

The apparition vanished almost as soon as he had deciphered the words. Rama fell back against the wall of his cell, and awoke.

It was long before he could collect his scattered faculties, and what were left to him seemed steeped in illusion; he could only wonder, and bow in mystified adoration before the niche in his cell.

CHAPTER XI.

THE HEROISM OF A CHILD.

IT was morning. All were assembled once more in the great hall, eager for a termination of their work.

Fresh troops of men to be enrolled and branded arrived every moment.

Then came Nai Dhamaphat; the Kromathan, or overseer; and lastly the Grand Duke, followed by an army of slaves, attendants, scribes, and cup and punka bearers. As he looked about him he saw, with a gleam of satisfaction, the veiled figure seated at her post, guarded by Amazons.

After a few minutes of conversation with the scribe who sat at his side, he ordered the prisoner Rama Singalee to be brought in.

No one remembered when the old, white-headed stranger was ushered in. But every one heard the wild cry of joy that seemed to die away on the lips of the strange girl, as, throwing off her saree, she sprang across the hall, and clasped the old man about the neck. After the first paroxysm of joy was over, she realized that her father was a prisoner; she looked still hopefully into his face, but, seeing no light there, laid her head upon the fetters that bound his feet, as if the iron had entered into her very soul.

Dhamaphat started, as if struck, and gazed sadly at the girl and her father.

Never scene so touching had been presented in that hall before. It arrested every eye, and filled every heart with sympathy; and it was no wonder, — the girl was a creature such as that country had never before produced.

Her beauty was of the purest Indo-European type, rich brown complexion, delicate almond-shaped eyes, finely arched eyebrows, nose almost Greek in the purity of its outlines. Her feet, which had never worn either sandals or shoes, were large and perfect in shape; her arms, slender as those of a very young girl, were set off to great advantage by the metallic and glass bangles she wore; her rich black hair hung in long braids over a coarse blue bodice, which revealed a form of faultless proportions; on her breast, suspended by a yellow cord, was a flat silver ring, on which some mystic characters were inscribed.

The wondrous beauty of the prostrate girl filled the father and the son first with pleasure, then with fascination, afterwards with rapture; drawn on by irresistible steps, they both arrived, unknown to the other, at that stage of passion which blinds the sensibilities to everything else.

But the desire of one was to possess, the other to rescue.

The old soldier did not attempt to raise his daughter, but, taking off his turban, buried his face in it.

The duke was transported, stupefied; he paused, hesitated, then, suddenly, without knowing what moved him, he said, in a gentle, tender voice: "Why, girl? Raise up your head. See! your father is now going to be set free."

Smâyâtee lifted up her head, and looked at the speaker with an expression of childlike gladness and trust that brought to the heart of the wretch before her the long-lost sense of shame, and he could not for the moment give utterance to the iniquity he was about to perpetrate against her; he beckoned to an attendant, however, a sort of treasurer, with a heavy box, who approached, crawling, and at his instructions counted upon the floor forty pieces of gold, — sixteen times the value of an ordinary slave-woman.

Rama still covered his face with his turban, so that none could have told what was passing within him. His daughter laid her hand upon his arm, saying: "O, my father, the good duke gives us all this gold and promises us freedom! take it, and thank him, that he may permit us to return home."

The unhappy Rajpoot turned a look full of mournful tenderness upon his child. At the same moment the scribe, who had been industriously writing, laid a paper before him, and said, in rather an authoritative manner: "Tham Khai khat thedeo" (make the sale good, i. e., sign the paper).

Even now it did not occur to the girl what the paper and the forty pieces of gold meant.

To her mind they brought visions of freedom, as her heart yearned for the hills and groves of her native land. She once more whispered to her father to "take the money, and thank the duke, that he may let us go back home."

But the old man looked at her in silence, seemingly unable to utter a single word; his breathing came quick and hard, and all at once he gasped out: "The gods forbid me to sell my daughter to thee, my lord. Indra, Agni, and the Maruts, at whose roaring every dweller upon earth trembles, forbid me. O, pardon thy servant, my lord, and let us depart hence in peace."

The duke was doubly enraged, because of his last night's promise and the forty pieces of gold with which he had hoped to bribe him into an easy parting with his child. He turned to the bewildered Smâyâtee, and said: " Come hither, girl." But as she only looked at him, and made no attempt to go nearer, he added: " One thing is certain; this old fool, thy father, is still drunk, and knows not his mind; he sold you to me last night, and now he refuses, saying the gods forbid it."

A YOUNG SIAMESE NOBLEMAN.

Smâyâtee turned from the duke to her father, her look changing from incredulity to surprise, from surprise to anguish, while the duke continued: "Now it is you who must decide for him; shall I hand him over to the royal judges to be tried and executed for the crime he is accused of, or will you consent to be my slave for life? I will make you rich and happy, and I will give him this gold, and he shall return in safety to his home."

He uttered these sentences in a loud, harsh voice, very different from that in which he had spoken to her a few minutes before.

When he had finished, the crowd cheered the speech.

The girl looked at them, and, not knowing why, began to cry.

This exasperated the duke.

He blew a small silver whistle; instantly a band of armed men entered the hall, and he gave orders that the prisoner should be conveyed to the supreme court to be tried for attacking the chief officer of the royal guard, with intent to murder him, while he was on duty.

At this instant the girl seemed to take her resolution; she crawled up to the savage duke's feet, laid her head down upon them and kissed them, saying: "I consent to be thy slave, my lord. O, give not my father up to the king's officers."

The duke countermanded his orders.

"Yes," said she, her face suddenly transfigured, beaming with the twofold radiance of beauty and nobility of soul, "strike off his chains, and let him go free, dear, good lord."

There were no longer any arms being pricked with lancet-shaped needles. There were no longer any scribes enrolling the people's names. There were only fixed eyes, listening ears, and beatings of sympathetic hearts. The crowd was dimly conscious of the sublimity of the

5 *

act; they were thrilled, awed, as much by her beauty as by the simplicity of her heroic self-sacrifice.

But Dhamaphat, who felt more deeply than the rest, noted how suddenly she had overcome her horror, how readily she had sacrificed herself for her father, and thought he saw in her face the effulgence of a heavenly light.

The order was given, and the Rajpoot was free. One final embrace, one look of triumph and despair from the girl, and she was led away by some female attendants.

Rama disappeared in the crowd, regardless of the gold, and the paper which his daughter had signed.

The work of branding and enrolling went on again, and the red light of the noonday sun shone upon the walls of the palace as if no young heart had been broken within its halls that day.

Dhamaphat left his work and went away, cursing the old priest, his tutor, and himself, in the impotency of his rage and sorrow.

CHAPTER XII.

THE INTERIOR OF THE DUKE CHOW P'HAYA MAND-
TREE'S HAREM.

EVERY harem is a little world in itself, composed entirely of women, — some who rule, others who obey, and those who serve. Here disinterestedness vanishes out of sight. Each one is for herself. They are nearly all young women, but they have the appearance of being slightly blighted. Nobody is too much in earnest, or too much alive, or too happy. The general atmosphere is that of depression. They are bound to have no thought for the world they have quitted, however pleasant it may have been; to ignore all ties and affections; to have no care but for one individual alone, and that the master. But if you became acquainted with some of these very women under favorable conditions, — very rare, however, — you might gather glimpses of recollections of the outer world, of earlier life and strong affections, of hearts scarred and disfigured and broken, of suppressed sighs and unuttered sobs, that would dispose you to melancholy reflections and sad forebodings, and, if you were by nature tender, to shedding of tears. Their dress and manners often betray all sorts of peculiarities, and yet all is harmonious outwardly. They are unconscious of the terrible defacement they have undergone. Yet it sometimes happens that this same little world has its greatness, and always when a woman becomes a mother her life changes; she passes from the ignoble to the noble; then she becomes pure, worthy, honorable.

The wall that surrounded the duke's palaces and

temples enclosed also about five hundred houses, with gardens and artificial lakes and fountains and aviaries. Most of the houses were built of solid masonry, with here and there a theatre of carved wood ; the streets were narrow, and the covered bazaars in no way remarkable except for the shops of female jewellers, gold and silversmiths. All the palaces and temples faced the river. The oldest Hindoo temple stood here, beside a Buddhist temple and monastery, from which the priests who officiated in the duke's household were supplied. The most remarkable edifice, however, was the duke's tower, or summer-house, of four lofty stories, opening all round into arches, made entirely of carved wood, and richly gilt. It commanded a magnificent view of the river, and overlooked more than one half of the city of Bangkok. When you mount the highest chamber, you open your eyes upon a scene too solemnly and mysteriously beautiful to be adequately described. You seem to be midway in the air, looking down upon a city of temples and palaces, gardens, lakes, minarets, pagodas and p'hra-chai-dees ; thousands of boats glide noiselessly over the silver floor that winds on forever. The great height hushes out even the joyous voices that are hushed nowhere else. In the gloom at the upper end of the river many a boatman, perched on the prow of his boat, seems like the Angel of Death guiding some helpless passenger to the silent shore. And overhead the sky looks like some blue door, such as must lead straight into heaven.

In every ducal or royal harem there are a great many buildings designed and built for the express purpose of training and educating the women, and every girl has to go through certain forms and observances before she is admitted among the favored ones.

The female teachers, physicians, and judges, who are placed over them, generally receive a careful professional education,—the best the country can supply. Mere children are often taken into these places and trained to be actresses, dancers, musicians, and singers.

Every department has a superintendent, who is generally a lady of high rank, and is responsible to the duke only.

The mode of teaching in the schools is peculiar; no books are used by the pupils, who are placed in rows, with female officers in attendance to administer the rattan in all cases of inattention. The teacher either reads or sings the first line of a poem, or plays the first bar of an air; the head pupil repeats it after her, and so on to the last girl in the class; then all together, until they have learned it by heart. Dancing and gymnastics are taught in the same way.

Often a hundred different airs and poems are committed to memory by very young girls, who are thus converted into walking libraries.

Smâyâtee was led into the adytum of the duke's palace, conducted to a small chamber, and left there; while her guards betook themselves to their dinner. Very soon, the rumor of her great beauty having spread, nearly all the lovely girls in the harem rushed in to get a glimpse of her; but finding her closely veiled, and that no persuasion could prevail with her to uncover her face, they gradually departed, one young woman only remaining behind, sitting apart in silent sympathy.

After a while two female physicians came in, talking in low tones one to the other. They then proceeded to question the girl, and to all of their questions she returned modest replies; after they were satisfied they bade her unrobe, which she did with some little hesitancy. When she laid aside her veil, her eyes met those of her silent visitor; an indescribable something beamed from every feature of the stranger, and they became friends.

The physicians then examined the girl, just as if she were an animal; having finished their inventory of her perfections and imperfections, they dropped a few pleasant words, and departed. Smâyâtee had no sooner dressed herself and taken her place close to her new friend, and they had in the brief moment exchanged names, when another batch of women appeared, and told her to follow them. She rose, and went out, holding her new friend's hand. After passing through a dark and silent street, they brought her to a marble building, with baths and fountains all round it. Here she was again told to undress, and take her place on a marble couch. With her eyes she pleadingly besought her friend to stay, who did so, seated, leaning against a pillar. The bathers then anointed Smâyâtee's person with a fragrant preparation; when she was completely besmeared they suspended their labors, in order to let the stuff dry on the poor girl, who knew no more what was going to be done to her than if she had been a little kitten; and as she sat there, her skin glowing and her heart palpitating, she heard herself discussed by the bathers, whose language she only partially understood. But she heard enough to realize the life in store for herself. After half an hour they seized her again, rubbed off briskly the dried paste, and showered buckets of hot and cold water upon her. Another set of women now took charge of the poor girl, and dressed her in beautiful silk robes, like those worn by the Loatian women of high rank. Her hair was combed, perfumed, and ornamented with flowers, finally she was conducted to a pretty little house, luxuriously fitted up, and left in the charge of a number of female slaves.

Smâyâtee now wore a new veil of Indian gauze, but she would rather have kept the old one. She cowered down in a corner, and laid her tired head in the lap of her new friend, who began patting and soothing her, without uttering a single word.

Most girls, as soon as they have overcome the horror which such a life must naturally inspire in the young and enthusiastic, begin to calculate on their chances of promotion to the highest place in the harem. As for Smâyâtee, no thought but of escape presented itself to her mind; her nature was too wild and untamed to be flattered by the luxuries that now surrounded her; she looked upon them only as so many fetters. All kinds of wild plans for running away took violent possession of her brain; but the soothing influence of the bath, combined with the exhaustion of the day, overcame her, and she was soon sound asleep.

CHAPTER XIII.

A NIGHT OF MYSTERIES.

MAI CHANDRA, Smâyâtee's new friend, redoubled her tenderness and sisterly love for the poor, forlorn girl when she found that she was asleep. As midnight approached, she gently placed her head on a cushion, and then went home to her supper, deeply in love with the beautiful stranger.

The Duke Chow P'haya Mândtree's pavilion was thronged, as usual, with courtiers and nobles. All manner of attractions and diversions were there. The duke himself, partly intoxicated, sat amidst them, boasting of the rare purchase he had made that day : " She is so beautiful," said he to one of his boon companions, " that she inspires me as this glass of English brandy does." And he filled and refilled the jewelled goblet out of which he drank.

This man, in his whole person, was a type of many who may be seen any day in Siam, — a human being sunk in the lowest depths of sensualism and savage barbarity. From his hair, which was a dull gray, his wrinkled brow, his livid lips and watery eyes, there breathed forth an atmosphere which would have repelled even the mother who bore him.

At one time it was his intention to have Smâyâtee brought into the pavilion, that his friends might judge of her beauty ; but, with his faculties already greatly enfeebled by the immoderate use of English brandy, he forgot his purpose.

At length the distant sounds of trumpets, conch-shells,

and the ringing of multitudinous pagoda-bells proclaimed
the last hour of day, — i. e. midnight. The nobles, courtiers, and friends retired and some elderly female attendants appeared; to them the duke gave orders to have the
new slave-girl conducted to the upper story of his summer tower.

The day had been hot and sultry; no clouds were to be
seen, except low on the eastern horizon, where they
stretched in lengthened ridges of gold and purple, like
the border between earth and sky.

As the women departed on their mission, a dark, heavy
mass of clouds rose in the black outline of the distant
hills. A sudden gust of wind, in fits and starts and
snatches, came sweeping up the river, and tossed its
waters wildly against the banks; then flashed incessant
lightnings, and the winds rang and roared as though they
heralded with joy the coming thunder-storm. Suddenly
the moon was blurred with clouds, and the tempest raged
outright. In the midst of the storm the poor terrified
girl was roused from her slumbers, led to the lofty chamber, and left alone, while the attendants retired to one of
the little alcoves to be in waiting.

Rama — who had that day made a circuit of the walls,
and had promenaded every nook and corner in the vain
hope of finding some means of getting, unseen, into the
duke's palace, had hired a boat, and was sailing wildly
up and down the river in front of it, laying desperate
plans of finding his daughter and carrying her off at
any risk and peril — was at the same moment, by one
mighty sweep of the water, dashed on the banks that
bounded on one side the gardens and temples of the palace. He staggered to his feet, and raised his head to the
dreadful sky. A sudden flash of lightning revealed the
gilded top of the lofty summer tower and the tapering
summits of the Buddhist and Hindoo temples.

H

With a dreadful purpose burning in his heart, he walked straight on to the latter building, which was dimly lighted, and stood open as if inviting him to take shelter under its sacred roof. He entered. Happy memories, every sweet emotion he had known, came crowding upon him, as he once more recognized, in the partial darkness, the faint outlines of the images of his long-forgotten gods, Dâvee and Indra and Dhupiyâ.

There is compensation in all things. He had lost his child, and found his gods. Joy and sorrow are bound up in every event of life, — even as opposite poles are inseparable in the magnet. The pity is that the night of trouble is at times so dark that the interwoven gold with which Providence relieves the woof of calamity remains undiscovered.

Thus it was with Rama; there was joy and sorrow in his heart as he bowed before the gods of his fathers, but there was hatred and revenge there too, mingled with dark and bloody thoughts.

"Life is now a useless gift, an insupportable burden," groaned Rama.

In how many lives there lurks a hidden romance or a hidden terror. No one was near to mark the secret workings of this terrible man's nature. He recalled his home on the hills of Orissa, the yearly sacrifice that his fathers had been wont to offer up on Dâvee's altar, and he suddenly resolved that he would himself be the sacrifice to his long-forgotten and neglected gods.

Only one person could have saved him from his rash purpose, and she was sitting up there alone, midway between earth and heaven. He slowly drew out from his cumberbund a glittering knife, and his expression became exultant as he felt its sharp edge.

Not all the gods, not all the love-lit eyes, not all the hills of Orissa, can move him from his purpose now. He

laid the knife upon the altar, and cried aloud to the insatiable Earth Goddess.

"O Dâvee, thou hast been unworshipped for years;
multitudes crowd thy sister temples, but thine they pass
unnoticed by. Behold my child now in the grasp of the
spoiler. Defend, preserve her, that her honor may shine
bright among men, and I will pour out to thee the life
of my heart. Drink of my blood, and be revenged on
the defiler of my house and my race."

Then, snatching up the knife, he waved it thrice over
his head, and thrust it into his side. Leaning forward, he
tried to picture his child's face, but could not for the light
that love threw around her, and the mist that death
wrapped round him; he drew nearer to his childhood's
God, and, drawing out the knife, fell down at its feet, turning up his face to it, reverently, lovingly; and there
was joy — joy of conscious strength, of victory — ming-
ling with the life-blood of the heart that was fast flowing
away forever.

It is two o'clock. The night is changed. The storms
and clouds and darkness are all dispersed. The blue sky
has thrown aside her veils, and the moon rides serenely
in limitless range, undimmed by a single fleck of cloud.
The very air breathes sweetness and perfume and peace.

But of all the mysteries of the night there is one yet
to be solved.

Smâyâtee still sits on one of the sills of the arches in
the topmost chamber of the summer tower, nearest to
where the women have retired out of sight. She hears
them whispering. She hears, too, some one slowly mount-
ing the stairs; the footsteps are heavy, and sound like
those of an aged man. She looks around to see if there
is any way by which she may escape. The tower has
but a single spiral stairway. She remains still and motionless. In a few minutes the sound of the footsteps

comes nearer; through the archway opposite, the totter-
ing figure of a dark, heavy man enters and approaches
her. In the dim light she looks up at him with a terror-
stricken, pleading face, daring neither to breathe nor speak;
she shrinks away to the other side, where the women are
in waiting. The duke, rather admiring her coyness,
laughs a drunken laugh, and attempts to follow her. In
crossing the threshold he stumbles. In trying to recover
his footing he is thrown back. His head strikes violently
against a massive gold spittoon.

A wild cry, and Smâyâtee rushes from her hiding-
place, springs across the prostrate figure, down the flights
of stairs, and through the labyrinths of flowering shrubs
and plants, to hide herself beside a low tank of water.

The attendants and slaves who were lying around
heard wild cries for help proceeding from the summer
tower, and hurried to the spot with lamps and lanterns.
All the piazzas, streets, gardens, and avenues are alive
with anxious faces and inquiring looks.

The duchess's fears are aroused. She too summons her
maidens with their lanterns, and sets out for the tower.

Suddenly she stops.

A few steps from her she sees an object dressed in
bright colors, crouching in a pool of rain-water by the
tank. She stooped to scrutinize the figure, and found it
was that of a young and strange girl. She bent over her
again, and said, gently, " Why art thou hiding here, my
child ? "

" I am afraid of him, dear lady," replied the girl, pointing to the lofty chamber.

" Afraid ! art thou, indeed ? " said she, a little coldly,
remembering the news of the day; "didst thou not sell
thyself to the duke in spite of thy father's wishes ? "

" O yes, I did, dear lady," replied Smâyâtee ; " but — "
and she began to cry bitterly, and could not say another
word for her tears and sobs.

The true woman triumphed in the "wife," for she put out her arms, and raised the forlorn stranger to her bosom, and comforted her with such words as women who have great and loving hearts only can. Then, confiding her to the tender care of her own women, she went on her way to find out the meaning of those dreadful cries.

Nai Dhamaphat, who had been watching in sadness and despair the marvellous expression of Nature's tears and smiles, was the first to mount the spiral staircase, to find his father in the last agonies of death. He takes him up gently, with the assistance of the women, and places him on his luxurious couch.

The duke is dead.

Everything is forgotten. He sees the pale face of the duchess, his mother, that silent woman, and, catching a glimpse of the bitter sorrow of that patient soul, who was so worthy of his father's love in her right of youth and beauty, — the foremost to love him, the last and only woman of all those whom he had wronged to mourn him, — he bows his head and weeps. The son and the mother are drawn closer than ever. They two had suffered in silence apart. Now they sorrowed together.

CHAPTER XIV.

"WEEPING MAY ENDURE FOR A NIGHT, BUT JOY COMETH IN THE MORNING."

A YEAR has passed since the occurrence of the fearful events here related.

The river in front of the palace is thronged with a numerous procession of gayly gilded boats and barges.

It is the morning after the cremation of the Duke Chow P'haya Mândtree.

The king, with sixty or more nobles and princes of the land, all armed and in regal attire, presides in the grand hall of the late duke's palace.

The duchess and her two sons, and a fair sprinkling of Siamese ladies and children, are here assembled. A vast number of serfs, soldiers, pages, and women are in waiting.

Around the deep embrasure formed by the windows in the massive wall, there ran a low seat, the space thus occupied being raised as a kind of dais above the general level of the floor. Here were seated on either side of the wall the principal officers, male and female, of the duke's household, headed by the priests of Brahma and of Buddha, who were to play a part in the important drama of the day.

The hall is hung with tapestry of the most original design, for the birds and beasts and flowers which are pictured there had surely never prototypes, unless in some lost geological formation, though patterns very like them seemed to be unanimously adopted as models by all the fair embroideresses of Siam.

In the middle of the dais were two ducal chairs of
state. On one was seated a young girl, very closely veiled,
on the other the young duke, now Chow P'haya Dhamaphat; over them is spread a canopy of white muslin, decorated with the sweetest white flowers.

The girl, beneath her white veil, thinks it all perfection,
and her eyes light up, and her cheeks burn, and her heart
beats in perplexing fashion; and Dhamaphat believes that
he alone holds the key to the temple of Elysium.

It is one of those rare occasions when the whole assembly is rapt in the regions of fancy.

The old priest, P'hra Chow Sâduman is there too, and
he often raises his eyes in admiration, and his heart in
prophecy of a propitious marriage. At length he begins
the grand, old, harmonious nuptial chant, and all the
priests of Buddha and of Brahma join in sonorous concert,
and through the canopy over the happy couple the typi-
cal waters of consecration, in which had been previously
infused certain leaves and shrubs emblematic of purity,
sweetness, and usefulness, are gently showered.

And now Smâyâtee's earnest friend, Mai Chandra, with
her tender mother-in-law, the duchess, conduct her, all
dripping, by a screened passage, to a chamber magnificent-
ly appointed, where she is divested of her former apparel,
and arrayed in robes becoming her now lofty station.

Then Chow P'haya Dhamaphat is ushered in. At the
moment of his entrance Smâyâtee rises to throw herself
at his feet, according to the custom of the country;
but he prevents her, embraces her in the European
manner, and presents her, standing upright by his side,
to his relatives, with which the ceremony for the day
terminates.

There is a general move towards the gateway by
which P'hra Chow Sâduman is to pass. All, even the
king, press to the front and fall on their knees to ask his

blessing. He blesses them in a broken voice; he is strangely moved to-day.

Yet another year, and in this same palace nowhere will you find a trace of either Dhamaphat, Smâyâtee, or the gentle duchess. A younger brother fills his place, and is lord over all, following closely in the footsteps of his late father.

Far away, near the suburbs of Bijree Puree, i. e. the Diamond City, stands a lovely little cottage, where the ex-duke, his mother, and his sweet wife reside. He has freely resigned all the splendor and state of his position for the quiet and peace of a country life; and nothing is wanting here. The grand old trees are dressed in tender green, and the bright sun touches with its golden-yellow light every nook and corner of the lovely scene around.

The cottage within is furnished partly in the European and partly in the Oriental style. There are here no slaves, but hired servants, who have an air of freedom, loyalty, and comfort about them very delightful to witness.

In an inner chamber is Smâyâtee, rocking a little boy to sleep in a rude Laotian crib, with a mystic Hindoo triform suspended over it, — she cannot make up her mind to put him into the European cradle which stands close by; she fears some secret evil influence may lurk about its pretentious aspect, — and the boy, with his finger in his mouth, looks at his mother as if he felt she was divinely beautiful, and could not bring himself to shut his dreamy eyes for the light upon her face.

Nai Dhamaphat has become a convert to the Roman Catholic faith, but his pagan wife cannot be persuaded to forsake the gods who have brought her so much happiness, to whom her father sacrificed his brave life, and therefore she has raised an altar in her nursery to Dâvee and Dhupiyâ and Indra. Her father's ashes, too,

SMÂYÂTEE.

rest here in a golden pagoda; but with the true, loving, tender veneration of her womanly nature, she has exalted over them all, in a niche on either side of the altar, an image of the Christ, and another of the Virgin Mary with her infant Son in her arms. These, in their symmetry and beauty, are to her the most beautiful of the gods upon her altar. In those porcelain images of the Christ, and the Mother with her tiny Infant, she feels that there is something higher, purer, loftier, than in the forms of her own dear gods, and she bows in worship, and trembles at the height to which her thoughts of that Mother and her Son elevate her soul.

Her religion, you can see at a glance, is not a gloomy one like that of her ancestors. There is a smile all over the chamber, and happiness all over her sweet face. Loving everything in her purity, worshipping everything in her humility, morning and evening she raises her eyes and her heart from those sombre old gods of hers to the tender ones of her husband; and this quiet pagan city has never before been lighted up with such a gleam of heaven upon earth as when her evening prayer bursts into song: —

> " To Thee are all my acts, my days,
>   And all my love, and all my praise,
>   My food, my gifts, my sacrifice,
>   And all my helplessness and cries.
>   Dâvee ! leave my spirit free,
>   And thy pure soul bequeath to me
> Unshackled. Let me in thine essence share,
>   Let me dwell in thee forever,
>   And thou, O Dâvee ! dwell in me."

6

CHAPTER XV.

THE FAVORITE OF THE HAREM.

THE morning on which his Majesty set out on his
annual visit to Pitchaburee was one of those which
occur in the climate of Siam at almost any season of the
year, but are seen in their perfection only in October.[15]
The earth, air, and sky seemed to bask in a glory of sunlight and beauty, and everything that had life gave signs
of perfect and tranquil enjoyment. Not a sound broke the
stillness, and there seemed nothing to do but to sit and
watch the long shadows sleeping on the distant hills, and
on the warm golden fields of waving corn.

Reluctantly quitting my window, I turned my steps
toward the palace, leaving all this beauty behind me in
a kind of despair; not that my temple school-room was
not in itself a delicious retreat, but that it always impressed me with a feeling I could never analyze; when
there, it seemed as if I were removed to some awful distance from the world I had known, and were yet more
remotely excluded from any participation in its real life.

Taking out my book, I sat down to await the coming of
such of my pupils as might not have accompanied the
king on his visit.

In the course of an hour, only one presented herself;
she was a young woman called Choy, a fair and very
handsome girl of about twenty summers, or perhaps not
so many, with regular features, — a very rare thing in a
Siamese woman; but the great beauty of her face was in
her large lustrous eyes, which were very eloquent, even in
their seeming indifference. Her hair, which was so long

that when unbound it covered her whole person, even to her feet, was tied in a large knot behind, and ornamented with the jessamine and Indian myrtle. She had a careless, and I might almost say even a wicked, expression in her face, which was slightly marked with the small-pox.

Choy was the youngest sister of the head wife (or concubine) Thieng, and had been my pupil for about six months. This morning she brought me a flower; it was a common wild-flower, that grew up everywhere in great profusion, making a lovely carpet, blossoming as it did in every nook and crevice of the stone pavements within the palace. It was just like her to snatch up the first thing that attracted her, and then to give it away the very next moment. But I received it with pleasure, and made a place for her at my side. She seemed to be out of humor, and, jerking herself impatiently into the seat, said abruptly: "Why don't you despise me, as all the rest of them do?" Then, without waiting for an answer, she went on to say: "I can't be what you wish me to be; I'm not coming to school any more! Here's my book! I don't want it, I hate English!"

"Why, Choy, what is the matter?" I inquired.

"I am tired of trying to do so much; I am not going to learn English any more," she replied.

"Don't say so, Choy," I said, kindly; "you can't do everything at once; you must learn by degrees, and little by little, you know. No one grows good or clever at once."

"But I won't learn any more, even to grow good and clever. There's no use, no one will ever care for me or love me again. I wish they had let me die that time," she continued. "Bah! I could kill that stupid old consul who saved my life. It were better to be quartered, and cast to the crows and vultures, than to live here.

Every one orders me about as if I were a slave, and treats me like a dog. I wish I could drown myself and die."

"But, Choy, you are here now, and you must try to bear it more bravely than you do," I said, not fully understanding the passionate nature of the woman.

"Mam," she said, suddenly, laying her hand upon my arm, "what would you do if you were in my place and like me ?"

"Like you, Choy ? I don't quite understand you; you must explain yourself before I can answer you."

"Listen, then," she said, passionately, "and I will tell you." [16]

"When I was hardly ten years old, — O, it seems such a long, long time ago! — my mother presented me, her favorite child, as a dancing-girl, to his Majesty. I was immediately handed over to that vicious old woman, Khoon Som Sak, who was at that time the chief teacher of the dramatic art in the palace. She is very clever, and knows all the ancient epic poems by heart, especially the Rāmāyānā, which his Majesty delighted to see dramatized.

"Under her tuition we were subjected to the most rigorous training, mentally and physically; we were compelled to leap and jump, to twist and contort our bodies, and bend our arms, fingers, and ankles in every direction, till we became so supple that we were almost like young canes of rattan, and could assume any posture the old hag pleased. Then we had to learn long passages from all sorts of poets by heart, with perfect correctness, for if we ever forgot even a single word, or did not put it in its right place, we were severely beaten. What with recitations, singing, dancing, playing, and beating time with our feet, we had a hard life of it; and it was no play for our instructress either, for there were seventy of us girls to be initiated into all the mysteries of the Siamese drama.

"At length, with some half-dozen of my companions, I was pronounced perfect in the art, and was permitted to enter my name among the envied few who played and danced and acted before the king.

"I would not have you think that the tasks imposed upon me were always irksome, or that I have always felt so depressed and unworthy as I do now. The study of the poets, and above all of the Rāmāyānā, opened to me a new world as it were ; and it was a great gain to have even this, with the half-smothered yearning for life in the outer world that it inspired. It helped me to live in a world of my own creation, a world of love, music, and song. Rama was my hero, and I imagined myself the fair and beautiful Sita, his wife. I particularly delighted to act that part of the poem describing Rama's expedition to Lanka* to rescue Sita from the tyrant Râwânâ, and their delicious meeting in the garden, where Rama greets her with those beautiful lines, —

'O, what joy ! abundant treasures
I have won again to-day,
O, what joy ! Of Sita Yanee †
Now the hard-won prize is mine.
O, what joy ! again thou livest, within this breast.
So mighty, armed with love, and with the wealth of heaven beyond ‡
Soon shall Sita, Indara's fairest daughter,
Stand by my side, as stands her matchless mother,
Aspārā, in heaven refulgent by the great Indara.'

"My face is slightly pock-marked I know ; but when painted and dressed in the court jewels I looked remarkably well as Sita, with my hair floating away over my shoulders and down to my feet, bound only by an exquisite crown of gold, such as Sita is supposed to have

* The Sanskrit name of Ceylon.   † Blessed.
‡ Highest heaven.

worn. On the very first occasion of my performing before the king I had to take part in this drama. As soon
as we had got through the first scene, the king inquired
my name and age. This set my heart beating in great
wild throbs all through the rest of the play. But after
this weeks passed by, and I heard nothing more from his
Majesty. He had forgotten me.

"I grew tired of reciting, and keeping time, and singing my sweetest songs for no one's amusement but that
of the old hag, who made me work like a slave for the
benefit of the rest of her pupils.

"I began to wish there would be some great *fête*
outside of the palace, where all the court, nobles and
princes, and the king, would assemble, and where I could
act Sita and sing like Narawèke,* and dance like Tha-
wadee.†

"Then father and mother might see me too, and O,
how pleased they would be! I thought. You do not
know how dull it is to be acting before women, and with
women only, dressed in robes of kings and princesses.
If it were only a real king, or a prince, or even a noble, it
would not be quite so bad; but all that mockery of love,
bah! it is too stupid. I was sick of my life. I wished
mother had kept me at home, instead of Chand. I could
then have done just what I had a mind to, and have been
just as gay and idle as she was.

"Well! the day came at last. I was all but sixteen
when that great and eventful day arrived. The *fête* was
in honor of the king's grandson's hair-cutting.

"Though I had performed several times at the court,
his Majesty had taken no further notice of me, and I was
sorely discontented with myself, piqued at the indifference of the king, and enraged against the old ladies, who
seized every opportunity to snub me, and take down my

---

* A famous singer.   † The goddess of motion.

pride, declaring that a pock-marked face was not a fit offering for the king.

"The longed-for day arrived at length. How elated I was! I had to represent the character of the wondrously beautiful Queen Thèwâdee in one of those ancient dramas of Maha Nagkhon Watt, whose beauty is said to have entranced even the wild beasts of the forest, so that they forgot to seize upon their prey as her shadow passed near them. My dress was of magnificent silk and gold, covered with precious gems; my crown was an antique and lovely coronet, one that had graced the brows of the queens of Cambodia. It was richly studded with rubies and diamonds. The first day of my rehearsal in this costume, all my companions declared that I looked enchantingly beautiful, that my fortune was made, and that, if I would only look and act thus, I could not fail to captivate the king. The bare idea of being elevated above my hateful old teacher, and above some of the proud women who domineered over me, half intoxicated me. In this mood I began to realize my future as already at hand, and, growing impatient with my doubts and fears, I sought at nightfall a crafty old female astrologer named Khoon Hate Nah. She took me into a dark and dismal cell underground, and, putting her ear to my side, numbered the pulsation of my heart for a whole hour; she then bound my eyes, and bade me select one of the dark books that lay around me. This done, she expounded to me my whole future, out of her mysterious book of fate, in which all my romantic visions of greatness were as clearly predicted as if the old fiend himself had revealed to her my secret and innermost thoughts. I was troubled only at one part of the old woman's revelations, which said, that, though I was destined to rise to the greatest honors in the realm, a certain malignant star which would greatly influence my destiny would be in ascen-

dency during the month of Duenjee,* and that if I neglected to pass the whole of that period in deep fasting,
prayer, and meditation, I should sink at once from the
highest pinnacle of my grandeur into the lowest and
most terrible abyss.

"I resolved that I would fast and pray for that entire
month every year of my life. How I wish now that I
had never consulted the old hag, because my confidence
in her predictions made me proud and defiant to the old
duennas, who are now my bitterest enemies!

"Alas! dear father and mother. It were better to
have cast your daughter Choy into the Mèinam than to
have given her to amuse a king.

"On the day of the *fête*, I awoke at five o'clock in the
morning, and began anointing my person with the perfumes and unguents provided for us at the king's expense.
I then spent the rest of the forenoon in making my hair
glossy and lustrous, which I did by rubbing it with the
oil of the doksarathe.† How I gloried and exulted to see
it floating away in long shining masses, waving over my
shoulders and covering my feet! The afternoon came,
and with it the old hags bearing my dress and the costly
jewels I was to appear in. They opened the box and
laid them before me. I had never seen anything so
beautiful. The boxes absolutely sparkled like the stars
of heaven in one blaze of light and beauty.

"When I saw these jewels I was seized with a fit of
temporary madness. I could not help skipping and dancing in a sort of frenzy about my chamber, saying all sorts
of absurd things and foretelling my future triumphs.
My slave-women looked on amazed at the wildness of
my spirits; and as for the old women who had the care
of robing me for the evening, they were wrathful and
silent.

* December.   † Flower of excellence.

A ROYAL ACTRESS.

" We were all ready at last. A small gilt chariot of a tower-like form, made of ivory and decorated with garlands and crowns of flowers, drawn by a pair of milk-white ponies, and attended by Amazons dressed superbly in green and gold, conveyed me, as the Queen Thèwâdee, to the grand hall where we were to perform. My companions, similarly attended, followed me on foot. His Majesty, the princes, and princesses, surrounded by all the courtiers, were already there. The king and royal family were seated on a raised dais under a tapering golden canopy.

" The moment the king saw me approach, my ponies led gently forward by Amazons, he rose and, before the whole court of lords and nobles and princes assembled, inquired my name of one of the duennas. This recalled me once more to his memory, for he said aloud, ' Ah ! we remember, she is the one who dances so beautifully.' O, what a moment of triumph that was for me! I felt as if my heart in its wild, ecstatic throbs would burst through its gorgeous fetters of silk and gold. I rose up in my chariot and bowed low before him three times. ' But, how now!' he exclaimed angrily, looking around ; ' where are the nobles who are to lead the ponies ? Let those Amazons fall back to the right and left.' In an instant there emerged from the crowd two most distinguished-looking noblemen, dressed in flowing white robes, threaded with gold and sparkling with gems ; they took their places beside the ponies on either side of my chariot. One was P'haya * Râtani, the other was a stranger to me.

" They did homage to me, as if I were a real queen, and stationed themselves at my ponies' heads.

" At this moment I was saluted with a burst of music and the curtain fell. P'haya Râtani bent his head close

* Duke.

6 *   I

to mine and whispered, 'How beautiful thou art!' I
turned a frowning look upon him for his presumption,
and replied, 'Have a care, my lord, a word from me may
be too much for thee'; but he immediately assumed so
humble and penitent an expression that I forgave him.
I was both flattered and piqued, however, at the other
nobleman's conduct; for though he looked admiringly at
me, he said not a word. I would have given my eyes if
it had been he who said I was beautiful; for there was a
majesty of youth, strength, and manly beauty about him
that made a blinding radiance around my chariot, and
excited an oblivious rapture in my heart. I panted, I
was athirst, for one word of recognition from him. At
length I became so vexed at his silence that I asked him
what he was looking at. He replied more cautiously
than his companion, 'Lady, I thought that I beheld an
angel of light, but thy voice recalls me to the earth again.'

"I was so enraptured at this speech, that I could hardly
contain myself. A flood of delight swept over me, my
breast heaved, my eyes glowed, my lips parted, my color
came and went through the maize-colored cream that
covered my face and concealed my only deformity.

"When the curtain rose, I, with this new life rushing
through my veins, looked triumphantly at the troop of
my companions who did me homage. This new existence
made me so joyous that I must have been beautiful.
Thus inspired I acted my part so wondrously well that a
deep murmur of applause ran throughout the hall. His
Majesty's eyes were riveted upon me in startled astonishment and evident admiration. I acted my part with a
keen sense of its reality, and gave utterance to the burning passion of my heart. As if I were really a queen, I
commanded my courtiers to drive away the suitors who
wooed me, declaring that anything beneath royalty would
stain my queenly dignity and beauty.

" But when the banished prince, my lover, appeared, I
rose hastily from my gilded and ivory chariot, and with
my hair floating round my form like a deep lustrous veil,
through which the gems on my robe shone out like
glorious stars of a dark night, I laid myself, like the
lotus-stem uprooted, prostrate at his feet. I pronounced
his name in the most tender accents. I improvised
verses even more passionate than those contained in the
drama : —

'Instantly I knew my lord, as the heat betrays the fire,
When through the obscuring earth unclouded
Shining out thou didst appear
Worthy of all joy ; my soul is wrung with rapture,
And it quivers in thy presence, as the lotus petals before a mighty wind.'

" The courtiers raised me up from the floor, and led me
back to the chariot. The prince, who was no other than
'Murakote,' took his, or more properly her, place beside
me, and the curtain fell. The play was over. With
nothing but the memory of a look, I returned to my now
still more dismal rooms. I disrobed myself of all my
glittering ornaments with a sigh, bound up my long,
shining hair, and sat down to enjoy the only happiness
left me, — my proud, swelling thoughts. I was just
losing myself in soft, delicious reveries, which illuminated as with a celestial light the whole world within me,
when I observed a couple of old duennas, who came
fawning upon me, caressing and praising me, while telling
me that his Majesty had ordered that I should be in attendance in his supper-chamber that evening.

" I listened in mute pain. The power of the new passion that now filled my heart seemed to defy all authority,
and the very thing for which I had so long worked and
longed had become valueless and as nothing to me. But
I dared not excuse myself, so I silently followed my con-
ductresses, and for the first time in my life ascended to
his Majesty's private supper-chamber.

" How changed I was! that which had been my sole ambition ever since I was ten years old came down upon me with a gush of woe that I could hardly have believed myself capable of feeling.

"I sat down to await the coming of the king; but I could have plucked out the heart that had rushed so madly on, casting its young life away at the feet of a man whose name even I did not know, whose face I had not seen till that day, but the tones of whose voice were still sounding through and through my quivering pulses.

"Well, my forehead, if not my heart, I laid at his Majesty's feet. ' I am your slave, my lord,' said my voice, the sound of which startled my own ears, so hollow and deceptive did it seem.

" ' Do you know how fascinating you were this evening?' said the king. ' Older by forty years than my father,' thought I, as, dissembling still, I replied, ' Your slave does not know.' ' But you were, and I am sure you deserve to be a queen,' he added, trying to play the gallant. ' My lord is too gracious to his slave,' I murmured.

" ' Why, Thieng!' he said, speaking to my eldest sister; ' why have you hidden this beauty away from me so long? Let her not be called Choy * any longer, but Chorm.' †
I would weary you if I tried to tell you how he praised and flattered me, and how before a week was over I was the proudest woman in the palace.

"I became a stranger to my dismal rooms in the street, to my slave-women as well as to my companions. I lived entirely in his Majesty's apartments, and it was only when he was asleep or in the council hall that I rushed down to plunge into the lotus-lake or to ramble in the rose-garden. But I never stopped to think. I would not give my heart a moment to reflect, not a moment to the past, not a moment to the future. I was intoxicated with

* Surfeit.   † Delight.

the present. Every day gifts rare and costly were brought
to me from the king; I affected to despise them, but he
never relaxed his endeavors to suit my taste, to match
my hair and my complexion. The late proud, insolent
favorite, who used to order us girls about as if we were
dogs, knelt before me, as half from *ennui* and half from
coquetry I feigned illness and inability to rise from my
master's couch. I cannot tell you how well I acted my
part; I was more daring than any favorite had yet been.

"In the tumult and excess of the passion I felt for a
stranger, I was able to make the king believe that he was
himself its object; and he was so flattered at my seeming
admiration and devotion, that he called me by the tender
name 'Look" (child), and indulged me in all my whims
and fancies.

"But at length I grew tired of so much acting, and the
intensity of my manner began to flag. I complained of
illness in order to escape to my own room, where I flung
myself down upon my leather pillow, and drove my teeth
through and through it in the after-agony that my falseness
brought upon me. I was worn with woe, more than wasted
by want of food. My sister observed my paleness, and said,
half in earnest and half in jest: 'Don't take it so much to
heart, child; we have all had our day; it is yours now, but it
can't last forever. Remember, there are other dancing-girls
growing up, and some of them are handsomer than you are.'

"'What do you mean?' I retorted, fiercely; 'do you
suppose I am sorrowing because of my grandfather?
Bah! take him, if you want him.' 'Hush, child,' she
replied, 'and don't forget that you are in a lion's den.'

"'Lion or tiger,' I said, laughing bitterly, 'I mean to
play with his fangs, even if they tear my heart, until I
am rich as you at least.' 'Do you, indeed?' she rejoined.
'Be quick, then, and give him a p'hra ong.'* With that

* Sacred infant.

she left me to my own wild, bitter, maddening, condemning self.

"Months of triumph, rage, agony, and despair wore away, and my day was not over   I was acknowledged by all to be the wilful favorite 'Chorm.' In the mean time I had one ray of comfort.   I found out the name of the man I loved, from a new slave-woman who had just entered into my service. It was P'haya P'hi Chitt. That very day I took a needleful of golden thread and worked the name into a scrap of silk which I made into an amulet and wore round my neck. This greatly solaced me for a little while, after which I began to crave something more.

"The new slave-woman who had entered my service, just because I was the favorite, seemed so kind and attentive, and was such a comfort to me, whenever I rushed to my rooms for a respite, that I determined to employ her in obtaining information of the outside world for me. 'Just to beguile me of my weary hours,' I said. She seconded the idea with great alacrity. 'To whose house shall I go first?' she inquired. 'O, anywhere,' I replied, carelessly; then, as if suddenly remembering myself, I said, 'O Boon, go to P'haya P'hi Chitt, and find out how the groom of the Queen Thèwâdee lives in his harem.'

" When she returned, which was close upon nightfall, I was impatient to hear all she had to tell me; but after she had told me all, I became more impatient and restless still. Her face lighted up as she expatiated on the manly beauty of P'haya P'hi Chitt, and her voice trembled slightly — she did it on purpose, I thought — as she went on to say that ever since the day he had met the lovely Thèwâdee he had become so changed, and had grown so melancholy, that all his dearest friends and relatives began to fear some secret distemper, or that some evil spirit had entered into him. This was ample food for me for months. It comforted me to think that he shared my misery.

"Then I drooped and languished once more, and began to long for some more tangible token of his love for me. I grew bolder and bolder, and the tender-hearted slave-woman sympathized with my passion for him. At last I sent her out with a message to him. It contained but two words, Kit-thung,* and he returned but two more, Rak-mak.†

"All this while I still visited the king, and was often alone with him; he continued to indulge me, giving me costly rings, betel-boxes, and diamond pins for my hair Every petition I made to him was granted. Every woman in the palace stood in awe of me, not knowing how I might use my power, and I was proud and wilful. My father was created a duke of the second rank in the kingdom, my brothers were appointed governors over lucrative districts. I had nothing left to wish for but a child. If I had had a child, I might have been saved. A child only could have subdued my growing passion, and given to my life a fairer blossom and a richer fruit than it now bears. At last, I don't know what put it into my head, but I began to solace myself by writing to P'haya P'hi Chitt every day, and destroying the letters as soon as they were written.

"My next step was to send one of these letters to him by Boon. He was very bold, and it makes my heart ache even now to think how brave and fearless he was. He wrote to me at once, and implored me in a depth of anguish and in words as if on fire to disguise myself in Boon's clothes, to quit the palace, and go out to meet him. I burnt the letter as soon as I had learned it by heart. My heart was set on fire; and I pondered over and over the proposition of my lover, until it became too fascinating for me to resist much longer.

"So I took Boon into greater confidence than ever, put

* I remember. † I love much.

a bag heavy with silver into her hands, and, moreover,
promised her her freedom if she would assist me to escape.
'Keep the silver till I ask you for it, lady,' she replied,
'but trust me to help you. I will do it with all my
heart.'

"Her devotion and attachment surprised me. It could
not have been greater had she been my own sister. Poot-
tho!* could I have seen the end I would have stopped
there. I saw nothing but the face that had kindled a
blinding fire in my heart.

"The faithful Boon served me but too well. It was all
arranged that I should go out at the Patoo-din† the next
evening at sunset, with my hair cut off, and disguised as
Boon. P'haya P'hi Chitt was to be there with a boat
ready to convey us to Ayudia, and Boon was to remain
behind until the whole thing should have blown over.
This last was her own proposition. I tried in vain to
urge her to accompany us in our flight. She said it would
be safer for us both to have a friend in the palace, who
could give us information of whatever took place.

"In the agitation in which I wrote these last instructions to my lover, I made so many blunders that I had to
write the letter all over again. Boon implored me to put
no name to it, for we still feared some discovery. I gave
it, sealed with my ring, to Boon, who carried it off in great
delight; and I laid myself down upon my couch to dream
of an overflowing happiness. In the blessedness of the
great love that absorbed every feeling of my heart, I loved
even the king, whom I had most injured and deceived,
with the loving devotion of a child.

"In the midst of my ecstatic dreams I fell asleep, and
dreamed a dream, O, so different ! As plainly as one sees
in broad daylight, I saw myself bound in chains, and
P'haya P'hi Chitt flung down a dreadful precipice.

---

* Pitiful Buddha.   † Gate of earth.

"My chamber door was thrown rudely open, I was seized by cold hands, harsh voices bade me rise, and I opened my eyes upon that woman who is called by us Mai Taie.* There was Boon, tied hand and foot, lying before my door. It was all over with us. 'If I could only save him,' was my only thought.

"They were putting chains on my hands, and jostling me about; for so benumbed and prostrated was I at the sight of Boon that I could not rise. I did not dare to ask her a single question for fear of implicating ourselves all the more, when my sister Thieng rushed into my room screaming, flung herself upon my bed, and clasped me around the neck.

"'Hush! sister,' I said. 'Make these women wait a little, and tell me how they came to find it out.'

"'O Choy, Choy!' she kept repeating, wringing her hands and moaning piteously.

"'Sister Thieng, do you hear me? I don't care what they do to me. I only want to know how much you know, how much *he* knows.'

"'A copy of a letter you wrote to some nobleman was picked up about an hour ago, and taken to the chief judge. She has laid it before the king.'

"Then, if that is all, he does not know the name,' I said with a sigh of deep relief.

"'Ah! but he'll find it out, sister,' said Thieng. 'Throw yourself upon his mercy and confess all, for he still loves you, Choy He would hardly believe you had written the letter.'

"'Has Boon said anything?' I next inquired.

"'No, not a word, she is as silent as death,' said my sister. 'But where did you get her? Who is she? She was taken on her return, because you had mentioned your slave Boon in your letter. Now I must leave you

---

* Mother of death, or female executioner.

and go back to the king,' said my sister. Then, weeping and abusing poor Boon, she went away.

"Boon and I were chained and dragged to the same cell you visited the other day.

"As soon as we were left alone, I asked Boon if she had confessed anything. 'No, my lady,' she replied with great energy, 'nothing in this world will make me confess aught against P'haya P'hi Chitt.' At the instant it flashed upon me that this woman, whoever she was, also loved him, and I looked at her in a new light. She was young still, and well formed, with small hands and feet, that told of gentle nurture.

"'Boon, châ,' * said I, in great distress, 'who are you? Pray, tell me, it is of no use to conceal anything from me now. Why are you so happy to suffer with me? Any one else would have left me to die alone.'

"'O my lady!' she began, folding her hands together as well as she could with the chains on them, and dragging herself close to me, 'forgive me, O, forgive me! I am P'haya P'hi Chitt's wife.'

"I was silent in amazement. At length I said, 'Go on and tell me the rest, Boon.'

"'O, forgive me!' she replied, humbly. 'I cried bitterly the night he returned from the grand *fête* because he told me how beautiful you were, how passionately he loved you, and that he should never be happy again until he obtained you for his wife. He refused to eat, to drink, or to sleep, and I vowed to him by my love that you should be his. But I found you were the favorite, and that it would be a more difficult task than I had at first thought; so rather than break my promise to my husband, nay, lady, rather than meet his cold, estranged look, I sold myself to you as your slave. Every ray or gleam of sunshine, every beautiful thought that fell from your lips, I treas-

* Dear.

ured up in my heart and bore them daily to him, that I might but console my noble husband. You know the rest. If I deceived you, it was to serve both you and him, while my heart wept to think that I was no longer beloved. Gifted with unnumbered virtues is my husband, lady; and my heart, like his shadow, still follows him everywhere, and will follow him forever.'

"I was so sorry for Boon, I had not the heart to reproach her. I crept closer to her, and, laying my head on her bosom, we mingled our tears and prayers together. And I marvelled at the greatness of the woman before me.

"Next morning — for morning comes even to such wretches as my companion and me — we were dragged to the hall of justice. The king did not preside as we had expected. But cruel judges, male and female, headed by his Lordship P'haya Promè P'hatt and her Ladyship Khoon Thow App. Not knowing what charge to make, they read the copy of my letter over and over again, hoping to guess the name of the gentleman to whom it was sent. Failing to do this, they subjected Boon to a series of cross-questionings, but succeeded only in eliciting the one uniform reply, 'What can a poor slave know, my lords?'

"Her feet were then bastinadoed till the soles were raw and bleeding. She still said, 'My lords, be pitiful. What can a poor slave know?'

"After a little while, Khoon Thow App begged Boon to confess all and save herself from further suffering. Boon remained persistently silent, and the lash was applied to her bare back till it was ribbed in long gashes, but she confessed not a word. At last the torture was applied to her thumbs until the cold sweat stood in great drops on her contorted and agonized brow; but no word, no cry for mercy, no sound of confession, escaped her lips. It was terrible to witness the power of endurance that sustained this woman. The judges and executioners, both male and female, exhausted their ingenuity in the vain attempt to make her betray the name of the man to whom she had carried the letter; and finally, when the lengthening shadows proclaimed the close of day, they departed, leaving me with poor Boon bleeding and almost senseless, to be carried back by the attending Amazons to our cell.

"I tried to comfort poor Boon. She hardly needed comfort; her joy that she had not betrayed her husband was even greater than her sufferings.

"Another day dawned upon us. Boon was borne in a litter, and I crept trembling by her side, to the same hall of justice. Boon was subjected once more to the lash, the bastinado, and the thumb-screws, till she fell all but lifeless on the ground. It was all in vain; that woman possessed the heart of a lion; if they had torn her to pieces, she would not by the faintest sound have betrayed the only man she had loved in her sad life.

"The physicians were sent for to restore her to life again. She was not permitted the luxury of death. Then, when this was over, they bound up her wounds with old rags, gave her something to revive her, and laid her on a cool matting. My turn came, and her eyes fixed themselves upon me with an intensity that fairly made me shiver. They seemed to cry aloud to my inmost soul, saying as plainly as lips could speak, 'What is suffering, pain, or death, compared to truth? Be true to yourself. Be true to your love. If you love another, you love not yourself. Flinch not. Bear bravely all they can inflict.' I shuddered as the judges began to question me, but I shuddered more whenever I met Boon's eyes, so fixed, so steadfast, so earnest, so appealing. I prevaricated. I told the judges lies. 'That letter was written as a joke to frighten my youngest sister.

I was only playing. I know no man in the world but my father and brothers and my gracious master the king.'

"My sister was summoned. If I could have spoken with her, she might have helped me in my strait; but the women who were sent to bring her questioned her before she knew what they were about, and she plainly exposed my lies to the judges.

" A messenger was despatched to the king. The judges feared to proceed to extreme measures with me, who had so lately been the plaything of their sovereign. After half an hour's delay the instructions were received, and I was ordered to bare my back. A feeling of shame prevented me. I would not obey. I resisted with what strength I had. 'You may lash me with a million thongs,' I said to them, ' but you shall not expose my person.' My silk vest was torn off, my scarf was flung aside, my slippers were taken from my feet. My arms were stretched and tied to a post, and thus I was lashed. Every stroke that descended on my back maddened me into an obdurate silence. Boon's eyes searched into my soul. I understood their meaning. My flesh was laid open in fine thin stripes, but I do not remember flinching. My feet were then bastinadoed, and I still preserved, I know not how, my secret. Then there was a respite, and they gave me something to drink.

" In fifteen minutes I was once more exhorted to confess. The judges, finding me still unsubdued, ordered the thumb-screws to be administered. Not all the agonies, not all the horrors I have ever heard of, can compare with the pain of that torture. It was beyond human endurance. 'O Boon, forgive me, forgive me !' I cried; ' it is impossible to bear it.' With Boon's eyes burning into my soul, I gasped out the beloved name. Boon threw up her arms, gave a wild shriek of terror, and became insensible.

" I was released from further punishment. Two of
the pha-koons * were despatched for P'haya P'hi Chitt.
He was betrayed to the king's officers for a heavy reward,
and before noon was undergoing the same process of the
law. When Boon was once more brought to life, she
saw her husband in the hands of the executioners. She
started upright, and, supporting herself on her rigid arms
and hands, cried out to the judges and to Koon Thow
App : ' O my lords ! O my lady ! listen to me. O, believe
me ! It was all my doing. I am P'haya P'hi Chitt's
wife. It was I who deceived the Lady Choy. It was I
who put it into his head. Did I not ? You can bear
testimony to my guilt ! ' An ineffable smile beamed on
her pale lips and in her dim eyes as they turned towards
her husband.

" There was profound silence among the judges.
P'haya P'hi Chitt, I, and even the rabble crowd of slaves,
listened to her with astonished countenances. There was
an incontestable grandeur about the woman. Khoon
Thow App, that stern and inflexible woman, had tears in
her eyes, and her voice trembled as she asked, ' What
was thy motive, O Boon ? ' There was no reply from
Boon. There was no need to torture P'haya P'hi Chitt.
He was chained and conveyed to the criminals' prison,
and we were carried back to our cell.

" The report of our trial and the confessions elicited
were sent to the king. That very night, at midnight, the
sentence of death was pronounced by the Secret Council
upon us three ; but the most dreadful part of all was the
nature of the sentence. Boon and I were to be quartered ;
P'haya P'hi Chitt hewn to pieces; and our bodies not
burned, but cast to the dogs and vultures at Watt Sah
Katè.†

* Sheriffs.

† The rite of burning the body after death is held in great veneration
by the Buddhists, as they believe that by this process its material parts

"My sister Thieng implored the king in vain to spare my life. My poor mother and father were prostrated with grief. As for Boon, she never uttered a single word, except, in answer to my inquiries if she were suffering much, she said very gently, 'Chan cha lah pi thort' (Let me say farewell, dear). Her pallor had become extreme, but her cheeks still burned; all the beauty of her spirit trembled on her closed eyelids. She appeared as one almost divine.

"On Sunday morning at four o'clock the faithful and matchless Boon was taken from our cell to undergo the sentence pronounced upon her and her husband. The day appointed for my execution, which was to be private, arrived, and I had no wish to live, now that P'haya P'hi Chitt and Boon were gone; but the women who attended me said that no preparations were as yet made for it. I wondered why I was permitted to live so long.

" After two weeks of cruel waiting to join my beloved Boon, I was removed to another cell, where my sister visited me, with the good Princess Somawati, her daughter, at whose earnest request, as I was told, the British Consul * had pleaded so effectually with the king that my life had been granted to his petition.

"Alas! it was Boon who deserved to live, and not I. I am not grateful for a life that is little better than a curse to me. God sees that I speak the truth. Woe still hovers over me. It is the doom of guilt committed in some former lifetime. I am an outcast here, and in this world I have no part, while every day only lengthens out my life of sorrow."

are restored to the higher elements. Whereas burial, or the abandonment of the body to dogs and vultures, inspires a peculiar horror; since, according to their belief, the body must then return to the earth and pass through countless forms of the lower orders of creation, before it can again be fitted for the occupation of a human soul.

* Choy's life was spared at the intercession of Sir Robert J. H. Schombergk, her Britannic Majesty's Consul at Bangkok. [17]

Here the poor girl broke off, laid her head on the table, and wept, as I never saw a human being weep, great tears of agony and remorse.

As soon as Choy left me, I hurried home and wrote down her narrative word for word, as nearly as I could ; but I encountered then, as always, the almost insuperable difficulty of finding a fit clothing for the fervid Eastern imagery in our colder and more precise English.

We became better friends. I maintained a constant oversight of her, and persuaded her gradually out of her griefs. She learned in time to take pleasure in her English studies, and found comfort in the love of our Father in heaven. Without repining at her lot, hard as it was, or boasting of her knowledge, but with a loving, humble heart, she read and blessed the language that brought her nearer to a compassionate Saviour.

RUNGEAH, THE CAMBODIAN PROSELYTE.

CHAPTER XVI.

MAY-PEÂH, THE LAOTIAN SLAVE-GIRL.

ON the evening of the 10th of August, 1866, I found myself suddenly and unexpectedly, and almost without being aware of it, involved in a conflict with the king, who thenceforth regarded me with distrust and suspicion, because I declined to affix my own signature to a certain letter which he had required me to write for him.

I began heartily to wish myself out of Siam, though still deeply interested and absorbed in my work of educating the prince, — the present King of Siam, — for I felt that, with regard to foreigners, there existed no laws and customs to restrain and limit the capricious temper and extravagant demands of the king, and I had everything, too, to fear from the jealousy with which certain royal courtiers and judges watched my previously growing influence at court. The heat of the day had been intense, the atmosphere was sultry and oppressive, and every now and then a low, rumbling sound of distant thunder reached my ears, while the parched trees and leaves drooped and hung their heads as if impatient of waiting for the promised rain. Nervous, and undecided what to do, I returned home, where I remained prostrated with a sense of approaching danger. From time to time I had had similar conflicts with the king, which very greatly disturbed my already too much impaired health. All manner of fears which the mind so prodigally produces on such occasions came crowding upon me that evening, and I felt, as I had never before, weighed down by the peculiar sadness and isolation of my life in Siam.

7   J

In this frame of mind I sat and pondered over and over again the only course remaining open to me, — to withdraw from the court, — when I was suddenly recalled to what was passing around me by what I at first imagined must be an apparition or some delusion of my own mind. I started up from the spot where for hours I had been seated like a statue, and, looking more attentively, perceived a pair of bright black eyes watching me with the fixedness of a basilisk, through the leaves of some flowering shrubs that grew over my window. My first impulse was to scream for help; but I was soon ashamed of my fears, and, summoning all my courage, I demanded, "Who is there ?"

"It is only me, your ladyship," said a strange, low voice. "I have been waiting here a long while, but your servants would not let me in; they say you have forbidden them to let any Siamese person enter your house after sunset."

"It is true," said I; "I don't want to see any one this evening; I am ill and tired. Now go away, and, if you have any business with me, come to me in the morning."

"P'hoodth thô !" said the woman, speaking still in the same low tones; "I am not a Siamese, and you do not know that I have rowed thirty miles against the tide to come and see you, or else you could not have the heart to send me away."[18]

"I don't want to know anything," I said a little impatiently; "you must go now, and you know it is not safe for you to be away from home at this late hour in the day."

"O lady ! do let me in; I only want to say one word to you in private ; please do let me in," whispered the woman, more and more pleadingly.

"Then say what you have to tell me at once, and from

where you are," I replied ; " there is no one here to over-hear you ; for I cannot let you in."

" Alas ! " said the voice, plaintively, as if speaking to herself, " I would not have come all this long distance but that I heard she was a good and brave woman, — some people indeed said she was not so, — still, I thought I would try her, and now she says she cannot let me in, a poor fugitive and desolate slave-girl like me ! O dear ! O dear ! "

" But I am afraid I cannot help you, whatever your trouble may be," I said more gently, touched by the woman's despairing tones. " The king is offended with me, and the judges know it, and I have no more influence with them now."

As I said this, the girl sprang through the window and came forward, and exhibited not only her bright eyes but her full figure and somewhat singular dress, for she was, as she had stated, not a Siamese, but a Laotian. She held her head erect, though her hands were clasped in the attitude of wild supplication. The symmetry of her form was enhanced by a broad English strap or belt which was buckled round her waist, and which had the effect of showing off her beautiful figure to the best advantage. She was unusually tall, and altogether a most pleasing-looking young woman.

The moment she stood before me she commenced talk-ing with a volubility and an amount of action which it would be almost impossible to describe. Her face became so animated, and her tears and sobs flowed so sponta-neously, that I stood bewildered, for, in truth, I had rarely seen so interesting and so natural a woman in Siam.

She watched my countenance during the whole time she was speaking, with the quickness of the native char-acter, and I began at length to suspect that she prolonged

her statements for the sole purpose of forming an idea of
her success, so that she might vary her line of action
according as circumstances revealed themselves; and
even while I had a glimmering perception of this, and
also that perhaps she was only acting, my interest in her
increased so rapidly that she became convinced in her
own mind, I think, of having gained my entire sympathy.

"Ah! I knew you had a kind heart," said the woman,
as she came forward with the graceful salutation of her
country, and laid a thick Oriental letter, enveloped in velvet and fastened with silken cords and sealed with English sealing-wax, at my feet.

She then dropped on her knees, and knelt before me in
an attitude of mute supplication.

I was never more embarrassed in my life, with that
mysterious letter, enveloped in crimson velvet, and written
on the outside in characters I had never before seen,
lying at my feet, and this woman kneeling there with
such strange, wild energy in her manner, such vehement
pleading in her dark, passionate eyes, imploring my aid in
a secret, daring scheme which I had neither the courage
nor the ability to undertake, nor yet the stoutness of heart
to refuse point-blank.

I therefore told the woman, with as much gentleness as
I could summon, that it was impossible for me to aid
her, and almost as much as my life was worth to become
the bearer of her letter to any prisoner in the palace. "It
is not for my own personal safety I fear so much, but for
my son's, whose young life depends on mine."

As I was speaking, the woman's face grew still and
cold, her features became rigid and fixed as stone, large,
dewy drops of perspiration broke out on her forehead, and
there fell upon her face such an expression of blankness
and utter desolation that I thought she was absolutely
dying from the pain of her disappointment.

This produced such a revulsion of feeling in me that I started from my seat in terror, and, taking her chilled, moist hands in mine, said, anxiously : " Does what I have said distress you so much ?   Why won't you speak ?   If there is any way by which I can help or comfort you, tell me.   Please tell me, and I 'll try to do my best for you."

The effect of this promise was immediate, but it was some time before the woman could recover her voice ; then, laying her hand upon my arm, she spoke hurriedly, but in the same soft, low tones and fervent manner.

" You have not asked me my name and who I am," she said.   " But I 'll tell you; I am sure you will not betray me, and it may be this is the last opportunity I shall have of serving my dear foster-sister."

As she uttered these words the hope and courage which had evidently been revived by the sympathy she saw in my face now seemed to forsake her ; tears and sobs burst from her afresh, and she crouched at my feet as if utterly overwhelmed with her grief.   At last, by a strong effort, she turned to me, and said : " My name is May-Peâh ; my home is in the city of Zienmai, i. e. Chiengmai ; my father, Manetho, is one of the most trusted councillors and friends, though a slave, of the Prince P'hra Chow Soorwang.[19]   My mother was a household slave in the family of the prince when my father obtained her for his wife, and I was only a month old when she was asked to be the wet-nurse and mother of the little infant daughter of the prince, whose wife had died in childbirth ; and thus it was that I became the life-long companion and friend and foster-sister of the young Princess Sunartha Vismita.   But alas ! dear lady, she is now, and has been ever since the death of her husband, the second king, a prisoner in the palace of the supreme king, and neither does her brother nor any one else know whether she is alive or dead.[20]

"This letter has nothing in it that will bring you into
any trouble. It is only one of greeting from her brother,
my master, the Prince O'Dong Karmatha. O, dear
lady, don't say no! the gods will bless and reward you,
if, sooner or later, you will put it into her hands; but it
must be done with the greatest caution and secrecy, and
it may be the means of saving her life. O, think of
that, of saving her life! for, if alive, she must be dying of
grief and pain to think that we have never yet replied to
a letter she sent us almost a year ago."

"And where is the prince, your master?"

"He is on a visit to the governor of Pak-lat."

Saying this, she almost instantaneously sprang out of
the window, and fled towards the river, as if conscious
of having delayed too long her return home; as she did
so, I noticed that she wore in the folds of her skirt a
small Laotian dagger attached to her English belt.

The storm which had been gathering in strength for
hours now burst forth, and for full three hours the
thunder and lightning and rain were the only things that
could be seen or heard; and I sat in the same spot, lost in
anxious fears for the safety of that solitary woman bat-
tling with the tremendous currents of the Mother of
Waters.

It was an awful night. Sick at heart, and full of natural
and unnatural fears, I locked up the letter at last in my
drawer, and tried to forget in sleep the disturbing events
of the day.

CHAPTER XVII.

AN ACCIDENTAL DISCOVERY OF THE WHEREABOUTS OF THE PRINCESS SUNARTHA VISMITA.*

FOR some time afterwards the mysterious letter remained locked up in my drawer, as nobody whom I knew seemed to be aware even of the existence of such a person as the Princess Sunartha Vismita, much less of her imprisonment in the palace, and I was afraid to open my lips on the subject before a stranger, lest I should inadvertently say something that might still more imperil her health and safety.

The king was once more reconciled to me, and had taken me into greater confidence than ever. Just at this time he was laid up with an illness which confined him to his topmost chamber, where I was summoned every day to write notes, or translate, with the help of the native female secretary, English documents into Siamese.

On one occasion, as I was at work in a room adjoining the royal bedchamber over a mass of perplexing manuscripts in the king's own handwriting, to be arranged for publication in the "Bangkok Recorder," the chief of the Amazons brought in the intelligence that the prisoner, Princess Sunartha Vismita, was very ill ; and, his Majesty being in the best possible humor, having just finished the above-mentioned manuscript, which completely refuted, as he fondly believed, Dr. Bradley's theory of Original Depravity, gave orders that the princess should take an airing in the palace gardens, and be removed to another

* See "The English Governess at the Siamese Court," p. 233.

cell, and that the chief lady physician should attend her without delay.[21]

The Amazon made haste to carry out her instructions, and I quietly left my desk to follow her.

I shall not attempt to enter into a particular description of the prison in the interior of this strange city. Indeed, it would be impossible to describe with any degree of accuracy so irregular and rambling an edifice. The principal features consisted of a great hall and two courts or enclosures, one behind the other, in which the prisoners were permitted to walk at stated times. Three vaulted dungeons occupied three sides of the enclosures; immediately below these were the cells already described in my former book.*

The upper cells were used more or less for the reception of women convicted of petty crimes, such as gambling, stealing, immodest language, etc. Besides these, there were other dungeons under the floor in various parts of the prison, some of them quite dark, and closed by huge trap-doors, designed for those whom it might be expedient to treat with peculiar severity. The prison was approached by two long corridors, opening into the courts; here were several small secret apartments, or cells, in which prisoners condemned to death, either by the Supreme Court or by the still more supreme will of the king, passed the last days of their existence. It was in one of these that the princess was confined.

The opening of the prison doors attracted, as usual, a crowd of idle slave women and girls, who hailed the slightest event that broke the monotony of their lives with demonstrations of the liveliest joy; and as I stood there a guard of Amazons appeared, marching in file, and in the centre was the Laotian princess, followed by two of her countrywomen. She did not seem to notice the

* See "The English Governess at the Siamese Court," p. 107.

general sensation which her appearance created, nor the eager curiosity with which she was regarded, but walked on wearing the depressed and wearied look of one who sought to meditate on her sorrows in silence and privacy. Her features were remarkably stern, however, and she moved along with a firm and steady step.

I followed with the crowd, who kept at a respectful distance.

When the procession arrived at one of the nearest gardens, laid out in the Chinese style, the princess, with a proud intimation that she could go no farther, took her seat on the edge of an artificial rock beside a small pond of water in which gold and silver fish sported merrily together. She hung down her head, as if the fresh air had no power to remove the smallest portion of her sorrows and sufferings.

A deep murmur of compassion now rose, not only from the idle crowd of women and girls, who gazed awe-stricken into her face, but from the " Amazonian Guard," those well-disciplined automatons of the royal palace of Siam.

I could see that she just raised her dark, sad eyes to us, and then cast them down again ; and that their expression, as well as that of her whole attitude, was one of mute and touching appeal against this most ungenerous usage.

After the lapse of an hour the procession resumed its course, and the crowd, who had by this time exchanged looks and whispers of sympathy to their hearts' content, — while some poor half-palsied and aged slave-women had lifted up their hands and prayed aloud for the happiness of the ill-fated princess, — brought up the rear, till they saw the same prison doors open and close once more on the noble lady and her attendants, when they dispersed to their various abodes.

7 *

When I returned home, the scene would constantly reproduce itself, and my thoughts would unceasingly revert to those sad eyes of which I had only caught a hasty glance; and that utter friendlessness, expressed in a few brief, slight actions, dwelt in my memory like the impressions of childhood, never to be wholly forgotten.

I could not help picturing to myself how those eyes would brighten if I could but put that letter into her hands, and tell her of one earnest friend at least whose love and sympathy knew no bounds.

This feeling at length urged me, now that with the restored favor of the king there could be no real danger to myself and my boy, to find some means of gaining access to the poor, sad prisoner.

I immediately put the letter into my pocket, and pinned it carefully there, and determined that after my school duties were over I would advise with my good friend Lady Thieng, of whom mention has already been made. Only one circumstance troubled my mind greatly, and it was how to broach the subject to her in the presence of the number of women who always attended her at all times and in all places.

CHAPTER XVIII.

LADY THIENG, THE HEAD WIFE AND SUPERINTENDENT OF THE ROYAL CUISINE.

LADY THIENG was a woman of about thirty, fair even to whiteness, with jet black hair and eyes; by nature enthusiastic, clever, and kind, but only partially educated when compared to many other of the cultivated and intellectual women of the royal harem.

She was the first mother, — having brought his Majesty four sons and eight daughters, — for which reason she was regarded with peculiar veneration and ranked as the head wife in the palace, the queen consort being dead. All these considerations combined entitled her to the lucrative and responsible position of superintendent of the royal cuisine.

She contrived to be always in favor with the king, simply because she was the only woman among all that vast throng who really loved him; though at no period of her life had she ever enjoyed the unenviable distinction of being the " favorite."

Her natural enthusiasm and kindliness of disposition made her generally loved, however; while, despite her immense wealth and influence, no woman's life had a truer and deeper purpose. She was always ready to sympathize with and help her suffering sisters, whatever their shortcomings might have been, or whatever the means she was obliged to resort to in order to render them the smallest assistance.

She reconciled all her little plots, intrigues, and deceptions to herself by saying: " Surely it is better for him not to know everything; he knows too much already, what with his Siamese and his English and his Pali and his Sanscrit. I wonder he can ever get to sleep at all with so many different tongues in his head."

It was after school that I accompanied one of my most promising pupils, the Princess Somawati, one of Thieng's daughters, to her mother's house. Being the head of the royal cuisine, Thieng had two houses. One was her home, where her children were born and brought up, — a quaint, stately edifice with stuccoed fronts, situated in the ladies' or fashionable part of the inner city, and in the midst of a pleasant garden. In the other, adjoining the royal kitchen, she spent the greater part of each day in selecting, overlooking, and sometimes preparing with her own fair hands many of the costly dainties that were destined to grace the royal table.

Thieng received me with her usual bright, pleasant smile and hearty embrace; to give me the latter, she put down her youngest baby, a boy about two years old, to whom I had, during my repeated visits to her house, taught a number of little English rhymes and sentences, and who always accosted me with, "Mam, mam, how do do?" or "Mam, make a bow, make a bow"; while he bobbed his own little head, and blinked his bright eyes at me, to the infinite delight of his mother and her hand-maids.

Little "Chai" settled himself in my lap, as usual, and the host of women, like children eager to be amused, gathered around to listen to our baby-talk; and great was the general uproar when Chai would mimic me in singing scraps of baby-songs, or thrust an orange into my mouth, or put on my hat and cloak to promenade the chamber, and say "How do do?" like a veritable Englishman; then his fond mother, in ecstasies of joy, would snatch him to her arms and cover him with kisses, and the delighted spectators would whisper that that boy was as clever as his father, and must surely come to the throne some day or other.

In the midst of these fascinating employments one of the lady-physicians was announced. Thieng retired at once with her into an inner chamber, carrying her beloved Chai in her arms, and beckoning me to follow her. Here she consigned Chai to me for further instruction in English, and laid herself down to be shampooed.

I felt that now was my opportunity; but I waited a little in order to make sure whether the doctor was to be trusted.

The ladies were silent for a little while; no word was spoken, with the exception of a sigh that now and then escaped from poor Thieng, partly to indicate the responsibilities of her position, and partly to show that the particular member which was being manipulated was the one most affected. Whatever might have been the question between the ladies, the doctor waited for Thieng to give the word, and Thieng evidently waited for the termination of my visit. But seeing that I made no attempt to go, she at length turned to the doctor, and said: " My pen arai, phöt thöe, yai kluâ " (Never mind, speak out, don't be afraid), all of which I understood as perfectly as I did English.

The doctor ceased her manipulations, and, after having cast a cautious glance round the room and shaken her head sorrowfully, remarked: " I don't think she 'll live many weeks longer."

Thieng sat bolt upright, and, clasping her hands together, said, " Phoodth thô !" *

" It is impossible," added the doctor, very earnestly.

* An ejaculation in frequent use among the Buddhists, and which means, " dear Buddha," or " dear God."

"It were better to put her to death at once than to kill her by inches, as they are now doing."

"P'hra Buddh the Chow,* help us!" cried Thieng, still more agitated. "What shall I do? What can I do to save her?"

"Something must be done, and at once," replied the doctor, suggestively.

"Well," said Thieng, "why don't you draw up a paper and give it to Mai Ying Thaphan?" (the chief of the Amazons.) "And now mind that you say she cannot live a day longer unless she is removed from that close cell and allowed to take an airing every day."

"Poor child! poor child!" repeated Thieng, tenderly, to herself. "With such a noble heart to perish in such a way! I wish I could find some means to help her to live a little longer, till things begin to look more bright."

"He has forgotten all about her by this time," rejoined the doctor.

The physician then took her leave of Thieng, and I inquired if they had been speaking of the Princess Sunartha Vismita. The good lady started and looked at me as if she supposed me to be supernaturally endowed with the art of unravelling mysteries.

"Why! how do you know the name," said she, "when we never even mentioned it?"

I then told her of the visit I had had from May-Peâh, and begged of her to help me to deliver the letter to the dying princess as soon as possible.

"We are all prisoners here, dear friend," said Thieng, "and we have to be very careful what we do; but if you promise never to say a word on this subject to any one, and in case of discovery to bear all the blame, whatever that may be, yourself, I 'll help you."

I gave her the required promise gladly, and thanked her warmly at the same time.

* One of the names of the Buddha.

" You must not think me weak and selfish, dear mam,"
said she, after a little reflection.   " You are a foreigner,
he has not the same power over you, and you can go away
whenever you like ; but we who are his subjects must
stay here and suffer his will and pleasure, whatever happens."

With that she told me to come to her after sunset, and
I bade her a grateful adieu and returned home.

CHAPTER XIX.

THE PRINCESS SUNARTHA VISMITA.

A N hour after dark I again sought the good and tender-hearted Thieng, who not only hurried me off,
telling me in a voice of great exultation that the physician's report had in a great measure ameliorated the
rigorous confinement to which the royal prisoner had
hitherto been subjected, but bravely sent two of her
women to tell the Amazons to show me the apartment
to which the sick princess had been removed.

The small apartment into which I was ushered was
dimly lighted by a wick burning in an earthen vessel.
The only window was thrown wide open. Immediately
beneath it, on a pair of wooden trucks which supported a
narrow plank, covered with a flowered mat and satin pillow, lay the wasted form of the Princess Sunartha Vismita. Her dress was that of a Laotian lady of high
rank. It consisted of a scarlet silk skirt falling in firm
folds to her feet, a black, flowered silk vest, and a long
veil or scarf of Indian gauze thrown across her shoulders;
some rings of great value and beauty and a heavy gold
chain were her only ornaments. Her hair was combed
smoothly back, bound in a massive knot behind, and confined by a perfect tiara of diamond-headed pins. She
was not beautiful; but when you looked at her you never
thought of her features, for the defiant and heroic pride
that flashed from her large, dark, melancholy eyes fixed
your attention. It was a face never to be forgotten. At
her feet were two other truckle-beds; on these were

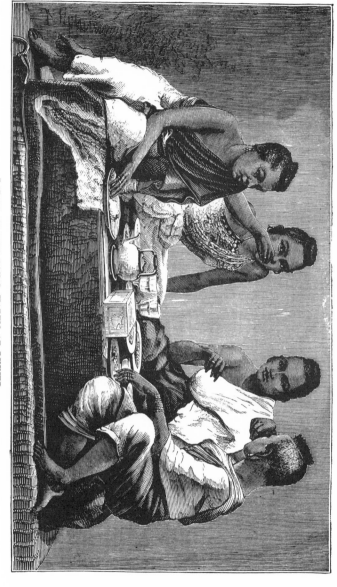

LADIES OF THE ROYAL HAREM AT DINNER.

seated the two young Laotian women who shared her captivity, and who looked very wan and sad.

Advancing unannounced close to this mournful group, I sat down near them, while the dark, depressing influence of the place stole upon my spirits and filled me with the same dismal gloom.

The princess, who had been gazing at the little bit of sky, of which she could only get a glimpse through the iron bars of the open window, turned upon me the same quiet, self-absorbed look, manifesting neither surprise nor displeasure at seeing me enter her apartment.

It was a look that spoke of utter hopelessness of ever being extricated from that forlorn place, and a quiet conviction that she was very ill, perhaps dying, yet without a trace of fear or anxiety.

The air was heavy and difficult to breathe, and for a moment or two I was silent, confounded by the unexpected bravery and fortitude evinced by the prisoner. But, quickly recovering my self-possession, I inquired about her health.

" I am well," said the lady, with a proud and indifferent manner. " Pray, why have you come here ? "

With a sense of infinite relief I told her that my visit was a private one to herself.

" Is that the truth ? " she inquired, looking rather at her women for some confirmation than at me for a reply.

" It is indeed," I answered, unhesitatingly ; " I have come to you as one woman would come to another who is in trouble."

" But how may that be ? " she rejoined, haughtily. " You must know, madam, that all women are not alike ; some are born princesses, and some are born slaves." She pronounced these words very slowly, and in the court language of the Siamese.

" Yes, we are not all alike, dear lady," I replied, gently ;

K

"I have not come here out of mere idle curiosity, but because I could not refuse your foster-sister May-Peâh's request to do you a service."

"What did you say?" cried the lady, joyfully rising, and drawing me towards her, putting her arms ever so lovingly round my neck, and laying her burning cheek against mine. "Did you say May-Peâh, May-Peâh?"

Without another word, for I could not speak, I was so much moved, I drew out of my pocket the mysterious letter, and put it into her hands.

I wish I could see again such a look of surprise and joy as that which illuminated her proud face. So rapid was the change from despair to gladness, that she seemed for the moment supremely beautiful.

Her lips trembled, and tears filled her eyes, as with a nervous movement she tore open the velvet covering and leaned towards the earthen lamp to read her precious letter.

I could not doubt that she had a tender heart, for there was a beautiful flush on her wan face, which was every now and then faintly perceptible in the flickering lamplight.

A smile half of triumph and half of sadness curved her fine lip as she finished the letter and turned to communicate its contents to her eager companions in a language unknown to me.[22]

After this the three women talked together long and anxiously, the two attendants urging their mistress to do something to which apparently she would not consent, for at last she threw the letter away angrily, and covered her face with her hands, as if unable to resist their arguments.

The elder of the women quietly took up the letter and read it several times aloud to her companion. She then opened a betel-box and drew out of it an inkhorn, a small reed, and long roll of yellow paper, on which she began a lengthy and labored epistle, now and then rubbing out the words she had written with her finger, and commencing afresh with renewed vigor. When the letter was finished, I never in my life saw a more unsightly, blotted affair than it was, and I fell to wondering if any mortal on earth would have skill and ingenuity enough to decipher its meaning. But she folded it carefully, and put it into a lovely blue silk cover which she took from that self-same box, — which might have been Aladdin's wonderful lamp turned inside out, for aught I knew to the contrary,— and, stitching up the bag or cover, she sewed on the outside a bit of paper addressed in the same mysterious and unknown letters, which bore a strong resemblance to the Birmese characters turned upside down, and were altogether as weird and hieroglyphic as the ancient characters found in the Pahlavi and Deri manuscript.[23] When all her labors were completed, she handed it to me with a hopeful smile on her face.

Meanwhile the princess, who seemed to have been plunged in a very profound and serious meditation, turned and addressed me with an air of mystery and doubt : " Did May-Peâh promise you any money ? "

On being answered in the negative, " Do you want any money ? " she again inquired.

" No, thank you," I replied. " Only tell me to whom I am to carry this letter, for I cannot read the address, and I 'll endeavor to serve you to the best of my ability."

When I had done speaking she seemed surprised and pleased, for she again put her arms round about my neck, and embraced me twice or thrice in the most affectionate manner, entreating me to believe that she would always be my grateful friend, and that she would always bless me in her thoughts, and enjoining me to deliver the letter into no other hands but those of May-Peâh, or her

brother, the Prince O'Dong Karmatha, who was concealed
for the present, as she said, in the house of the Governor
of Pak Lat.

I returned her warm embraces, and went home somewhat happier ; but I seemed to hear throughout the rest
of the night the creaking of the huge prison door which
had turned so reluctantly on its rusty hinges.

CHAPTER XX.

PAK LAUT, OR THE MOUTH OF THE OCEAN.

PAK LAT, or, more properly, Pak Laut, is situated a few miles above Pak Nam, and is in itself a picturesque village containing from six to seven thousand inhabitants. The most important portion of the town faces a beautiful bend of the great river Mèinam, and is rather irregularly built, and surrounded by a great many rude houses and shops, some of them quite old, and others quite new.

A magnificent new Buddhist temple is seen gradually raising its head close by the side of an ancient one which has so far crumbled to decay that the bright sun pours down unchecked a flood of golden light on the tapering crown of a huge brass image of the Buddha, which sits with its hands folded in undisturbed and profound contemplation on its glittering altar. On the other side, as far as the eye can reach, stretch unlimited groves of bananas and extensive plantations of cocoanut and betel-nut palms. The mango, tamarind, banyan, and boh, or bogara, trees here are of wonderful size and beauty, ponderous and overshadowing, as if they had weathered a thousand summers and winters, and would live unimpaired through a thousand more ; and as you wander through the deep cool shade which they afford, you find that many of them must have served hundreds of years ago — before Buddhism was introduced into Siam, and at a period when both the " Tree " and " Serpent " worship prevailed here, as in other parts of the Old World — as altars to a generation long gone by.

Many of their huge old trunks have been hollowed out and carved in the form of oriel chapels or windows, in the inmost recesses of which may still be traced the faint remains of what was intended to represent the cobra-de-capello, or hooded snake of India, now covered over with tender leaves and brilliant flowers, and forming at once the cosiest and most delicious of couches for the weary traveller to rest upon.

Pak Laut, with all its ancient splendor and attractiveness, had one drawback, and that was a very serious one. Among the village edifices was an open sala, or hall, which had long been the favorite place of rendezvous for all the rough and riotous seamen, English and American, the crews of the merchant vessels trading to Bangkok; and it was in consequence set down in the code of etiquette observed by the dozen or so of the *élite* of the English and American foreigners who resided at Bangkok "as a dreadfully improper place for a lady to visit alone."

Thus it was quite out of the question that I should go there without an escort, and not be tabooed by those good people as one utterly outside of the pale of their society.

Luckily, at this time Monsieur M——, an *attaché* to the French consulate, had been sent by Dr. Campbell to Pak Laut for change of air, and Monsieur L——, the commander of the king's guard, and his wife, were going to see him.[24] Being acquainted with the invalid, I obtained their permission to make one of the party.

Notwithstanding the perplexity of friends, who could not imagine my motive for going there, and who made themselves quite merry at my expense, I found myself in a boat, with the blue letter pinned in my pocket, my boy at my side, and Monsieur and Madame L—— opposite me, at five o'clock one morning, sailing down with the tide to Pak Laut.

When I arrived there, I made a hasty breakfast with the sick man and his friends, and leaving my boy at play in charge of the lady, I hurried off in the direction of the governor's palace.

P'haya Keean, the governor, was a Peguan prince by birth, and the father of my dear friend, whose name, translated into English is "Hidden Perfume."[25]

He received me so kindly and looked so benevolent that I felt encouraged to tell him the object of my visit at once.

Taking my hand in his, and keeping the smile of appreciation on his honest face, he led me through several long halls and corridors, which brought us at length to a very queer-looking old tower, covered with moss and black with age, with narrow loopholes for windows, and surrounded by a deep moat or ditch full of stagnant water.

From the roof of this extraordinary building descended two flights of steps built in the wall, and leading directly to two ruinous old drawbridges that· spanned the moat. The one communicated with the governor's palace, while the other led to a low arched gateway which opened immediately on a canal, and thus had access to the river.

What the moat was intended for I could in no wise imagine, unless it were especially designed to connect the tower, independent of the bridges, with the river, and thus, in cases of necessity, afford the inmates an opportunity of immediate flight by water.   There were two boats on the moat, ready for any such emergency.

The governor left me standing outside of the low wall that skirted the moat, crossed one of the crumbling old bridges, and entered the tower through an arched doorway, solemn and ponderous as if it had withstood the storms of many a dreadful siege.

In a few minutes May-Peâh, the Laotian slave-girl, came

running out, crying, " O, I love you dearly ! I love you dearly ! I am so happy. Come in, come in and see the prince ! " So saying, she pulled me after her into that singular, toppling-down-looking old edifice, which I must confess inspired me with a dread that I could not overcome, nor could I divest myself of the feeling that I was under the influence of some wild, fantastic dream.

The only floor of the old tower (for there was but one) consisted of three rooms ; one was rather large, and might have been in its best days of a vermilion color, but was now utterly discolored by great patches made by rain-water, which had changed it to a dull, yellowish, muddy hue. It was an ancient and gloomy-looking apartment, with all manner of rusty and antique Indian armor, shields, banners, spears, swords, bows and arrows, and lances ranged along the wall, which seemed to have been wielded by men of gigantic stature, and pointed to an epoch beyond the memory of the present race. Passing through this hall, we entered another and smaller room, the walls of which had also once been painted with gigantic flowers, birds, and beasts, among which the figure of the crocodile was most conspicuous. It contained a bed of state which looked like Indian, i. e. Bombay, workmanship, lifting to the ceiling a high, solemn canopy of that ponderous flowered silk called kinkaub.

I cannot depict the scene : how the glimmering light within and the changing lights without, reflected from the dark green waters, touched upon and singled out for a momentary illumination one after another the picturesque arms and the gigantic pictures on the walls, and diffused an air of mystery over the whole.

"Welcome, welcome, brave friend ! " said one of the three dark young men I found seated within, who rose and came to meet me with a singular gesture of courtesy and respect, and whom I at once recognized, from his

A LAOTIAN.

strong likeness to the Princess Sunartha Vismita, to be
the Prince P'hra O'Dong Karmatha. The prince, for it
was he, with an excitement he could not quite control,
inquired if I had seen his sister. As I spoke, May-Peâh
drew near and listened to what I said, with intense interest and anxiety expressed in her fine face. But when
I handed the prince the letter, they were all inexpressibly
delighted. All the others waited anxiously, turning silent
looks of sympathy and affection on him, as he read it first
to himself, and then aloud to the party.

"May-Peah" were the only two words I understood of
its contents; but I saw two big drops like thunder-rain
fall suddenly from the eyes of P'hra O'Dong on the
blotted yellow paper, and his voice died away in a hoarse
whisper as he concluded the strange epistle.

After which the party were silent, saying nothing for
nearly a whole hour, as it appeared to me, and absorbed
each with his own thoughts.

Then P'hra O'Dong cast an upward glance as if in
prayer, and May-Peâh crept quietly to his side and looked
at him with the calm, deep determination of high and noble
resolve depicted on her fine face. The two faces presented
the strongest contrast possible, — the one dark, troubled,
impetuous, and weak; the other resolute, passionate, un-
changeable, and brave. I wanted no further proof of the
nature of the friendship which May-Peâh bore to the young
prince and his sister. There are times when one almost
knows what is passing in the mind of another. Thus it
was that I was able to form some glimmering conception
of the elevated character of the slave-woman before me.

It was time for me to go. The prince begged me to
take something from him by way of compensation, but I
declined, thanking him all the same, and carrying away
with me only loving words of comfort and hope to his
long-imprisoned sister and her companions.

8

May-Peâh followed me out, and her fine face — for the oftener I saw it the finer it looked — was never more expressive than when she thanked me, and bade me tell her beloved mistress to keep a stout heart, adding, in a whisper : " I do not know what I am going to do, but something shall be done to save her, even if I die for it."

It was in vain that I urged her to be patient, and not to do anything so rash as to attempt the rescue of the princess ; nothing that I could say would move her from her purpose.

The day, though it commenced brightly, now began to be overcast, and the tide was turning for Bangkok, so I left her. As we parted, she was standing in one of the long corridors, with her hands folded and raised high above her head, and a flood of tender emotions brimming over into her eyes.

CHAPTER XXI.

NARRATIVE OF THE PRINCESS OF CHIENGMAI.*

MY good friend Thieng arranged another interview for me with the princess, who seemed wonderfully improved in health and spirits, and who related to me, almost word for word, the following narrative.

"The Prince P'hra O'Dong Karmatha and I are the only children of the Prince P'hra Chow Soorwang, the brother of the present king of Chiengmai. Chiengmai is now tributary to Siam. But there was a time when my ancestors were the independent sovereigns of all the land lying between Pegu and Birmah on the one hand, and Siam and the mountains of Yunan on the other.

"It was the Prince P'hra Chow O'Dong Karmatha, after whom my brother was named, who founded the beautiful city of Chiengmai, and built those stupendous works which bring water to its inhabitants.

"My poor mother died at the time of my birth, and May-Peâh's mother brought me up as if I were her own child ; and thus May-Peâh and I became sisters in the flesh, as we are indeed in spirit.

"My brother, the Prince O'Dong, is just seven years my elder. He was fond of pleasure, but he loved glory and honor and independence still more, and it was ever a source of mortification to him that our house should be obliged to pay the triennial tribute which the sovereign of Siam exacts as our homage of fealty.

"It was on one of these occasions, when my brother became the representative of our uncle, and the bearer of

* Chiengmai is the capital of Laos country.

the gold and silver trees to the court of Siam, that he met with his Royal Highness P'hra Somdetch Pawarendr Ramasr, the second king of Siam. Being both fond of the chase, and experienced hunters, they formed a strong friendship the one for the other.

" God forbid that I should disparage the supreme king of Siam, but every one who knows them will admit the superiority of the younger brother," said the lady, proudly.

" Soon after this the second king came on a visit to our home, and accompanied my brother on many a hunting expedition. I cannot describe to you my first meeting with the prince, whose praises had already inflamed my imagination. If I could coin words of deeper meaning, or if I could learn from the angels some new language wherein fitly to clothe the higher and purer joy that fell upon me in his presence, I might reveal to you something of the charm and the spell of that hour.

" When he at length returned to Sarapure, I was as one who had lost the key-note of her existence.

" My brother, apprehending the cause of my grief, sent May-Peâh, unknown to me, to Sarapure, to serve in any capacity whatever in the palace of the prince, and to discover, if possible, the state of his affections.

" May-Peâh and her mother set out for the palace of Ban Sitha. Having arrived there, she contrived to get admission into the harem of the prince, in order to visit some of her friends. While there, she drew out of her vest a silver flute, and played it so exquisitely — for she is the best musician in our country, and can perform on ten different instruments — that she charmed her hearers, who at once introduced her to the chief lady of the ' harem,' Khoon Klieb, who purchased her from her mother, and presented her to the prince, her master.

" She was then invited to perform before the prince ; he too was delighted with her wonderful skill and power,

and being at the time in ill health and feeble in body, he
hardly ever left his palace, and retained her almost always by his side.

"On one occasion, seeing that she had soothed and
charmed the unhappy and suffering prince with her
melodies, she begged permission to sing him a song of
her own composition, set to his favorite air of 'Sah
Mânee Chaitee' (The Lament of the Heart).* The prince
.smilingly assented, not without, as he afterwards told me,
surprise and wonder at the singular hardihood and fearlessness of the young stranger. 'But,' to use his own
words, 'she sang her wonderful song with such power,
such a sweet mixture of the fragrance of the heart with
the melody of touch, that the memory of it lingers still
with me as a dream of a day in Suan Swarg (paradise). Then I snatched from her hand the lute, and
struck on it in wild and imperfect utterances the burden
of my love for thee, dear Sunartha Vismita.'

"Just three months from the time of May-Peâh's de-
parture, when I had become weary and disconsolate because of her unaccountable absence, she returned home,
bearing letters and presents from the prince; and a month
afterwards I set out, a happy bride, for the beautiful palace
of Ban Sitha.

"When we arrived at Sarapure, my brother went on
before to announce my arrival to the prince —" Here
she ceased suddenly, and gave way to a burst of passionate tears.

After a little while she resumed her story, saying:
"And so we were privately married. The prince, however, had long been failing in health, and after a few
short months of unalloyed happiness he again fell griev-
ously sick, and exhorted me to return home to my father,

* The late second king was passionately fond of music, and was himself a skilful performer on several of the Laos instruments.

lest by his death I should fall into the power of his elder brother.   But I refused to leave him, and followed him to his palace at Bangkok, where he sickened rapidly and died.   His last words to me were : ' Fare thee well, Sunartha ! thy presence has been to me like the light of the setting sun, illumining and dispersing the dark clouds which have hitherto obscured my sad life.   Fear not ; I will keep the memory of thy face bright and unclouded before my fading eyes, as I pass away rejoicing in thy love.'

"A short time after my husband's death I found myself a prisoner in his palace, and as time passed on I was removed to this palace, where a residence befitting a queen was appointed to me, and where I first had the honor of receiving and entertaining the elder brother of my husband, the great king Maha Mongkut, who, ignoring my deep sorrow and deeper love for my late husband, offered me his royal hand in marriage.

" Openly and proudly I rejected the cruel offer, for which reason I am here again a prisoner, and perchance will remain forever."

She ceased speaking, and the Amazon entered to say it was time to shut the prison door.   With her lips firmly pressed together, her nostrils quivering, and her head bowed in her strong grief, she motioned me her adieux.   I saw her once or twice afterwards, sitting leisurely among the palace gardens, under the watchful eyes of the Amazonian guard, as self-absorbed, but, I thought, more hopeful than she used to be.

CHAPTER XXII.

"BIJREPUREE," OR THE DIAMOND CITY.

MEANWHILE his Majesty was better, and it was the last day of October. So the court and I, with my boy, and all the most favored of the royal family, set out for our annual visit to Bijrepuree, — leaving the Invincible City and the disconsolate princess with her pale-faced companions to the care of the high officials Mai Ying Thaphan within, and the Kroma Than Song Wang without.

Bijrepuree, or Petchabury, as it is commonly called, is the third city in size, and second in importance, in Siam, and is situated nearly one hundred and fifty miles in a south-westerly direction from Bangkok, on a river of the same name, which waters a country a thousand-fold more picturesque and beautiful than that around Bangkok. As you ascend the river, a chain of mountains varying from seventeen to nineteen hundred feet in height rises above the surrounding country, the loftiest of which is called Khoa L'huang, or Royal Mountain. This is one of his Majesty's most favored country residences. A splendid palace has been built on its summit, on which five hundred laborers have been employed daily for ten years, and it is still (1866) unfinished. A winding path which leads up to it has been admirably contrived amid the volcanic rocks which cover the surface of this mountain district. I climbed to no such favored spot during my residence in Siam.

On the hither side far away stretches from north to south a chain of mountains called Khoa Dèng, and inhabited by many rude and independent tribes of the primitive Kariengs. Beyond these again rises another chain of lofty hills, the outlines of which appear like misty clouds in the distant horizon.

On the slopes and in the valleys are immense forests of magnificent trees, hiding in their dark recesses myriads of unknown plants and lesser forests of ferns, with palm-trees, rice-fields, tobacco and sugar plantations looking intensely dark in the setting sun, and dividing the lights and shades into numberless soft radiating shafts which fall in a red haze of different degrees of strength on the pellucid river that flows gently through them.

Then to the south and east stretches another plain, and beyond this lies the Gulf of Siam, on whose waters, fading away in the distant horizon, were sometimes sparkingly revealed a few scattered sail, outward and homeward bound.

On the peaks of several mountains adjoining the royal residence rise stately temples and p'hra-cha-dees. All over these mountains the workmen are still toiling, laying out the grounds into gardens and shrubberies. In the centre of many of them may be seen beautiful stone vases of Egyptian form, cut out of the selfsame rock, and filled with gorgeous flowers. Attached to the palace is a school-house and a residence for the teacher, with a private chapel for the ladies ; but no distinct " harem," or woman's city, as at Bangkok. Those of the women who accompany the king on his annual visits have rooms allotted to them in the western wing of the palace, which is only curtained off by a wall and guarded by Amazons.

We, that is the young Prince Somdetch Chow Fa, my boy, and I, made the most of our visit to this delightful region, rambling over the hills and forests, gathering wild flowers, and visiting the hot springs, caves, and

CRENELLATED TOWERS OF THE INNER CITY.

grottos, which form some of the more interesting features of the neighborhood. In the foreground, near the school-house, stood a clump of ferns full of pictures; a little farther on was a cave, over the mouth of which trailed huge convolvuli; and immediately above it an overhanging rock variegated with natural tints and colors, the effect of which was most wonderful.

From this spot there were tempting walks through groves of dark green trees, opening upon wide terraces which commanded exquisite views of the country, rich with cultivation or dotted with houses and gardens, or the still more fertile valleys, winding amongst which might be traced the silvery thread of the Diamond River.

Not far from the Royal Mountain are several grottos, two of which are of surprising extent and great beauty, an exact painting of which would be looked upon with incredulity, or as an invention of fairy land.

Whatever may have been the origin of these grottos, owing to the moisture continually dropping through the damp soil of the rocks they have been clothed with the richest and most harmonious colors, and adorned with magnificent stalactites, which rise in innumerable slender shafts and columns to support the roof and walls. The setting sun reveals a gorgeous mass of coloring, ending in dark blue and purple shadows in the distant chambers and hollows.

I never witnessed such wonderfully illusive transforma-tions as the sunlight effected wherever it penetrated these subterranean halls. No human hands have as yet touched their marvellous walls and roofs and pillars. All that has been done by man is to cut a staircase in the rock, to aid the descent into the grottos, and enable the visitor to see them in all their regal beauty.

The largest grotto has been converted into a Buddhist temple; all along the richly tinted rock-walls are con-

8 *   L

templative images of the Buddha, and in the centre, just
where is concentrated the richest depth of coloring, lying
on a horizontal bed of rock, is a large sleeping idol of the
same inevitable figure, with the same mysterious expression about the closed eyelids, as if he were in the habit,
even in sleep, of penetrating distant worlds, in his longing
to gaze upon the Infinite.

Lower down the mountain lies a calm lake, with its
smooth silvery surface ever and anon broken by the leap-
ing of a fish, as if to prove that it is water and not glass,
and beyond the lake are more mountains rolling up into
the sky in purple and green folds, with the faintest of
blue borders and crimson-tipped edges, for they are many
miles off.

It was evening, and we had just spent a delicious fortnight here, teaching in the mornings and rambling in the
evenings, and his Majesty had assured me, to my great
delight, that we should stay yet another while among the
mountains ; my boy and I had retired to our little rocky
nest, around which there was an impression of savage
grandeur and of loneliness almost overpowering, and
where I used to imagine the "Hill Giants," of whom I
had heard so much, lurking in secret in the caves and
hollows, as ready to tear the Royal Mountain from its base
and cast it into the gulf beyond, for the pitiless way in
which the monarch doomed those poor five hundred slaves
to toil on and on, without any prospect of ever coming to
an end, in smoothing and shaping its rugged sides.   And
it was here that I first realized and appreciated the belief
of the simple people about me in ghosts and spirits,
pleasant and unpleasant : —

> " Genii in the air,
> And spirits in the evening breeze,
> And gentle ghosts with eyes as fair
> As starbeams through the twilight trees."

But in spite of them all we were sleeping soundly that night in the third story of our little eyry, when, about three o'clock in the morning, the sound of tocsins, gongs, and trumpets was flung out all over the distant hills and mountains, and re-echoed tauntingly, like the cry of so many demons full of mad sport, in the multitudinous voices of the rocky solitudes.   We were suddenly transported from deep sleep to wide-awake realities, to find the royal palace all alive with lights and sedans and horsemen, and torch-bearing, shadowy phantoms, issuing from dark portals, gliding hither and thither among the rocks, and coming towards us.

What did it all mean ?

The whole thing looked so mysterious that I at first thought the king was dead, or that the palace was beseiged, or that the " favorite," Peam, taking advantage of the mountain fastnesses, had run away.

The torchlight phantoms proved to be veritable brawny Amazons, who came to inform us that the court would return to Bangkok within an hour.   "What ! not stay another fortnight ? " I inquired, sadly.

" No, not another hour.   Get ready to follow," was the peremptory order.   And so, on the third day succeeding, we were all settled down in our respective places at Bangkok.

CHAPTER XXIII.

THE DEAF AND DUMB CHANGELING.

IN the next morning's cheerful daylight I set out to re-
sume once more my school routine within the sombre
walls of the "invincible" city. But, as we proceeded on our
way, we were surprised to see knots and clusters of people
reading with absorbing interest huge placards written in
Siamese, Pali, Cambodian, Birmese, Peguan, and every
other language spoken by the many distinct peoples who
inhabit the mountains and valleys watered by the great
river Mèinam, and posted all along the imperial walls.

Here was another mystery.

I could read printed Siamese and Pali tolerably well.
But the written characters, wherein every scholar in-
vents an orthography of his own, baffled all my lin-
guistic efforts, and not a glimmering of light could the
numberless questions I put to many of the curious
readers procure for me ; they were as afraid to speak of
royalty as of the devil, lest he should appear. So I went
on to school to find the same mysterious announcements,
which had sprung up like mushrooms during the night,
running zigzag over all the walls, and playing hide and
seek along the dark, narrow lanes and streets, only to
elude my strictest inquiries.

Now, to tell the truth, as I was treasonably disposed
against slavery and polygamy and several other gross
abuses that grew out of them, and had stoutly set my face
against them from the very first day of my installation
as teacher in the palace, I began to fear that these
placards might concern me and my teachings ; so when

school closed I went to see my friend, Lady Thieng. But she was even more mysterious than the unintelligible hieroglyphics on the walls, looking at me curiously, and shaking her head in a solemn manner, and feeling me all over in a pathetic way, so as to reassure herself that I was not a spirit, but made of flesh and bones like herself, and could not have been, as she had begun secretly to suspect, at Bijrepuree and at Bangkok at the same time.

She then gravely asked me if I had ever practised sorcery or witchcraft. My lips trembled with irrepressible laughter as I assured her I had not as yet enjoyed the good fortune of knowing a real witch; but that nothing in the world would please me better than to be introduced to one who would give me lessons in that art. She admonished me sternly for my levity, and went on to say that there had really been a very powerful sorceress in the palace during the king's absence at Bijrepuree, who had, unseen by human eye, conjured away the beautiful and disconsolate princess, and left in her place a rustic deaf and dumb slave-girl.

Amazed and altogether taken by surprise, I looked into my friend's face in unspeakable sorrow. My heart whispered to me the last words of May-Peâh, "I do not know what I am going to do, but something shall be done to save her, even if I die for it." I could not bring myself to ask another question, I was so afraid of confirming my worst fears. I had learned to love that slave-woman better than her mistress, and would have braved a thousand perils if I had thought I could save her through them.

"I wish," cried Thieng, at last, in a sudden burst, as if her thoughts had been going on in this strain and only broke from her when she could restrain herself no longer, — "I wish that this deaf and dumb slave-girl could be exorcised and made to speak, and then we would know how it happened, and how the old witch looked.

"O dear! O dear! I am afraid for my life and the lives of my poor children; and even the very stones out of which this dismal city is built inspire me with dread and horror," said poor Thieng, ruefully; " and do you know?" she added, — her eyes growing rounder and rounder every moment, as the awfulness of the situation presented itself to her mind, — " his Majesty has shut himself up in his topmost chamber, and guards are set at all the doors and windows, lest any suspicious-looking person should enter, and no one but only the old lady-physician, Khoon Maw Prang, is allowed to see him to serve his meals, and he won't come down till the palace and whole city has been exorcised. And there will be no school to-morrow,' she continued, growing more and more communicative, " for he has ordered all the royal children to be shut up in their homes until noon, when the old devil shall have been driven out by the priests of Brahma ; and the priests of Buddha will then purify the city with burning incense and sprinkling the houses, walls, and all its inhabitants with holy water."

Up to the last moment a natural cause for the disappearance of the Princess Sunartha Vismita never even presented itself to the mind of my simple-hearted friend, and I was not a little comforted, for the sake of the strange Laotian woman, to find that it was thought so absolutely the work of some supernatural agent. For Thieng also told me that the court astrologers and wizards were trying to unravel the mystery; that large rewards had been promised to them if they could throw any light on the subject; and, lastly, that the two Laotian captives, with the deaf and dumb changeling, were to be exorcised and examined in the ecclesiastical court on the following day by the " wise " men and women in the country.

After which the poor unhappy lady laid her head down

upon her pillow, utterly grieved and terrified by her fears. I tried in vain to comfort her. But what between her dread of the supernatural and her misgivings that to-morrow the chances were that certain accusations against herself and me, as secret agents of some devilish sorceress, might be brought forward with unanswerable logic, she was quite inconsolable and greatly to be pitied.

I believe she would have been content to give her life, ere day broke, only to catch a glimpse of the poor unfortunate princess whom the demon had thus maliciously kidnapped and carried off.

The only thing I could say, that seemed in the slightest degree to soothe her, was that I would endeavor to be present at the ecclesiastical court at the time appointed for the exorcism, and obtain such intelligence of its proceedings, and the facts elicited during the trial, as my imperfect knowledge of the technical language and formalities of the Siamese courts would enable me to gather for her.

CHAPTER XXIV.

WITCHCRAFT IN SIAM IN EIGHTEEN HUNDRED AND SIXTY-
SIX, COMPARED WITH WITCHCRAFT IN ENGLAND IN
SEVENTEEN HUNDRED AND SIXTEEN.

IT might be difficult, at the present time, anywhere in
any enlightened Christian community, to find persons
of the most ordinary intelligence who entertain the
smallest faith in witchcraft.

But yet there are thousands upon thousands who implicitly believe in spirit-rapping and in table-turning, in
mesmerism and animal magnetism, and in Mr. Joseph
Smith and Brigham Young, his successor, who exhibits
such extraordinary powers in prophecy and sensualism
at Utah ; and in fact it would seem that the doctrine
of " Credo quia impossibile " never had more earnest disciples than it now numbers.

Yet we all alike, with one accord, profess our utter dis-
belief in witchcraft.

This scepticism on our part, however, is of very modern
date ; for even in the early part of this century the belief
was not quite eradicated in England, and we have only
to step back a century more to find it acknowledged
without shame by a civilized and highly enlightened
people, and at a time, too, when the literary intellect of
England shone as brightly as ever in her history ; when
the memory of Dryden was still fresh in the minds of
many of his most cherished friends and admirers ; when
Pope had risen, and Addison was painting his genial
portrait of Sir Roger de Coverly ; when the bewitching
" nightingale at Twickenham " poured forth his sweetest

AN AMAZON OF THE ROYAL BODY GUARD.

songs, and kind-hearted Steele and Swift, stern, incorrigible, and lonely, domineered over the proudest of English peers and statesmen. Nothing can ever be more touching than the sad record of those dark days when the fair Eleanor Cobham, the wife of a duke, and the aunt of a king of " Great Britain," did penance for her " witchcraft," and walked " hoodless save her 'kerchief " through all the crowded streets of London and Westminster, taunted and hooted at by a ragged crowd, to offer a " consecrated taper " at the high altar of St. Paul's, and thence to her cruel, life-long imprisonment at Kenilworth, while her wretched accomplice, Bolingbroke, expiated his crime on a gibbet at Tyburn. And there are those seemingly darker days when Archbishop Cranmer, a high-priest of the tender Jesus, directed his clergy at large to make " strict inquiry into all witchcraft and such like craft invented by the devil " ; and when that very honorable personage, the Lord Chief Justice Coke, uttered these memorable words : " It would be a great defect in government if so great an abomination had passed with impunity." Then no one cast even the shadow of a doubt on the existence of witchcraft, or even questioned the extraordinary powers which were at the time imputed to a witch. And one becomes sensible of the dark superstitions that must have pervaded even the general atmosphere of the immortal poet Shakespeare, when he makes Ford lay his cudgel across the shoulders of Falstaff, supposing him to be the " wise woman of Brentford," and embodies the grander and more terrible idea of witchcraft as no man has ever done before or after him in the tragedy of " Macbeth."

Almost every page of ecclesiastical history of ancient times is full of monstrous relations of the powers of the dèvil, or of those who had entered into copartnership with him ; and, emerging thence into the light of more recent times, we shall find the same superstition in such men as Matthew Hopkins, the "witch-finder"; in Matthew Hale, presiding at the trial of the Bury St. Edmunds witches; and in Sir Thomas Browne, author of the " Religio Medici," and of the " Inquiry into Vulgar Errors," giving the evidence on which so many wretched old and young women were sent to the gallows. But, alas! what shall we say when we hear such holy men as Baxter and Wesley asserting that the belief in witchcraft was essentially connected with Christianity, and one of its most important points; and, down almost to our own day, find Johnson half doubting and half believing in the existence of witches and in their supernatural powers?

It was not until the close of 1763 that the statute which made witchcraft a felony punishable by death was repealed; and so lately as 1716 the curious reader will find in Gough's Brit., Vol. I., p. 439, an account of a substantial English farmer, named Hicks, who publicly accused his wife and child — a girl of only nine years of age — of witchcraft; and, what seems more incredible still, that they were actually tried at the assizes at Huntingdon before a learned judge, and visited by pious and God-fearing " divines " to whom the poor victims confessed the belief — which was forced into their own convictions by the strong current of public opinion, and still more by the unnatural conduct of a father and a husband — " that they were witches "; for which the unhappy wife and tender child were hanged at Huntingdon, on the 28th of July, 1716.

Can any page in the history of Siam be more appalling than this? Let the reader turn from England in her light and glory, her civilization, refinement, and power, from her altars raised to the true God, and centuries after her baptism in the matchless name of Christ, to benighted Siam still bound in the iron fetters of paganism, idolatry, and slavery, and he will find there in many respects just such a picture as England presented in the seventeenth and eighteenth centuries.

Nothing can be more appalling than the incurable superstition of the Eastern mind, and even while their belief in the supernatural inspires them with perpetual horror, they cannot be brought to give it up. In fact, it seems a part of their nature to cherish in their secret hearts the belief that there are spirits, good and bad, who walk the earth unseen, and delight either to bless or to cheat and abuse mankind; and that there are witches and wizards in the country who have the power of turning men into any shape they choose.

Rational and reasonable on all other points as the Siamese are, the moment you try to approach them through their religious senses they appear like a world coming suddenly under an eclipse of the sun; slowly and surely the disk of their mind is darkened, and the gloom and perplexity increase, till it becomes completely obscured.

CHAPTER XXV.

TRIAL FOR WITCHCRAFT.

NO one who has had the good or bad fortune to alight in the northeastern portion of the city of Bangkok can ever forget the temples and monasteries of Brahmanee Wade. They are situated by themselves, at the northeastern extremity of the city walls, where not a modern building is to be seen, for even the few houses which were erected as lately as yesterday have been fashioned after the ancient model prescribed by the Hindoo architect ; and in no part of the world is there seen so perfect an historical picture of the ancient Brahminical architecture as in this part of the city of Bangkok. The varied gables, the quaint little windows, the fantastic towers and narrow doorways, with the endless effects of color, make this spot a perpetual delight to the curious traveller ; and the Brahmins who occupy this part of the city, allotted to them from time immemorial by the kings of Siam, still preserve the ancient costume of their forefathers, which makes the picture complete.

On the morning of the 20th of November, 1866, three women, half stupefied by the foul air of the damp cells in which they had been immured, were conducted through the silent, sleeping streets of the palace and city to a small room or "black hole" adjoining the great courthall of the temple of Brahmanee Wade, and locked up therein, while the file of Amazons and the troop of soldiers in charge took their places around it.

While the Invincible City was being disenchanted by one set of Brahmins to be purified by another set of

Buddhist priests, I set off on horseback, attended only by my Hindostanee syce, or groom, to the scene of the trial.

November here is the pleasantest month in the year; and the morning sun shone brightly, but not too warmly, as we approached the walls of the temples and monasteries of Brahmanee Wade, — so wild, so isolated, so set in contrast by oddness of architectural effects to the general order and appearance of the rest of the town, as to seem, indeed, to belong to another age and another world. The dark walls and huge trees were covered with parasitic plants.   A deep, narrow valley, through which a tiny streamlet runs, over a stony bed, betwixt sloping sides of grass and furze-clad steeps, is crossed by a stone bridge, black with time, which leads to the portals of Brahminism.   The little mad stream roared and fled darkly on, as it will perhaps forever.

There was a dreadful loneliness about the place, and a sort of darkness, too, whether in my mind or in the place I cannot say, but it spoke of all kinds of magic and witchcraft, and even of devilcraft.

Deep in the glen, sloping down to the stream, amid picturesque and romantic surroundings, stood the old temple of Kalee Durga; and running along, like a huge, jagged shadow, dark even in the brightest sunlight, rose the roofs of the monastic dwellings of the Brahmin ascetics, from which the place is named.

I alighted, and told my syce to wait outside for me; but he, being a pious Hindoo, bestrode the pony and rode off, to return in a quarter of an hour with oil and fresh flowers and sweetmeats enough to propitiate a great many dark goddesses.

There was not a soul to be seen anywhere, whether of Brahmanic or Buddhistic faith.   So I followed my syce into the temple, and while he prostrated himself at full length before each one of his gods, I took out my note-book and occupied myself in making sketches and memoranda of the strange scene before me.

Vishnu, Siva, Krishna, and the goddess Kalee, were the chief deities of the place, and figured as the heroes and heroines among the numerous grotesque and monstrous myths sculptured on the walls.

Here was Vishnu lying comfortably on the thousand-headed snake Shesha, or sporting as a fish, or crawling as a tortoise, or showing his fangs as a wild boar, or shaking his head in his last and fifth *avatar* as a dwarf, all admirably executed. Here too was Krishna, like another Apollo, whipped out of heaven for playing tricks on the lovely shepherdesses of Muttra, whose tender hearts he stole away, and whose butter he found so tempting that he perpetually ran off with it in secret, and whose jars of milk it was this madcap's pleasure roguishly to upset. In another compartment, crumbling with age, he is seen again in his last mad prank, perched on a stony tree with the milkmaids' stony habiliments under his arm, and an unmistakable grin on his stony, greasy * face, while the owners of the dresses are standing below in various attitudes of bashfulness imploring their restoration. Before them in different places stands the Lingam. Here was also a beautiful sculpture of Siva and his wife Parvati, with the sacred bull Nandi lying at their feet, and Kalee in combat with the monster Mahashasura; and close by again she is seen caressing a Nylghau,† that is looking up to her.

The figures of the goddesses are wonderfully spirited, and of exquisite symmetry, conveying the idea of perfect and beautiful womanhood. And yet Kalee is represented elsewhere in the same temple as a black and

---

* The Hindoos besmear these sculptures with oil on festive occasions.

† A large short-horned antelope found in Northern India. The males are of a beautiful slaty blue, and the females of a rusty red.

terrible being, covered with symbols of the most ferocious cruelty.

Having finished my notes, I passed out by another entrance, and tried to quiet my fears for May-Peâh by continuing my rambles and explorations until breakfast-time. Instead of returning home for that meal, I despatched the syce to buy from the small Hindoo village close by an earthen lota of milk and a flat cake of Bâjree bread, of which I made a pleasant repast, sitting under the deep shadows of the temples and trees dedicated to Brahma, of whom there is rarely, if ever, any representation.

Very soon I was repaid for my patient waiting, for I heard the sound of drums beating and martial music playing; and, rushing to the side whence it proceeded, the queerest and most weird-looking procession met my astonished eyes, — old women dressed in scarlet and yellow, and old grayheaded men in every variety of costume, combining all the known and unknown fashions of the past, some on foot and others on horseback, with embroidered flags of the same multiplicity of colors flying before the wind; and in the centre of all, clad in black and crimson vestments, riding on white mules, a band of about twenty men and women, some quite young and others extremely old, advancing with slow and solemn steps. These were the royal astrologers, wizards, and witches who, incredible as it may seem, are supported by the supreme king of Siam, and receive from the crown large and handsome salaries. I observed that the whole procession was composed of persons of the Hindoo religion.

In the rear came some Chinese coolies hired for the occasion, carrying two boxes and two long planks, which excited my curiosity. As they drew near they were joined by large numbers of well-dressed Siamese and a host of ragged slaves, which completed the motley scene.

I stepped out of the solemn shade of the boh and peepul trees, and took my seat on a broken stone pillar, still under shelter, and commanding a view of the grand hall. The roof, which was fast crumbling away, was an inferior imitation of that of the wondrous temple of Maha Nagkhon Watt, and had scarcely been touched for centuries, for there still figured the inevitable Siva and Kalee, and all the rest of the Hindoo gods and goddesses, dismantled and broken, but still in sufficient preservation to show the wild grotesqueness of the Hindoo imagination, which seems to have grown riotous in the effort to embody all its imperfect conceptions of the Divinity.

When this strange and solemn procession entered the portal of Brahmanee Wade they suddenly halted, threw up their arms and folded their hands above their heads, and repeated one of the most magnificent utterances of Krishna: "O thou who art the life in all things, the eternal seed of nature, the understanding of the wise and the weakness of the foolish, the glory of the proud and the strength of the strong, the sacrifice and the worship, the incense and the fire, the victim and the slayer, the father and the mother of the world, gird thy servants with power and wisdom to-day to slay the slayer and to vanquish the deceiver," * etc. After which they marched to the sound of music into the temple, and offered sacrifices of wine and oil, and wheaten cakes and fresh flowers, and with their eyes lifted to the dark vaulted roof they again prayed, calling upon Brahma the father, the comforter, the creator, the tender mother, the holy way, the witness, the asylum, the friend of man, to illumine with the light of his understanding their feeble intellects to discern the devil and to vanquish him.

At length the astrologers, wizards, and witches took

* A prayer from the "Hindoo Liturgy," embodying some of the remarkable formulas of the Brahminical worship.

their places in the hall, with eager crowds all round them, standing in rows on all the steps of the building. Then came two officers from the king with a royal letter, — one was the chief judge of the Supreme Court, and the other his secretary to report the trial. After this lordly personage had taken his seat, the prisoners — the two handmaids of the princess and my friend May-Peâh, who, as I feared, was the deaf and dumb " changeling " — were brought in. She was deadly pale, and there was a wild light as of madness or intense suffering in her eyes. They were placed at the end of the hall, strongly guarded by as many as fifty Amazons, while the soldiers scattered themselves all round about the building. Not a word was spoken, and the strange assembly looked into one another's faces, as if each knew his neighbor's thoughts. I trembled for the unhappy prisoners; and the crowd, who seemed to look upon poor May-Peâh as a veritable witch, were silent in breathless expectation.

It was a frightful spot, and a still more indescribably terrifying scene, where one might indeed say with Hassan of Balsora, " Lo! this is the abode of genii and of ghouls and of devils." I had half a mind to slip down from my rocky perch and run away. But very soon my anxiety for poor May-Peâh absorbed every other feeling.

The three prisoners sat profoundly silent, waiting in sadness to hear their doom.

But why did they not begin the trial? There were the boxes and the planks with little niches cut into them, deep enough to enable any nimble person to climb with the tips of their toes, and scale any wall against which they might be placed. I turned to a soldier who was standing close by, and asked him why they still delayed the trial.

" They are waiting," said he, as if he knew all about it,

9   M

and had witnessed many such scenes before, "for the 'sage,' or holy man of the woods; it is for him that they have blown the conch-shells these three times." There was, to me, nothing improbable in the soldier's story. He told me that this holy man, or yogi,* lived in a cave, in the rocks adjoining, all alone, and that he rarely issued from his unknown retreat during the day, but that pious Hindoos, while performing their ablutions in the stream after the close of their labors, could see him moving in the moonlight, and hear him calling upon God. Feeding on tamarinds and other wild fruits, he slept during the day like a wild animal, and prayed aloud all night, oppressed by his longing and yearning after the Invisible, as by some secret grief that knew no balm. Even the cool evening air brought him no peace; for,

> " At night the passion came,
> Like the fierce fiend of a distempered dream ;
> And shook him from his rest, and led him forth
> Into the darkness, to pray and pray forevermore."

By and by a man appeared on the opposite banks of the stream, plunged into it, and emerged on the hither side ; shook the wet from his hair like a veritable beast, and made his way towards the hall, where he sat himself shyly down near the prisoners. This strange mortal, who lived the life of an "orang-outang," had a remarkably fine, sensitive face, and a noble head, around which his long, matted, unkempt hair fell like dark clouds. He was meagrely clad, and his wiry frame gave evidence of great muscular power. There was, to my thinking, a gleam of a better and higher humanity in his fine, dark face, that shot out in irrepressible flashes, and convinced me, in spite of his filth and nudity, of a noble and impressive nature.

The soldier assured me, in a tone of the utmost rever-

* A Hindoo mystic.

ence, "that this man's eyes were opened, that he could see things which the paid mercenaries of the court could not begin even to comprehend; and that therefore they always made it a point to invite him to aid them in their spiritual examinations."

I somehow drew comfort from the yogi's shy and fascinating face.

And now the trial commenced by the judge reading the king's letter, which spoke of the mysterious and important nature of the accusation made against some unknown person for the abduction of a state prisoner, a lady of high rank and unflinching integrity, and called upon the assembly to do their utmost to unravel the inexplicable affair.

After the royal letter had received its customary salutations, and at the command of the judge, the two Amazons who were on duty on the night of the abduction of the princess testified to the following facts : " That on the night of the 12th, on a sudden a strong wind arose that extinguished their lanterns, leaving them in utter darkness, and immediately afterwards they were sensible that a tall, dark figure enveloped in a black veil entered the hall, and that as she approached them they saw, somewhat indistinctly, that she held a short dagger in one hand and a ponderous bunch of keys in the other; that never before having known themselves liable to any illusion of the senses, the horror which fell upon them at the moment deprived them of all power of speech or action; that, as the strange being stood over them brandishing her glittering knife, there flashed all round about her a hideous light; that by this light they saw her proceed to the cell in which the Princess Sunartha Vismita was confined, open it with one of her mysterious keys, and lead the princess forth, pulling her forcibly along by the hand, and as the flashes died away a double darkness fell upon them; that after an interval of nearly two hours, as they were still paralyzed and unable to move from the spot, the strange figure reappeared, pallid, and more ghastly than before, but without the veil, or the dagger, or the bunch of keys; that she passed quickly by them into the cell, and drew the prison door so forcibly that it closed upon her with a dismal cry of pain."

Then the two Laotians stated "that on the night of the 12th they were awakened by the slamming of the cell door, and, on looking in the darkness towards the bed on which the princess slept, they saw a figure sitting on it; on which they lit the lamp, and found it was not their mistress, but a dumb slave-woman in her place, and that they instinctively shrank away from her in fear and horror lest she should metamorphose them also into some unnatural beings."

As for the Amazons, it could readily be seen that their imaginations had been so vividly impressed that they were prepared to swear solemnly to their having seen a supernatural being twice the size and altogether unlike the deaf and dumb creature before them. The unnatural light of pain or madness or frenzy, or whatever it was, burned still more brightly in May-Peâh's eyes. Her reddish-brown dress seemed to be stained here and there with darker spots, as if of blood, and her face grew more and more colorless every moment. But to all the numberless questions put to her by every one of the crafty wizards and witches, she returned no reply. Her lips were of an ashy whiteness, and they really seemed to have been closed by a supernatural power.

I recalled her volubility of speech when I first met her, and her impassioned song, by which she won for her mistress the acknowledgment of a deep and undying love; and I asked myself the question over and over again, "Is it possible that she can be acting?" At a signal, an alarm-gong was struck, and so suddenly and immediately behind her that the whole assembly started, and May-Peâh, taken by surprise, turned to see whence the sound came. " Now," shouted the wily judges, " it is plain that you can speak, for you are not deaf."

No sooner was this said than the feeling against the accused ran high, on account of her obstinacy, and she was forthwith condemned to all the tortures of the rack. But the humane yogi, on hearing this, raised his bare arms on high, and uttered the wild cry of " Yah" (forbear) so commandingly that it rang through the temple, and arrested the cruel process.

He then turned to the poor girl, and, placing his huge, bony hands upon her shoulders, tenderly whispered in her ear something which seemed to move the prisoner for she raised her burning eyes, now filled with tears, to his face, and, shaking her head solemnly and sadly to and fro, laid her finger on her mouth to indicate that she could not speak.

A tender light kindled the dark face of the yogi, as he informed the assembly that " the woman was not a witch, nor even obstinate, but powerless to speak, because under the influence of witchcraft."

The tide of feeling was again turned in the prisoner's favor. " Let her be exorcised," said the chief judge of the Supreme Court, whose secretary was making minutes of all that took place during the trial.

On which the queerest-looking woman of the party, an old and toothless dame, drew out a key from her girdle and opened the wooden boxes, from which she took a small boat, a sort of coracle,* — such as are still found in some parts of Wales, made by covering a wicker frame with leather, — a long gray veil of singular texture, an earthen stove, whereon to kindle a charcoal fire, and some charcoal ; out of the second box she produced some

---

* Similar boats were used by the ancient Egyptians.

herbs, pieces of flint, cast skins of snakes, feathers, the hair of various animals, with dead men's bones, short brooms,. and a host of other queer things.

At any other time I should have been highly amused at the grotesqueness of the figure, and the comically ludicrous manner in which she drew, one after another, her mysterious ingredients out of her boxes ; but now I was too anxious, and too much pained by the situation of May-Peâh, and by what seemed to me diabolical jugglery, to think of the comical side of the scene.

With the charcoal the old woman proceeded to light a fire in her earthen stove ; when it was red-hot she opened several jars of water, and, muttering some strange incantations, threw into them portions of her herbs, repeating over each a mystic spell, and waving a curious wand which looked like a human bone, and might have been once the arm of a stalwart man.   This done, she seated the prisoner in the centre of the motley group, covered her over with the veil of gray stuff, and handing the short handbrooms to a number of her set, she, to my intense horror, began to pour the burning charcoal over the veiled form of the prisoner, which the other women, dancing around, and repeating with the wildest gestures the name of Brahma, as rapidly swept off.   This was done without even singeing the veil or burning a hair of May-Peâh's head. After this they emptied the jars of water upon her, still repeating the name of Brahma.   She was then made to change her clothes for an entirely new dress, of the Brahminical fashion.   Her dressing and undressing were effected with great skill, without disclosing her person in the least.   And once more the yogi laid his hands upon her shoulders, and whispered again in her ears, first the right, and then the left.   But May-Peâh returned the same intimation, shaking her head, and pointing to her sealed lips.

Then the old wizard, Khoon P'hikhat, — literally, the lord who drives out the devil, — prostrated himself before her, and prayed with a wild energy of manner; and, rising suddenly, he peremptorily demanded, looking full into the prisoner's face, "Where did you drop the bunch of keys?"

The glaring daylight illuminated with a pale lustre the fine face of the Laotian slave, as for the third time she moved her head, in solemn intimation that she could not or would not speak.

To see her thus, no one would believe but that, if she willed, she could speak at once.

"Open her mouth, and pour some of the magic water into it," suggested one of the "wise women."

But they who opened her mouth fell back with horror, and cried, "Brahma, Brahma! an evil fiend has torn out her tongue." And immediately the unhappy woman passed from being an object of fear and dread to one of tender commiseration, of pity, and even of adoration.

So sudden was the transition from fear and hate to love and pity, that many of the strong men and women wept outright at the thought of the dreadful mutilation that the fiend had subjected her to.

Now came the last and most important question, "Was the exorcism effectual?" To prove which a small taper was lighted and put into the witches' boat; and the whole company betook themselves to the borders of the stream to see it launched. The boat swept gallantly down the waters, and the feeble lamp burned brightly, without even a flicker, — for it was a calm day, — till it was brought to a stand by some stones that were strewn across the stream.

Then the yogi raised a shout of wild delight, and all the company re-echoed it with intense satisfaction and pleasure. And, in accordance with the king's instructions, being fully acquitted of any complicity with the devil in the abduction of the princess, the prisoners received each a sum of money, and were set at liberty.

The planks, which in any other court would have been one of the most tangible evidences that some person had thereby scaled the palace walls, were never even thought of during this singular trial. So irrational and so superstitious is the native character, that they preferred to believe in the supernatural rather than in any rational cause for the disappearance of the princess ; and for once in my life I was led to rejoice in their ignorance.

It was sunset before this inconceivably grotesque and self-deluded and deluding set of maniacs dispersed. The yogi went back to the solitude of his unknown cave to sleep by day and pray alone by night. And I sent my syce home, and remained behind under a jamoon-tree, to which my pony was tied, in the hope of getting an opportunity of speaking alone with the women who still lingered with May-Peâh in the hall.

When May-Peâh at length saw me, she rushed into my arms, and laid her head upon my shoulder, uttering the most doleful and piteous of cries ; they were not cries of sorrow, but of the wildest joy ! I embraced her with something of the tenderness and sorrow with which a mother takes a brave but reckless child to her heart.

May-Peâh's friends then told me, what I had all along surmised, that it was she who scaled the walls by means of the two planks, terrified the Amazons, opened the prison doors with the keys she had provided, and led her mistress forcibly out. After assisting her to climb the walls on the inner side, she sat on the top of the outer wall until she saw her safely on the other side. She then dropped the keys to her, to be flung into the river. Here the prince and his two friends received the princess, and led her to a small craft that was ready to convey them to

Maulmain. In vain they entreated May-Peâh to come down from the wall and join their flight. She resolutely refused to leave the companions of her beloved mistress in peril, and, full of dread lest, by the dreadful torture which she knew awaited her, she might be forced to betray those who were dearer to her than her own life, she with one stroke of her sharp dagger deprived herself forever of the power of uttering a single intelligible sound.

"O, but why did you not all go off with the princess?" I inquired.

"Because we were too many, and we should have only delayed and perhaps imperilled the success of the enterprise," said the women; "and May-Peâh had promised not to leave us to bear the penalty of her doings."

It was difficult to tear myself away from her. I was at once proud to be loved by her, and heart-broken to think that she would never speak again.

But at length we parted, and she, raising her hands high above her head, waved them to and fro, and smiled a joyful adieu, in spite of the pain she still suffered from her cruel mutilation.

They took the way to the river to hire a boat for Pak Laut, whence they were to sail to Maulmain to join the fugitive prince and princess.

Assuredly, so long as men and women shall hold dear human courage and devotion in what they believe to be a just cause, so long will the memory of this brave and self-sacrificing slave-girl be cherished.

9*

CHAPTER XXVI.

THE CHRISTIAN VILLAGE OF TÂMSÈNG, OR OF THOMAS
THE SAINT.

IT was on a bright Sunday morning in the month of May that a handsome boat with four young women at the oars conveyed me and my boy to the residence of Mrs. Rosa Hunter, situated in the village of Tâmsèng.

My friend Mrs. Hunter was a native of Siam, but of Portuguese parentage. Her husband, Robert Hunter, was private secretary to the supreme king.[26] She had two sons, who had been taken away from her in their infancy by their Protestant father, — lest they should be brought up in the Roman Catholic faith, — and shipped off secretly to Scotland, in order that they might be educated under the influences of the Free Church of Scotland, in which he had himself been brought up. This occasioned a breach between the husband and wife which led to their ultimate separation, and Rosa returned all but heart-broken to the home of her childhood, where I visited her at short intervals to write the long, loving letters which she dictated to me in Siamese, and which I wrote in English to her absent boys.

A day at her house was always a pleasant change. On one of these visits, which I remember well, the table had been spread by the window that looked up the river, and lost it amid high banks and the projecting spires of the Roman Catholic and the Buddhist temples adjoining.

I had finished and sealed her loving messages to her absent children ; the moon was rising, and we needed no other light, as the conversation between us, often shifting and often pausing, had gradually become grave, and we fell into confiding talk of what we hoped and what we feared, as we saw the future of our children stretched before us in deep shadows.

"There is so much power in faith," said Rosa, "even in relation to earthly things, that I am surprised you are not a Roman Catholic. I believe in my church; when I go to confession and receive the holy communion, I am filled with peace and trust, and have no fears for the future."

"There is a great deal in what you say, Rosa," I replied; "but I am afraid that I should not make a good Catholic, since I am disposed to question everything that does not accord with my own perceptions of the right and the true."

"Well, I suppose," said Rosa, "that our natures differ; all my life has its roots in the Roman Catholic Church. I never doubt, therefore I never question. The Holy Virgin and her Son are sufficient for me, and the good priest who absolves me from my sins. My only one sorrow is that my children are cast out of the pale of salvation by the foolish prejudices of their father."

This was said in a voice of much feeling, and tears gathered to her eyes. I moved to her side, and tried to comfort her by saying, "After all, Rosa, you seem to let your fears for your children cloud your faith in that Saviour who died for them as well as for you."

While I was speaking, my eyes fell upon a long, narrow canoe, called by the natives Rua Keng, in which was seated a tall, slender, and shapely young girl, who was slowly, with the aid of two short paddles, making her way towards us through the water, while her face was raised to the moonlight that fell brightly upon her. It was nearly high tide; a fleet of canoes, boats, and barges was moving in all directions over the broad waters.

We watched the girl as her paddles rose and fell softly and slowly, silver-tipped by the moonlight, now dipping into the water, now rising above it, like the white wings of some lazy bird. Nearer and nearer came the long boat, and clearer shone the fair face that was still uplifted, and reflected back the moonlight, till it almost looked as if divinely inspired. It is impossible to do any kind of justice to this beautiful moonlight picture. Gently the boat shot under our window, and was lost to our sight.

I bade my friend adieu, and hastened to the pier, where I met the girl again. She had fastened her canoe to one of the posts that supported the quay, and was crossing the street : in one hand she held a bunch of lilies, and in the other a lotus-shaped vase full of flowers.

Yielding to the impulse of the moment, instead of stepping into my boat I took my boy's hand and followed her graceful figure.

It was not yet seven o'clock. A number of people were in the squalid, dirty streets of Tâmsèng. The twinkling evening lights were stealing out one by one, and the girl drew over her face a veil or covering which was attached to her hair by a large and beautiful pin. A dozen or more steps, and we stood in the porch of the Roman Catholic chapel dedicated to "Tomas the Saint."

Lights were burning on the altar, over which were two figures of the Christ : one suspended above it with a crown of thorns, bleeding, and nailed to the cross ; the other, of magnificent stature, was enveloped in a costume as gorgeous as the coronation robes of an emperor, the vestment being a sort of Indian brocade of woven gold arabesqued with jewels and scented with spikenard ; a diadem lavishly adorned with emeralds and diamonds pressed its forehead, in some measure confining the hair which streamed down in abundant tresses upon the shoulders, and mingled with a beard no darker than the glossy hue of the chestnut. On either side of the altar were two other figures, one of the Virgin Mother, in the same regal attire, and crowned as the queen of heaven; while the other was the patron saint, with a flowing beard and a benevolent face. Suspended over the altar was a grand Japanese lamp.

The priest, a dark, heavily built man, a native, but of Portuguese parentage, was standing before it, with his cap on his head and his back to the congregation.

The moment the girl beheld the glory of the altar and the lights that shot up and quivered and were reflected in a thousand beautiful tints upon the magnificent figure of the Christ, she dropped on her knees and held down her head in mute adoration. After a little while she rose, and, advancing a few steps nearer, placed her golden lotus-shaped vase of flowers on the bare floor, dropped on her knees again, and, holding the white lilies between her folded hands, seemed absorbed in her devotions.

In her attitude and bearing there was a depth of feeling which, harmonizing with her beautiful figure, arrested the eye of the observer, and cast every other object in the shade.

I withdrew reluctantly and returned to my boat, wondering who she could be. On my way home I gathered from the women at the oars that she was known by the name of Nang Rungeâh (Lady Rungeâh); * that her parents were Buddhists and Cambodians, proprietors of a large plantation east of Tâmsèng. Her father, Chow Suah P'hagunn, was a distinguished noble, and her mother a Cambodian lady of high birth, who claimed to be descended from the rulers of that ancient and almost unknown kingdom, and that her only brother was a Buddhist priest. But the Nang Rungeâh had become deeply impressed with the beauty of the Christian re-

* Rungeâh, a sort of magenta-colored lotus, found in the pools and marshes of Siam.

ligion, and was at this moment the only candidate who had offered herself, for a number of years, for baptism into the Roman Catholic Church.

"Tomas Saint," the founder of the beautiful church around which had grown up this Christian village, was a Portuguese gentleman renowned for his piety and his wealth. He had obtained the title of "saint," even in his lifetime; but the good people, fearing to arouse the jealousy of the Apostle of Christ, after whom he was named, placed the title after, instead of before, his name, and out of it had grown the name of "Tâmsèng."

On the very next Saturday following, it being the first holiday that offered itself to me, I set out with my boy very early in the morning to explore the village of Tâmsèng.

We chose for our head-quarters one of the most beautiful Buddhist temples in the neighborhood, the grounds and monasteries bounded the Catholic village on the northeast side of the river.

This temple, called Adi Buddha Annando, i. e. The First Buddha, or The Infinite, was embowered in a grove of trees of luxuriant growth, affording a delicious shade. It must have been, in its best days, a magnificent building; for even now, though much of its beauty was obliterated, it was covered from its massive base to its tapering summits with sculptures, and frescoed within and without with marvellous effect, so that wherever you turned your eyes the impression of a more subtle and a finer spirituality dawned upon you, as it was meet it should, in a temple dedicated to One whom the pious Buddhists will never even name, so great is their reverence for the First or Supreme Intelligence.

After a simple breakfast of fruit and milk, we strolled about the village and its surroundings, making notes and sketches of all that could be seen.

It was surprising to me that it looked so well in the early sunshine. The places that had struck me as foul and repulsive in the dim twilight now wore a different aspect, as if bent on looking their brightest and best in acknowledgment of the prodigal sunlight.

But the farther we penetrated into the heart of the village the more we were disappointed, and my first impressions were more than realized. We soon came upon scenes of the most squalid misery and filth, poverty and destitution, amid heaps of refuse and puddles of mud that caused us to shrink aside with disgust.

It is natural to demand that beautiful ideas should be clothed with beautiful forms. It was therefore to me an outrage on the name of Christianity to find that while all around lay scenes of luxuriant beauty which brightened the eye and cheered the heart, the only Christian village in the vicinity of Bangkok, which should have been an embodiment of all that is pure and lovely, had been transformed by the greed and oppression of the local officers to a pestilential spot to fester and poison the pure air of heaven. Some few native Christian women were about milking their goats, others were seated on their doorsteps, unwashed and uncombed; they seemed even to have lost the virtue of personal cleanliness, which with the Indian covers a multitude of sins. Stray packs of pariah dogs and herds of swine were barking and grunting in the ill-kept streets, and all kinds of poultry were picking a scanty breakfast from the heaps of garbage. Every now and then we were compelled to cross a stagnant pool or a muddy gutter alive with insects.

I never saw anything like the mud; it was a black liquid, sticky, slimy, and yet hard, hurting like hail when it struck the flesh.

And now we reached the quaint little chapel of " Tomas Saint." Its glories were sadly obscured by wet and damp, and the painting and gilding on the outside looked cold and dull.

A colored priest, a descendant of the renowned Tomas, was officiating. It was some saint's day. An assemblage of men, women, and children was seated on the floor, some in groups and some on rude benches. The priest bends over his missal, and pours forth in execrable Latin the exquisite prayers of the Church of Rome ; and all the congregation, in their silks, and in their rags and wretchedness, are hushed and silent, with bent heads and folded hands, while the sound of the prayers — which they do not understand, beyond that it is the voice of prayer — fills their unenlightened but reverent hearts with mysterious dread and worship.

On quitting the chapel, we were at once beset by a numerous horde of beggars. It was not food or money that they craved, but, strange to say, it was justice. They followed us all the way back to the temple, importuning me to redress their wrongs and find a remedy for their grievances. Some of the poor wretches were half-witted, and not a few were crazed. An elderly lady, evidently once of superior rank, came crawling up to me, and clasped my feet, making a painful noise in a language that I could not understand, and piteously gesticulating some incomprehensible request. The people of the place denied all knowledge of her. At last she insisted on my giving her a leaf out of my note-book full of writing, which she apparently considered as a charm, for she attached it to a cord round her neck, and seemed to be perfectly happy in its possession. God only knows what the poor thing wanted to tell me, but likely enough her story was one of some great wrong, of some cruel injustice. If the smallest details of what I heard that day might be credited, the wrongs of these people were of the most harrowing nature, and altogether without hope of remedy under the twofold and inverately vicious system of Siamese and Portugo-Siamese administration that prevailed there.

I was alarmed when I found that my visit was thought to be one secretly intended "to spy out the land," in the service of the king of Siam, and that I was expected to wipe away the tears from all eyes. In vain I protested to the contrary; no one would listen to me, but the crowds kept coming and going, and pleading and praying, and promising me fabulous sums of money if I would only see their wrongs redressed.

Many a heart-rending tale was told to me that day, with quivering lips and streaming eyes, as I rested beneath the porch of the temple of Adi Buddha Annando, by women who had been plundered of all they once possessed, their children sold into slavery or tortured to death, their habitations despoiled, merely because they happened to have property, and presumed to live independently upon lands which their more powerful neighbors coveted.

The greater number of these depredators were Siamese of influence, who had enrolled themselves as Christians under the French or the Portuguese flags, and unless the sufferer could claim the protection of either the one or the other, it seemed a cruel mockery to refer them for redress to any existing local authority, so long as P'haya Visate, a high but unprincipled Roman Catholic dignitary, was the governor of this district; and the saddest part of it all was, that the sufferers themselves felt there was no use in applying for justice to him.

In talking with some Buddhist men and women who were land proprietors in the vicinity, they told me that they were afraid of their Christian brethren, and would not, if they could prevent it, permit them to lease farms on their estates.

N

" Why ? " I asked.

" Because, if they once get hold of a house or a farm, they manage in time to turn us out."

" But how ? "

" Well, they lease small bits of land, year after year, expend money on it, and then, when they have a sufficiently large plantation to settle upon, they refuse to pay rent, go to law, and bring false witnesses to prove they have purchased the land of the owners, while the local authorities either take the part of the wrong-doers or imprison both parties until they have squeezed all they can out of them.   The Buddhist does not dare," said they, " to lay his hand upon the sacred tree * and swear falsely, because the god who lives in it sees all, and he dreads his vengeance.   But the Christian may swear to as many lies as he pleases, for the priests of the P'hra Jesu will give him absolution for them.   Where, then, is the harm to him ? "

I observed among the crowd a highly respectable looking and handsomely dressed woman, who sat apart, taking no share in the conversation, but listening with apparent interest to all that was said.   Her eyes were very dark and very fine, but filled with rather a sad expression.

Towards evening she rose to go away, but, as if on second thought, she turned to me and greeted me in a peculiarly sweet voice, that sounded like music to my ears after all the voices of the crowd, inviting us to go and take our evening meal at her house, to which she at once led the way.

A narrow, gravelled walk led to the house, situated in a lovely garden, and separated by a wilderness of wild plants and prickly-pears from the neighboring Christian village.   A long veranda with stone steps led down to the gravelled path.   Just in front stood an old banyan-tree,

* Boh, or bogara-tree.

lusty and burly in the full strength of its gnarled trunk, and vigorous, long boughs and branches forming arched and leafy bowers all round it.

The pathway ran through a shrubbery luxuriant with oleanders, jessamine, roses, laurel, and the Indian myrtle. Beneath these small wild rabbits had formed a colony, and it was curious to see a leaf moved upwards mysteriously, a head and ears protrude themselves, or a tail and legs, and then disappear as suddenly. This road ran to a great distance behind the house, and led through nearly three miles of ground, laid out in sugar, rice, cocoanut, and tobacco plantations. A small stream trickled through these, stagnating here and there into deep, green pools.

In passing near one of these pools I noticed that my hostess turned away her face, and in answer to my questions, she told me that it was once a large tank, but was now called Tâlataie, the Pool of Death. On further inquiry, I learned that this name had been given it from a tragic circumstance which had happened in her family ; that shortly after her eldest daughter's engagement to a young Siamese Christian, the betrothed pair went out for a ramble along the banks of the streamlet. Night descended, and the shadows deepened into midnight, but her daughter and her lover did not return. At length her fears were aroused, and the whole household set out with lanterns to search the grounds ; but nowhere could they find a trace of the absent couple until morning dawned upon their fruitless search, when her daughter was found lying on her face in the dark pool, stripped of all the beautiful jewels in which she had arrayed herself on the previous evening ; and her Christian lover was never seen or heard of again. " But her spirit still haunts the spot," said the sad mother to me, " and on moonlight nights I see her pale form floating in the pool and crying to us for help."

The lady then wiped away her tears with her black p'ha hom, or scarf, and led us into the house. Her husband, a much older and more melancholy-looking person, now appeared, and the slaves brought us a great many delicacies on silver trays.

While we partook of them, our hostess asked me a number of questions about my home, friends, children, and relatives. She then informed me that her family now consisted of one son and a daughter, and that the former was a Buddhist priest, serving in the very temple where she had met me.

"Where is your daughter now?" I inquired.

She pointed to a window which opened into an inner chamber. I looked in, and to my glad surprise saw seated on a low stool, holding an open book in which she seemed wholly absorbed, the same girl who had so attracted me on the Sunday evening previous.

Her face was very fine and seemingly full of spiritual beauty, and her figure surpassingly beautiful. While we stood gazing at her, some sudden and apparently painful emotion flitted rapidly across her face as she read in the book, like the shadow of a dark cloud over the quiet water.

The mother was silent, evidently making an effort to master the feelings which this sight occasioned in her breast, so as to speak calmly about it.

I sat down again, and inquired the name of the book in which her daughter was so absorbed.

"It is a book called Beeble," said the woman. "What kind of a book is it?"

I assured her that it was a very good book, the Book above all others ever printed; that her daughter did well to read it, and that it would help to develop her into a lovely and beautiful character.

I then left my kind hostess, satisfied and yet saddened by my trip to Tâmsèng.

CHAPTER XXVII.

NANG RUNGEAH, THE CAMBODIAN PROSELYTE.

TÂMSÈNG presented a picture of the sea at the moment when the tide is on the turn: there is always a lull, and sometimes a profound calm, before the mighty currents shift and set in another direction. The eager child who is piling up castles of sand one upon another on its shores pauses in wonder and astonishment at the sight. That strong angel, the tide, that he had watched in breathless delight advancing resistlessly, ever onward, nearer and nearer, rushing on to kiss with its foaming mouth his wayward feet, then rolling back, and "laughing from its lips the audacious brine," is suddenly arrested. The dull, surging roar that filled his ear, as if it were the voice of some mysterious sea-god, is hushed; the great sea has become silent and still, and the strong angel has expired. His last faint effort, and his feeble dying moan, fall upon the child's attentive eye and listening ear like a death-knell, for he has been told that this " tide " keeps the salt sea fresh and its shores healthful. He sets up a shout of despair, and prays the strong angel to return and trouble again the still waters, to renew the life which has passed away, and prevent that in-setting of stagnation that must bring with it mortal disease to the earth.

Religions have their tides as well as the ocean, and all life has its grand cyclical currents, whether in the church, the state, the individual, or the nation. Thus this little village of Tâmsèng seemed long since to have arrived at the period of that reaction which marks the disappearance of the tide from the sea, and the influx of that sluggish insensibility which foretells the beginning of the stagnation, which, if not removed, must inevitably end in mortification and death.

But now, after the torpor of nearly half a century, and through the death-like stagnation of the decaying village, there is heard a voice of general rejoicing. The main features of the place undergo a slight change; a gentle flow of life stirs its corpse-like visage; a beautiful and wealthy Cambodian heiress, the Lady Nang Rungeah is a candidate for baptism in the Roman Catholic Church.

On the 25th of June, it being the morning of her first confessional, the bells are set in motion and ring all day till sunset, as is the custom for a new convert, resounding in the glens and hollows and amid the spires of the Buddhist and Roman Catholic temples.

The chamber into which I had looked at a young girl reading with her heart and eyes a copy of the New Testament — translated, not by a Roman Catholic, but by an American Presbyterian missionary, the Rev. Mr. Mattoon — is now the centre of a most animated scene. Khoon P'hagunn and his wife Jethamas are seated in the little room in earnest conversation. They are interrupted by their daughter Rungeah, who comes quietly in, throws her arms around her mother, kneels before her and lays her head in her lap. The mother folds her arms tenderly around her child, and caresses her lovingly, smoothing her soft hair.

" Ah! Rungeah, art thou dressed already? Thou dost not need much adornment." And the old man's eyes brightened with pride and love as they lighted on the pleasant beauty and the graceful proportions of his daughter.

Nang Rungeah, the bright lotus-flower, was indeed pleasant to look upon. Hers was the half Indian and half Cambodian beauty so rare in Siam, — the large, long, drooping eye, round, oval face, and clear complexion, with a touch of healthful ruddiness in her cheeks, purple-black hair, soft and rich, falling loosely in long curls over her shoulders. The charms of her face and feature, however, were as naught to the brightness and kindliness that played over them like a sunny gleam. Her figure was remarkable, tall and lithe, yet perfectly rounded, and swelling fairly beneath the graceful bodice and the full skirt that fell in soft folds to her sandalled feet. The pin by which her veil was fastened was set off with a number of brilliants ; her arms were ornamented with gold bangles, and on her neck she wore a new chain, a gift from her sad and loving mother, a rosary of gold and black coral beads, to which was attached a massive gold figure of the Christ on the cross.

"Alas ! my child," said the mother at length, "I pray P'hra Buddh the Chow that no harm will come to thee through this new religion."

"I wonder to hear you speak thus, dear mother," replied the young girl, lifting her eyes reproachfully to her mother's face. "O, I wish you could be brought to see how much more beautiful this religion of P'hra Jesu is than that of Buddha; and then think of the beautiful ' Marie,' his Holy Mother, who is ever at his side, ready to whisper words of tender love and pity in behalf of such poor sinners as we are. I feel as if I should never go astray, or do any evil thing, now that I have the good priest to pray for me, and the Holy Mother and her Son to be my gods."

"P'hra Buddha forbid that I should mistrust your gods, my child ; but I do mistrust the priests and my own heart," said the anxious mother.

In spite of her love and her faith, Rungeah's cheek grew pale and her eyes filled with tears as she reached the chapel of Tâmsèng. With a palpitating heart she

knelt at the confessional-box, waiting for the priest to
take his place within, and open the small window through
which he heard the confessions of the congregation.

She hears a footstep on the other side. The priest enters, he shuts the door upon himself and takes his place;
he then pulls a cord which opens the little window of the
confessional-box, and shuts at the same time the door
which she had left ajar as she came into the chamber.

The confessional window is open, and the priest coughs
a slight cough; but Rungeah kneels there with her heart
beating and her hands folded, gazing on that ideal and
perfect manhood who has given up his life to save hers.

After a long interval of silence, the voice of the priest
breaks upon her ear, like the boom of a cannon amid a
garden of flowers.

" My daughter," said the voice, " confess your sins."

" My father," replies Rungeah, her love and joy breathing from her heart and struggling for utterance on her
lips, " whenever I think of Him, His goodness and His
love, of which I never tire reading, I am filled with gladness and praise; I am now never weary, never cast down,
never afflicted, nor does my heart or my pulse ever fail
me in loving and adoring Him."

" My daughter," interrupted the priest, suddenly, " this
is not confession; you must tell me of your secret sins,
the guilty thoughts, words, and acts you have cherished,
spoken, or committed, when you were still a believer in
the false and horrible doctrines of the Buddha."

A deep flush of pride, which the girl herself does not
quite understand, overspreads her beautiful face, and her
lips, still quivering, remain parted in surprise. Her secret
sins and guilty thoughts! Why blame her for not remembering them?

She was as pure as the snow-flake upon the mountain-
top.

She turned her thoughts upon herself, and tried to recall some sin; she would have given the world to find
some grave fault which she could justly own as hers, to
pour into the ears of the impatient priest. But she could
not recall a single one.

"My memory is treacherous, good father," said she ; " I
cannot now recall any one of my sins in particular, though
I must have done many, many wrong things, unless, indeed, it is the one I have committed in forsaking my dear
old god Buddha, whom I did truly love and reverence
until I heard and read of the beautiful P'hra Jesu."

"This is not satisfactory," said the priest, dryly ; " you
will have to do penance for such thoughts as these ; and
where did you read of P'hra Jesu ? "

"Ah ! " said the girl, " I have a beautiful book which
tells me all about him."

"But who gave it to you ? " persisted the priest.

"I found it in the temple of Adi Buddha Annando,
where it was left for my brother by an American priest."

The priest of Tâmsèng turned uneasily in his seat, and
coughed a low cough preparatory to what he was going
to say.

"My daughter," said he at length, in a voice of grave
reproof, " this last is a dreadful sin. That book is dangerous, and those American priests are our enemies.
They lie in wait to deceive the children of the true
Church. They deny the divinity of the Holy Mother
of God, and they go about the country preaching their
false doctrines and giving away their books only to de-
lude the simple-hearted natives. Be sure that you never
listen to them, and that you abstain from looking into
that book again. Bring the book to me, and you will be
saved from this great temptation."

The girl listened, abashed, hanging down her head, and
with tears of repentance in her eyes.

10

He then proceeded to state the penance she would have to perform.

To repeat fifty *paternosters*, walk, on the following Sabbath morning, barefooted, and dressed in her meanest garb, to the chapel of Tâmsèng, and be admitted thus by baptism into the true Church.

The priest again pulled the cord; the window was shut, the door stood ajar, and the girl rose and passed out to join her attendants. Her bright face was overcast, unbidden tears were in her eyes, and all her love and joy in the beautiful Saviour she had found blighted like autumn leaves before the wind. When she gained her boat, great black clouds lowered in the sky, the winds rose into a squall, and the waves tossed and tumbled and rolled high upon the banks. It was one of those sudden hurricanes that are so common in Siam. The boat proved unmanageable, and, in spite of all the combined efforts of the three women, she was capsized in the middle of the angry, surging waters. Long and desperately the women struggle for life, again and again they try to swim towards the bank, but the stronger waters carry them away in their irresistible grasp.

The high-priest of the temple of Adi Buddha Annando has taken shelter beneath the porch of his temple. He sees the empty boat and the struggling women; he hesitates. His vows forbid him to touch a woman, even his own mother, and still hold his office as a priest of Buddha. He sees the women throw up their arms as if imploring his aid. He casts aside his upper yellow robe, and plunges in to their rescue, regardless of his vows, his office, of everything else.

And now a sudden dizziness veils the eyes of the Nang Rungeah; while her companions are safe on the bank, she relaxes her efforts; a sickness like that of death overcomes her, and she sinks. But again the strong man plunges and dives deeper and deeper, and at last holds her firmly in his herculean arms. She hears, or she thinks she hears, the voice of the priest reproving her, and the jubilant chimes of Tâmsèng clang at her fainting heart as she is borne out of the dark waters and laid upon the flowery bank; but at length she opens her eyes on Maha Sâp, the chief priest of the temple of Adi Buddha Annando, her brother's tutor and guide. A slight shudder, and then a blush of shame passes over her as she recognizes her early religious teacher. But he, stooping, gathers a handful of flowers, hands them to her, and says: "Sadly and heavily did my heart ache to see thee in the grasp of the strong demons of the storm, and to save thee I have violated the vows of my order. But if thou wilt return to me one of these flowers as a token, I will neither regret the loss of my sanctity nor yet of my priestly office, but rejoice in the fates that have blessed me with a new life."

To the sonorous rushing and wild dash of the waters is joined the deep melodious voice of the priest, urging her to give him a token from his flowers; and the chimes now seem to swell into joyful choruses of jubilant anthems as she gives him the sweet token.

After the fury of the storm had abated, the priest left them and set off to confess himself to the Archbishop of the Ecclesiastical Court; and the women returned home.

The first thing Nang Rungeah did was to relate to her mother all that had befallen her from the time she entered the chapel of Tâmsèng to her return home. She then took the "dangerous book" from under her pillow and laid it on a high shelf out of her reach, but put in its place her crumpled flowers. Then she knelt down and repeated her fifty *paternosters* with lessening fervor, and tried to believe that she was a better woman. But how was it that her thoughts would stray from the morrow's bright vision, when she would publicly be baptized into the Church of Christ, to the dark face of Maha Sâp and the tenderness she had seen in his eyes.

She shut herself up in her chamber to weep and pray in agonizing doubts and fears, because of that something which has come between her and her beautiful P'hra Jesu.

CHAPTER XXVIII.

AD OGNI UCCELLO SUO NIDO È BELLO, — "TO EVERY BIRD
ITS OWN NEST IS CHARMING."

WHEN Rungeah awoke on the following morning, it seemed to her that she had just thrown off some wondrous and powerful spell that had somehow girt its strong and mysterious illusions about her heart. A new soul from within that inmost chamber had started into life. She faltered, hesitated, and dropped on her knees and raised her eyes towards heaven, and felt as she had never done before.

In her visions — strange contradiction of human nature — and in her holiest thoughts of the beloved Mother and her Son, the face of the priest of Buddha would intrude.

Her prayers finished, she put on her most faded and meanest robe, laid aside all her customary adornments and jewels, save only her veil and her rosary, and, attended by a host of fond relatives and slaves, and among them the priest her brother, and Maha Sâp in a layman's dress, went her way barefooted to the chapel, where she solemnly recanted the errors of Buddhism, and was baptized into the church of Christ.

Again the merry bells were rung, and on the dark face of the priest of Tâmsèng might be seen

> "The slow wise smile, that round about
> His dusty forehead dryly curled,
> Seemed half within and half without,
> And full of dealings with the world."

A month after her baptism, Mariâ, as Rungeah was now named, was selected, on account of her great piety and devotion, to be one of the female wardens of the chapel.

This distinction she enjoyed with six other girls, whose duty it was to dust and sweep the chapel, clean the lamps and the gold and silver candlesticks, and to dress the altar with fresh flowers.*

Saturday was the day appointed to Mariâ to serve in the chapel, and a lovely warden was the gentle Cambodian girl. She had given up the dangerous book to her father confessor. But the handful of crumpled flowers still nestled under her pillow, and her secret preference for Maha-Sâp was deeply hidden in her heart; and yet it proved an impenetrable barrier, as long as she lived, between her and her confessor.

It was touching to see this girl at her duties in the chapel. After the floor had been swept, and the candlesticks polished and replenished with fresh candles, and the flowers arranged in the vases in the niches, and the garlands hung over the images of the gods and the saints, she would kneel at the foot of the sad Christ, after having touched with her lips the nailed and bleeding feet, praying to him to make her as noble and as self-sacrificing as himself, and to the tender Mother to intercede for her at the throne of grace.

One Saturday evening, Mariâ, having spent a comfortless day within herself, repaired to the chapel as usual, attended only by the oars-women, to open it for the evening service. She opened wide the doors, and sat herself down under the cross. There were rays of comfort emanating from that figure nailed on it forever, that had now become very precious to her.

Long after the congregation had dispersed, she knelt on

* This is one of the Buddhist customs adopted by the Catholics for the purpose of securing the daughters of rich natives as servants of the Church.

the floor of the sanctuary. All the religion of the place and the hour came over her, and a strange yearning sorrow, for which she could not account. And as she knelt there she fancied that a shadow darkened the lights that streamed down from the altar upon her, but only for a moment, for the next found the shadow gone, and tears gathering in her eyes. "Alas! what is it that steals my thoughts from Thee to Buddha, and the temple in which I once loved to worship?" muttered the girl, conscience-stricken at her own depravity.

The chapel bell suddenly "flung out" the hour of five, i. e. ten o'clock. She rose from her knees, put out the lights, and, locking the doors, turned into the dark deserted street; but somehow a sudden fear overcame her, and a feeling that somebody was watching her, perhaps following her. She drew her veil over her face and ran breathlessly towards the river, where she gained her boat and returned home for the night.

The Roman Catholic Missionary Society at Bangkok consisted of one bishop and from fifteen to twenty priests, besides a number of proselytes from the Siamese and the Chinese, who also were admitted into the priesthood. Of the former, most of the priests were endowed with every talent that a strict collegiate education could furnish; but the latter were particularly useful, because, besides being professing and, some of them, sincere Christians, they possessed the power of expounding the doctrines of the Church to their native brethren in a language natural to themselves from their birth. Nor was this all; they were nearly all well skilled in medicine and surgery, which gave them more power than the French priests in winning over the discontented followers of the Buddha to lend a willing ear to the marvellous facts of the Christian faith. And, moreover, as the teachings and ceremonies of the Roman Catholic Church are in many respects almost identical with the Buddhist teachings and ceremonies, the Roman Catholic priests are more successful in making proselytes than their Protestant colaborers in the same field.

When a poor ignorant Buddhist goes into his temples he sees the images of the Buddha, and he sees certain forms and prostrations practised, the burning of incense, the bowing before the well-lit shrines, and hears prayers uttered in an unknown tongue, and he knows also that the most heinous sin that can be committed by the Buddhist priest is the violation of his oath of celibacy. And if from idle curiosity he should be induced to enter a Roman Catholic chapel or church, to his surprise and delight he observes not only forms and ceremonies very nearly approaching to those used in his own temple, but also images and pictures far more beautiful and attractive than those of his own gods. On inquiring he finds that the priests of this faith also do not marry, that they have the marvellous power to absolve the transgressor from the consequences of his deadly sins, and that the only thing necessary to escape the irresistible " wheel of the law " is faith in Christ. So the poor, timorous, trembling soul, that feels a certain consciousness of a fearful retribution awaiting his sins, and yet knows not where or to whom to fly, hails with joy the name of Christ, the all-atoning sacrifice, as a rock on which to rest his weary wings, and fears no more the inexorable "wheel" of the Divine vengeance.

It is not to be wondered at, then, that the Siamese, Peguans, and Cambodians readily give ear to the native Catholic priests, and particularly when even the French and Portuguese priests adapt themselves, in many instances, to the usages and customs of the natives themselves, the most striking of which are in employing the children of the rich as wardens and keepers of the churches, and of never wearing any covering on their heads.

On the morning following the night on which Mariâ had lingered so late in the chapel, Khoon Jethamas had risen at daybreak; for ever since the day of the eventful thunder-storm she had troubled dreams accompanied with signs and omens that foretold approaching calamity; and now she sat alone on the doorstep, meditating sadly on the future of her dear child.

It had been predicted by a wise old man, in the days of Rungeah's infancy, that " she was born under the fatal star Sathimara, who would assume the form of a fair and beautiful angel to lead her on to her own destruction."

The pagan mother could not discern between the heavenly and the earthly church of Christ, nor between the true and the false ministers of the gospel. And now the prophecy seemed in a way of being fulfilled, but, like all prophecies, in the most unlooked-for manner.

Suddenly the dark priest of Tâmsèng with a band of officers appeared on the gravel walk. The lady gave a cry of alarm that brought nearly the whole household to her side, and, as the priest with the officers persisted in forcing an immediate entrance into the house, there ensued a violent scuffle between the officers of the law and the slaves of P'hagunn.

" Very good," said the padre, doggedly; " it is certain, however, that the chapel of Tâmsèng has been plundered by Mariâ and a vile pagan who was seen lurking in its vicinity last night."

On hearing this the blood rushed violently to the mother's temples, and she fell back in a death-like swoon.

P'hagunn and his numerous attendants were also stupefied by horror and dismay at this dreadful accusation; and the officers, headed by the padre, proceeded coolly to search the house for the missing jewels and the gold and silver

10 *

candlesticks, censers, and vases that had ornamented the altar of the chapel of Tâmsèng.

At last they reached Mariâ's chamber. She had just risen, and was now on her knees before the open window. The door was burst open, and she turned, still kneeling and holding her breath, her fixed and terrified gaze upon the intruders.

The chapel and the convent bells struck six. It was the hour when she usually set out to perform her small round of sacred offices and to open the church doors. But she had no power to move. She saw the padre dash aside her pillow and then her mattress, and with it her crumpled flowers. One of the men came towards her and demanded the key of the chapel. But she could not open her lips to speak; she knelt there petrified in the morning sunlight.

"To think that *you* should have connived at such an outrageous sacrilege upon the altar of God!" said the padre; and he ordered the men to handcuff her and carry her away to the prison at Tâmsèng.

She made no resistance, but let them do whatever they wished with her; she seemed even to have lost the power of comprehension. She sees the trees, the thatched roofs, the plantations, the fields, the tapering spires of the Temple of the Infinite, and a thousand small objects; she hears voices and cries that would have escaped her at another time, as she is dragged from the home of her parents to the prison cell of the doomed, but she cannot speak, or cry, or even think where she put the key. She knows that her mother is seated outside of the prison door, wailing and crying, and protesting that her child is innocent of the dreadful crime of which she is accused; and this is all that is clear to the stricken girl.

Twilight was falling just as I was coming out of the palace, — for I had been detained there all day helping the secretary to despatch the royal mail, — when Khoon Jethamas came running up to me, took both my hands in hers, and told me the story of her daughter's imprisonment.

What was to be done ?   The woman was frantic with grief, and I was almost as much confounded as she.

" You must come with me to-night, dear lady, this very evening.   I cannot rest till I get her out of that dreadful place."

I at last persuaded her to come to my house and take a cup of tea, and when I had soothed her so that she could make herself intelligible, I thought the affair did not look quite so hopeless as she supposed, and I tried to make her take a more cheerful view of the matter. The only thing that seemed strange was that Mariâ could give no account of what she had done with the key of the chapel door.

Whoever robbed the chapel had got possession of the key.   The locks on the chapel were of European manufacture, and there were only two keys that could open them, one in the possession of the padre Tomas, and the other in the keeping of the young wardens, who transferred it to the next person on duty after the morning service.

In a short time Khoon Jethamas and I were rowing against the tide for the village of Tâmsèng.   On cross-questioning the lady, I discovered that the late priest Maha-Sâp had been seen prowling about the chapel when Rungeah, as the mother still called her, was at her devotions, and that on the following morning he was going towards the same spot when he was taken prisoner.

I confess that now I began to feel anxious, for the value of the jewels, etc., that were stolen was fixed at several laks or millions of ticals, an incredible sum which no person could pay.   I hardly knew what to think.

Amid hopes and fears, and innumerable plans, which were abandoned as soon as formed for new ones that seemed equally impracticable, we reached the prison of Tâmsèng.

What a dreadful spot it was in the night-time! And the very darkness was aggravated by the people around, who looked more savage and fiercer than wild beasts. Before and behind and on all sides there were rags and filth and wretchedness crowding upon us with the double darkness of night and misery. Some hideous women were jailers; for a few ticals and a promise not to tell upon them, they allowed us to go in and see the girl.

Rungeah sat as one entranced, with her eyes fixed upon the ground, as if she expected Jesus or the Mother to rise up out of it to vindicate her cause. We could not get her to say a word, to utter a cry or even a moan. We were almost as much overwhelmed at her grief as she was by the padre's accusation.

What was to be done?

Leaving Rungeah, we set off for the convent of Tâmsèng.

The clock had long before struck eight, when we came to the convent gate, and we were full of hope. But no light was to be seen, and a high wooden fence ran all round the house. Groping our way, we came to a gate at last, but it was locked. We began to knock, and we knocked loudly for a quarter of an hour, and then we waited to see if any one would come to open it. No one came. We were uncertain what to do, the night came on full of clouds, clothing with darkness even the star-filled depths. The convent clock struck nine, and the thought of poor Rungeah struggling with her anguish came with redoubled force upon the mother's heart, and again we both knocked together more and more loudly. At length lights appeared amid the gloom, and three women with lanterns approached and demanded who we were and what we wanted. On hearing that I was a Christian woman, they opened the gate, and after surveying us carefully, passing their lanterns up and down our persons from head to foot, they led the way to the apartments of the Lady Abbess. When we entered, we found a morose-looking old lady of Portuguese descent seated on a tall high-backed chair, with nine or ten young women, mostly Siamese, sewing scapulars. All round the room were dreadful pictures of the Christ and the Mother in all kinds of agonizing attitudes.

We proceeded to make our business known, which was only to go bail for Rungeah until the trial should come off, and to ask the Abbess's influence with the padre Tomas in urging our request.

The old lady coolly replied that it was her duty to wait upon the Lord Jesus, and not to rush about the country, as some folks did, intermeddling with other people's business.

We left her with clouded hearts, and set out for the house of the padré. As we were women, which we in our distress of mind had quite forgotten, the servants or slaves of this holy individual drove us from the doorstep with scorn and contemptuous language for our indelicacy in going there at all.

We then, but less hopefully, turned our almost fainting steps to the house of the Governor P'haya Visate. Khoon Jethamas was afraid to enter, but I was not going away without seeing him. I climbed the steps and entered the veranda ; two slaves went before to report our arrival. I saw the great man seated on a cushion in a room adjoining, with women and men crouching in all sorts of abject attitudes before him. I walked in, ready, at the mother's request, to double and treble the bail if necessary. As soon as he saw me approaching, the governor rose, retired

to his bedchamber, and shut the door violently in my
face.

I came away completely cast down and defeated ; as
for the poor mother, she wrung her hands and wept
piteously. It was now nearly eleven o'clock, and we
went back to the prison. The unhappy Khoon Jethamas
took up her abode near the only window of the cell where
her daughter was immured. I left her sitting on a strip
of matting, with her hands over her face, shutting out the
outer darkness, in order to realize the utter darkness that
had fallen upon her life and upon the light of her home.

Nights and days succeeded each other in regular succession, and day after day I went to the prison to find
the patient, loving mother living under the shadow of
its roof, so as to be ever near her child, and once a day
she was admitted to see her loved one visibly wasting
away. The only change that had taken place in the prisoner, that was hopeful, was, that now it was she who
comforted her mother every day, by relating to her her
bright visions, and assuring her that she felt the time
was not far distant when the Mother and her Son would
come down from heaven to proclaim her innocence ; that
the holy angels descended at night to bless and comfort
her with loving promises of speedy justice, and that now
the prison-house had been transformed by them into a
paradise.

There are mysteries in all religions, which the uninitiated cannot penetrate, and we stood abashed and silent
on the other side of the veil that was lifted for the spiritual consolation of this strange girl.

The burning July sun shone daily on the tiled roof of
the prison of Tâmsèng. The ground on one side was full
of muddy pools, and the river on the other was the cess-
pool of the village, — a liquid mass of poison from which
rose the pestilence and the cholera that brooded with their

deathlike wings over the inhabitants of Tâmsèng.   The
evening air was either heavy with noxious vapors or it
came in fitful burning gusts across the river, and brought
no balm to the suffering prisoners within.

Rungeah languished day after day, for the case was to
be tried before the International Court of Siam, and the
days and the weeks and the months passed away like

> "A stream whose waters scarcely seem to stray,
> And yet they glide like happiness away."

With them poor Rungeah's bright faith began to grow
dim, and her nightly prayers to the Mother and her
holy Son were less and less hopeful, but yet she still
strove with each returning day to revive her drooping
spirits, and with sweet self-deceit " to paint elysium "
upon the darkness of her prison-walls.

The mother bribed the jailers to take to her daughter
some little delicacies every day, for the coarse prison food
disgusted the girl, and she was gradually being starved
to death; and now a low cough and a hectic fever had
set in.

The judicial courts of Siam, one and all included, were
neither better nor worse than that of other Oriental and
despotic kingdoms; and the judges of the outer city, with
the exception, as far as I know, of only one man, his
Highness Mom Kratai Rajoday, were very far from being
model judges.   They aimed no higher than the traditional
policy of the empire, "the good old rule" that "might
makes right," which had guided the rulers of Siam ever
since Siam began to exist as a kingdom and a nation; so
that everybody preyed upon his weaker neighbor, and
everybody was obliged to suffer, without hope of redress,
the wrongs which one stronger than himself could inflict.

Meanwhile the mother grew more and more impatient
for her daughter's trial, which seemed to her as if purposely delayed, and in an unguarded moment she accused

the padre Tomas of having secreted the jewels and ornaments of the altar of Tâmsèng, and of having made a false accusation against her daughter for the sole purpose of laying claim to her estate. The padre became exasperated and brought a charge of libel against the mother; and poor Rungeah was more and more hopelessly a prisoner.

The timid P'hagunn shut himself up in his house, and left it to his brave wife to threaten the Christian officials, and to haunt the courts with her complaints, expending large sums of money, but without result.

At length, as Rungeah was really very ill, and I feared she would die, I accompanied Khoon Jethamas on a private visit to his Highness Mom Kratai Rajoday, the chief judge of the International Court, taking with me a private letter from the king, which simply stated that I wished to be made personally acquainted with him.

The judge received us very cordially indeed, and the unhappy Jethamas threw herself at his feet, and with tears and sobs implored of him to hasten the trial of her child, which he most kindly promised to do.

It was now December, and three days after our visit to the chief judge the trial came on.

I could not attend on the two first days, but on Saturday, the 10th of December, 1864, I accompanied Khoon Jethamas and the feeble and wasted Rungeah to the court, where I was rejoiced to see his Highness Mom Kratai Rajoday presiding in person. All the preliminaries had been gone through with on the two previous days. The court-house was crammed with native Christians, Buddhists, and Cambodians, so that there was not even standing room to be had anywhere.

After going through a great many forms and ceremonies, such as laying the right hand on a branch of the boh-tree, and thence on his left side, and taking the

Buddhist's oath, Maha-Sâp's innocence was clearly proved. He confessed, however, that he was in the habit of repairing to the chapel morning and evening, but that his sole motive was to be near by to protect Rungeah from any danger that might threaten her.

The judge then turned and asked Rungeah to relate again all that she had done on the night of the robbery.

All her natural grace of feature, all her excellences of mind and soul, shone out as she calmly repeated her story; the only thing she could not account for was where she had dropped the key. " But," said she, " my soul and my conscience acquit me of this sin. How then shall I plead guilty to that which I have not done ? Will it not be accounted a sin against myself by P'hra Jesu and his Holy Mother in heaven ? "

The beating hearts of the crowd were suspended in breathless expectation; some being interested for and some against the prisoners. The next moment the judge declared that Rungeah and Maha-Sâp had been imprisoned on insufficient grounds; that their innocence was quite apparent, even without or rather before the trial, and that the case was dismissed.

Scarcely were these words articulated, when a shout like that of a great hurricane broke from the excited masses of the people; the boarded floor seemed to thrill and ripple as with the throes of an earthquake, and the crowd staggered to and fro as if inebriated with the sudden paroxysm of joy. It was to them not so much the cause of a young and beautiful Cambodian lady of high rank, as the cause of Buddhism against Roman Catholicism.

I was stunned with their deafening roar. But poor Rungeah was too feeble to bear the sudden and overwhelming joy of her acquittal; an exclamation of the wildest delight broke from her pale lips, and she fell back insensible.

The excited crowd unable to master their now as sudden agony at the sight of the apparently lifeless girl, were hushed, and a lull as profound as death succeeded. They bore her to the boat and laid her down in it, and her mother implored me to go home with them. In the fresh air, as we rowed slowly along, the girl soon revived, and, putting out her arms, drew her mother down to her, and held her firmly to her breast.

Maha-Sâp, her brother, both noble-looking men, and a crowd of people, followed in another boat.

As we approached the temple of Adi Buddha Annando, Rungeah whispered to her mother to take her in there to rest; that she was weary, and that it would comfort her to enter its sacred precincts once more.

The sun is near his setting, and broad lights and shadows are lying upon and veiling the grand proportions of the temple of the " Infinite."

Now the boats are fastened to the pier, and a little group follows the women who are bearing the form of Rungeah into the temple.

It is the hour of the Buddhists' evening prayer. They bring a small mat, and she is laid in the middle of the temple, while the bonzes are seated on either side, waiting for the high-priest to open the vesper service.

During the service the girl lies there with her eyes closed.

Sunshine is reflected in wonderful glory from the head of the great silver image of the Adi Buddh. Sunshine is flooding the temple, glorifying the stolid idols that are standing around, and streaming on the floor and over the quiet figure of the girl. Her face assumes an ashy hue, and she again puts out her arms and draws her mother down to her.

"O mother, pray to the Virgin Mother for me," says the girl, "to tell P'hra Jesu that I am innocent."

The pagan mother makes no reply, but bends an agonized look on her dear child's face, and the girl's face becomes grayer in the floods of sunlight. Her fingers twitch and quiver around her mother's neck.

The priests are hushed, and the temple is more and more flooded with light; and the faint, sweet, pleading voice of the girl is again heard: "Mother, dear mother, pray to P'hra Jesu that he shut not the heavenly gates upon me"; and the strong love of the mother conquers her religious scruples, and, lying there with her head cushioned on the bosom of her dying child, she raises her voice and prays: —

"O thou who art called P'hra Jesu, free my child from sin. O forgive her, sacred One. She has loved thee to the last. She believes in none but thee. Be thou her God, and shut not, O shut not thy heavenly gates upon her, even though they shut her out forever from my sorrowing heart and eyes."

At the utterance of those strange syllables falling from the lips of a Buddhist mother in the most solemn of the temples of the Buddha, a marvellous change passed over the face of the dying girl; the gray pallor of death gave place to a heavenly light, and a faint but lovely smile irradiated her pale lips. She opened her eyes and gazed enraptured upon some vision that seemed to float before her. "O mother, mother," cried the exulting voice of the girl, "I see P'hra Jesu and P'hra Buddha; Ph'ra Jesu is above and P'hra Buddha is below, and the two mothers, Marie and Maia * are sitting side by side, and they are all smiling and calling me upward, upward." And Rungeah stretched out her arms and closed her eyes, the gray pallor returned; her spirit fluttered for a moment,

* One of the names of the mother of the Buddha.

and then was gone forever.   But the smile never left her lips.

She was buried with the rites of the Roman Catholic Church, with her rosary and the golden image of Christ on her bosom, by a French priest from the other side of the village of Tâmsèng.

Two years after, a man was taken in the act of plundering the jewels of a princess of Siam, as she was travelling in her boat to Ayudia, and on his trial he confessed that he was a Christian, that he had been betrothed to Rungeah's sister, whom he had murdered for the sake of her jewels, and then fled to Ayudia, whence having gambled away all the proceeds of his spoils, he once more returned to Bangkok and robbed the chapel of Tâmsèng.   He offered to deliver up the jewels, etc., if his life should be spared.   His request was granted, but he was condemned to lifelong imprisonment, while the crown and the diadem are once more to be seen on the brows of the figure of the Christ and the Virgin Mary, and the gold and silver candlesticks again light up the altar of the little chapel of Tâmsèng.

CHAPTER XXIX.

STRAY LEAVES FROM THE ROYAL SCHOOL-ROOM TABLE.

THE three temples around which the city of the Nang Harm had taken root and gradually grown to its present dimensions were especially remarkable. The one in which I taught, Watt Khoon Chom Manda Thai, — Temple of the Mothers of the Free, — was formerly dedicated to the mother of the Buddha, as its ancient name Manda Maia Goudamana clearly shows; and the other was dedicated to the "Buddha Thapinya," Buddha the Omniscient, and the third and most beautiful to the "Buddha Annando,"* Buddha the Infinite, — all names from the Pali. The general effect of each of these buildings is that of some great church in the southern part of Europe. The basement story is a square mass of about two hundred feet on each side, with double rows of windows flanked by pilasters and crowned with a curious flamboyant spiral canopy, in what may be called the French-Gothic style. These pilasters and this canopy are the two most marked and universal features in the Buddhist architecture; at the middle of each side of the basement rises a lofty porch or ante-hall, terminating in an immense gabled façade, pilastered and canopied like the windows. These halls or vestibules convert the temple into a vast Greek cross. Over the basement rise a number of diminishing terraces with small pagodas at the angles, the

---

* I would here remark that all intelligent Buddhists make a very marked distinction between the Buddha and the Buddh. Buddh, or as he is sometimes called, Adi Buddha, is the Supreme Intelligence, from whom Buddha is only an emanation, has existed from all eternity.

whole culminating in a pyramidal steeple like the Hindoo shivala; and lastly the steeple itself is crowned with a chayatree, or tapering umbrella of gilt iron-work, rising to nearly two hundred feet from the ground.

The interior consists of two great concentric corridors with large recesses for the images. Most of the images are standing figures; the Buddha alone is either seated or reclining, in various attitudes of benediction, or preaching on elevated lotus-shaped pedestals. The vaulted cells in which the Buddha is seated reach up to the second and sometimes to the third terrace, and from a small window in the roof there streams a flood of sunlight downwards on the head and shoulders of the colossus, with wonderful effect.

There is great uncertainty about the dates and builders of these three temples, and I know nothing more interesting and beautiful than the legend which is attached to the spot on which they stand. In the Siamese annals, however, it is stated that these temples have stood here for nearly twelve hundred years, embedded in what was once a sacred grove of olive, palm, and boh trees, before Bangkok was ever settled, and in the palmy days of the ancient and beautiful city of Ayodhya or Ayudia; that they then attracted pilgrims from all parts of the world, particularly women, who came to perform vows or to offer votive sacrifices at their shrines.

It was P'hra P'huthi Chow L'huang, a usurper, who, in order to establish more securely his throne, selected the vicinity of these triad temples as the seat of government, removed his palace from the west to the east bank of the Mèinam, founded a city, surrounded it with triple walls, and called it the abode of the beautiful and invincible archangel.

As often as I sat in the porches of these temples, the chanted prayers of the worshippers boomed through the aisles and inspired me with feelings of the deepest devotion; and whenever I passed along the dim, silent corridors, and came unexpectedly in front of one of the great golden images with its folded arms and drooping eyelids, looking down upon me in monitory sadness, with the wisdom of ages stamped upon its brow, amid the gloom of a never-ending twilight, while the head and shoulders were illuminated by a halo of light from the unseen source above, the effect was strangely mystical, solemn, and profound.

The character of these buildings I do not exaggerate in calling them sublime; they prove unmistakably that the architect, whoever he was,

> "Wrought in a sad sincerity;
> Himself from God he could not free;
> He builded better than he knew:
> The conscious stone to beauty grew."

This impression was deepened every time I visited them, and, though I knew every inch of the temples and their surroundings, the meanings of some of the symbols remained mysterious and incomprehensible. If I succeeded in unravelling one portion, the remainder was lost in inextricable perplexity and doubt.

My pupils in that wonderful city numbered from twenty to twenty-five boys and girls, the loveliest and most remarkable of whom were the heir-apparent, the Prince Somdetch P'hra Paramendr Maha Chulalonkorn, his younger sister, the little fairy-like creature Fa Ying,* the Princesses Wanee, Ying-You Wahlacks, Somawati, the Prince Kreta-Bhinniharn, the only son of Hidden-Perfume, P'hra Ong Dwithwallabh, and Kabkranockratin, the sons of the child-wife; and in addition to these were several gentlewomen of the harem.

We always began school immediately after the Buddh-

---

* See "English Governess at the Siamese Court," Chap. XIII. p. 116.

ists' morning service, which I was obliged to attend, so as to muster my pupils together in good order, and which was held precisely at nine o'clock in the temple of the Chom Manda Thai. The long inlaid and richly gilt table on which we pursued our studies day after day was the same on which had been laid every morning for hundreds of years offerings to the priests of Buddha, and whereon stood the bronze censers and the golden vases from which ascended clouds of fragrant incense amid the perfume of still more fragrant flowers, while the brilliant colors of the silks, satins, diamonds, and jewels that adorned the regal worshippers relieved the gloom.

The studies that took the most absolute possession of the fervid Eastern imaginations of my pupils were geography and astronomy. But each had his or her own idea about the form of the earth, and it needed no small amount of patient repetition to convince them that it was neither flat nor square, but round.

The only map — and a very ancient one it was — which they had ever seen was one drawn and painted about a century before, by a Siamese who was thought to possess great scientific and literary attainments.

This map was five feet long by three wide; in the centre was a great patch of red, and above it a small patch of green. On the part painted red — which was intended to represent Siam — was pasted a comical-looking human figure, cut out of silver paper, with a huge pitchfork in one hand and an orange in the other. There was a crown on the head and spurs on the heels, and the sun was shining over all. The legs, which were of miserably thin dimensions, met sympathetically at the knees. And this cadaverous-looking creature was meant for the king of Siam, — indicating that so vast were his strength and power they extended from one end of his dominions to the other. In the little patch of green, intended to rep-

QUEEN OF SIAM.

resent Birmah, was a small Indian-ink figure, consisting
of a little dot for the body, another smaller one for the
head, and four scratches of the pen for the legs and arms;
this was meant for the king of Birmah.[27] A legion of little
imps, in many grotesque attitudes, were seen dancing about
his dominions; and these almost unintelligible hieroglyphics were to show to the uninitiated in what a disturbed
state the Birman Empire was, and what an insignificant
personage in his own dominions was the king of that
country. On the north side of the green patch was
painted a huge Englishman, sporting a cocked hat with
red feathers, clasping in his arms what was meant for a
vast tract of land. This was marked as British Birmah,
and the Englishman was Lord Clive, holding on to it. The
rest of the map was all blue, and all around the Siamese
territories richly painted and heavily freighted ships were
sailing to and fro. But the poor Birmese monarch had
not a boat to display. My simple pupils knew just so
much as this map taught them, and no more. Birmah on
the north, and Siam on the south, and the sea all around,
— this was the world to them.

But of their celestial geography they could tell me a
host of interesting particulars, all of which they would
relate with the accuracy and picturesque vividness of a
fairy tale; and whenever a dispute arose as to the height
of some of the mountains or the depth or breadth of
the oceans in the celestial worlds, they would at once
refer to a Siamese book, called "Tri Loke Winit Chai,"
— a book which settles all questions about the three
worlds, of angels, of demons, and of gods, — and find
therein a satisfactory solution of their difficulties. In
their celestial chronology they were all equally well
grounded. A little fellow of nine years old, when speaking of "time," stood upright in his chair and informed me
that he was "time." His name signified a period of time

11   P

appointed for the creation or the destruction of a world.
He then proceeded to tell me with wonderful clearness for
one so young, "that the first time, or Kâp, is reckoned by
the Siamese from the appearance of a certain cloud called
god-thirst, which was the harbinger of a creative rain, and
which brought into existence the worlds and their attendant suns and moons; that the second Kâp, or time, is the
period between the creation of these worlds and the coming
of another great cloud denominated the dissolving cloud,
and which is the third Kâp and the forerunner of the dis-
solution of the worlds; and the fourth Kâp is the period
when matter remains in a chaotic mass, waiting for the
generative cloud, — god-thirst, — which again pours forth
the creative rain, and life once more springs into being.
These four periods added together make a Maha-Kâp."

When I pressed him to state the number of years contained in a Maha-Kâp, he became indignant, and replied,
"that as the length of a single Kâp could not be com-
puted by the gods themselves, it was unreasonable for me
to suppose that he could give me any correct estimate of
their actual duration."

I soon found that my pupils were in some respects
much wiser than I, and thenceforth we exchanged
thoughts and ideas. I gave them sound realities in return for their poetic illusions and chimeras, which had
for me a certain charm and a great deal of odd reason-
ableness, for it was their way of explaining the incomprehensible.

When a large English map and globes of the celestial
and terrestrial spheres arrived, they created quite a sensation in the ancient temple of the "Mothers of the Free."
His Majesty caused the map to be set in a massive gold
frame, and placed it with the globes on ponderously gilt
supporters in the very middle of the temple, and for nine
days crowds of women came to be instructed in the sci-

ences of geography and astronomy, so that I found my hands quite full. It was hard for them to see Siam reduced to a mere speck on the great globe, but there was some consolation in the fact that England occupied even a smaller space. After the first excitement had worn off, my pupils began to enjoy their lessons; they would cluster round the globes, delighted with the novel idea of a world revolving in space, and some of them were as keen as any Arctic explorer for the discovery of the North Pole, where they could some day sit astride, as they thought, with perfect ease and security, and satisfy their doubts about the form and the revolution of the earth.

I found them always full of eager inquiry, unlike most Western children, about the sun and moon and stars; but they preferred to have them peopled with demons, ghosts, and hobgoblins, rather than to have them uninhabited.

On one occasion, when I informed them that the moon was supposed to be uninhabited, all the little eager faces were clouded, and their interest flagged, and little Wanee declared, "that for her part she was convinced that the moon was the beautiful daughter of a great king of Ayudia, who lived many thousands of years ago, and the head wife of the sun, and not a great stupid ball of earth and rock rolling about in the sky to no purpose but for the sun to shine upon."

One day the steamer "Chow P'haya" brought his Majesty a box of ice from Singapore, and I obtained some for an object-lesson.[28] The women and children found no difficulty in believing that it was water frozen; but when I went to tell them about snow, the whole school became indignant at what they considered an evident stretch of my imagination, and my dear simple friend, Hidden-Perfume, laid her hand gently upon my arm, and said, " Please do not say that again. I believe you like my own heart in everything you have taught to me, but this sounds like the story of a little child who wishes to say something more wonderful than anything that was ever said before." So my lesson of the snow proved a stumbling-block to me for several days; my pupils' imaginations had taken alarm, and they could not be brought to believe the simplest statements.

I informed his Majesty of my dilemma; he came to my aid, and assured the royal children that it was just possible that there was such a thing as snow, for English books of travel spoke frequently of some phenomenon which they designated as " snow."

On another occasion, as we were all busily engaged in tracing the river Nile on an ancient map of Egypt, there fell suddenly from the vaulted roof above our heads, and upon the very centre of our chart on the table, a coil of something that looked at first like a beautiful thick silk cord neatly rolled up; in another instant, however, the coil unrolled itself, and began to move slowly away. I screamed, and fled to the extreme end of the temple. But what was my surprise to see all my pupils sitting calmly in their seats, with their hands folded in veneration and their eyes fixed in glowing admiration on the serpent as it moved in tortuous curves along the entire length of the table. With a blush of shame and a sense of inferiority I returned to my seat and watched with them the beautiful creature; a certain feeling of fascination dawned upon me as I looked into its clear, bright, penetrating eyes; the upper part was of a fine violet color, its sides covered with large scales of crimson edged with black; the abdominal parts were of a pale rose-color edged likewise with black; while the tail terminated in tints of a bluish ash of singular delicacy and beauty. As the snake slowly dragged itself to the end of the table I held my breath in terror, for it dropped on the arm of the chair on which the Prince Somdetch Choufa Chulalonkorn was seated, whence it fell on the floor, trailed itself along through the dim corridor and down the steps, and finally passed out of sight under the stone basement of the temple.

On the moment of its disappearance my pupils jumped up from their seats and clustered around me in the wildest joy, caressing me, and declaring that the gods loved me dearly, else they would not have sent me such an auspicious token in favor of my teaching. I was told that the gliding of the snake all over the table was full of happy omens, and that its dropping on the arm of the Prince's chair was an unmistakable sign that he would one day become famous in wisdom and knowledge. All the old and young women congratulated me, as did even the king himself, who, when he heard of the singular visitor we had had, caused the circumstance to be made known to the wise men and women of the court, and they all united in pronouncing it to be a wonderful and inspiring recognition of favor from on high. From this time I was treated with great consideration and respect by the simple-hearted women and mothers of the harem, but I nevertheless felt not a little uncomfortable for days after the sudden descent of the snake, and secretly hoped I might never again be so signally favored by the gods.

I afterwards learned that this snake has three names. In Sanskrit it is celebrated as the Sarpa Rakta, the red snake, who brings secret omens from the gods; in Pali, as the Naghalalvana, the crimson snake of the woods, who carries on his person in glowing letters the name of his great master; and in Siamese, Gnuthongdang, the crimson-bellied snake, who brings with its appearance all that is good and great to the beholder.

I leave it with my readers to decide which is the better, our inherited dread of and desire to destroy the serpent race, or the Siamese custom of idealizing, though with a certain superstitious reverence, the meanest of the works of nature.

Among the ladies of the harem, I knew one woman who more than all the rest helped to enrich my life and to render fairer and more beautiful every lovely woman I have since chanced to meet. Her name translated itself — and no other name could ever have been so appropriate — into "Hidden Perfume." Her clear, dark eyes were clearer and calmer, her full lips had a stronger expression of tenderness about them, and her brow, which was at times smooth and open, and at others contracted with pain, grew nobler and more beautiful as the purposes of her life, strengthened by new elements, grew deeper and broader each day.

She had been deprived of her opportunity of loving as a wife and a woman, and the sorrow that had broken up the fountains of her nature now caused them to flow into deeper channels, for she had become an earnest and devoted mother.

Our daily lessons and talks had become a part of her happiest moments. They gave her entrance into a new world, without requiring that she should abandon any part of the old world she had known, or that she should accept any new religious feelings or dogmas. Her aim was to find out all things that are pure, noble, brave, and good, and to adopt them, whether Pagan or Christian in their origin, and to leave dogmas, creeds, and doctrines to those who were inclined. to them by temperament.

One day, it being the Siamese Sâbâto (Sabbath), I called at her house on my way home. In passing into the little room that she had fitted up to receive me, and which we had dignified with the title of "the study," I saw that my friend, in the room adjoining, was at prayer, kneeling before her altar, on which was a gilt image of the Buddha, while on either side hung pictures of the king and her little son. The room in which she knelt was a gay one, covered with Birmese paper, on which were seen

huge trees, some standing, and others uprooted and carried away by the inundation of a mighty tropical river,
here and there drifting along passive and lifeless, and
anon covered with gay flowers. Thousands of miles distant the sun left open his golden gates, that his waves of
light might rest in benediction and with protecting fond-
ness on her dark, upturned face and colored brow. There
was a mysterious joy in her worship, which transfigured
by its soft inner light her otherwise not beautiful face,
and she seemed as if she were holding direct communion
in her inner soul with the Infinite Spirit. I stepped into
the study and waited until her prayer was offered up.
In a little time after I heard her clear voice calling me,
and in another moment I was seated beside her at the
foot of her pretty little altar. She then asked me to look
at her paper, which I did, telling her that I thought it
was a very gay one indeed for her little oratory.

"I see you do not understand the meaning of it." And
she proceeded to explain the allegory to me in her quaint
and broken English.

"That big green tree there," said she, "is like unto me
when I was young and ignorant, rejoicing in earthly dis-
tinctions and affections; and then I am brought as a gift
to a great king, and only think how grand and how rich
I may become; and there you see that I am drooping and
my leaves are all withering and begin to fall; here I am
shattered and uprooted by a sense of sorrow and humilia-
tion, drifting along an impetuous river, but by and by a
little flower stops my downward course. That little flower
is my child; he springs out of the very waters which
threatened my destruction; and now he grows into a garden of flowers, to hide away from me that which would
make me sad and sorrowful again; and now I am always
glad."

After a little while, desirous of knowing what the glittering image of Buddha really was to her, I said kindly: "Sonn Klean, you were praying to that idol?"

She did not reply at once, but at length, laying her hand gently upon my arm, said: "Shall I say of you, dear friend, that you worship the ideal or image which you have of your God in your own mind, and not the God? Even so say not of me that I worship the golden image up there, but the Great One who sent me my teacher Buddha, that he might be the guide and the light of my life."

On another occasion when she read and translated the Sermon on the Mount, she suddenly exclaimed with great emotion: "O, your sacred P'hra Jesus is very beautiful! Let us promise one another that whenever you pray to P'hra Jesus you will call him Buddha, the Enlightened One; and I, when I pray to my Buddha, I will call him P'hra Jesu Karuna, the tender and sacred Jesus, for surely these are only different names for the one and the same God."

Her favorite book, however, was "Uncle Tom's Cabin," and she would read it over and over again, though she knew all the characters by heart, and spoke of them as if she had known them all her life.

On the 3d of January, 1867, she invited me to dinner, and she sent to me, in the course of the day, so many messages, telling me to be sure to come, that I began to suspect it was going to be a very grand entertainment. So I put on my best dress, and made myself as fine as I could.

My friend was looking down the street, with her head and shoulders out of her window, as we appeared, and the moment she saw us she rushed to greet us in her own sweet, cordial manner. Dinner was served in the study, for it boasted of one table and five chairs; but our party numbered six in all, so my boy and the Prince Kreta

B'hiniharn were obliged to squeeze themselves into one chair, and then there was one apiece for the rest of us. We were served by Peguan slave-girls in the Peguan fashion, on little silver plates, the slave-girls kneeling around us. Fish, rice, jelly, and a variety of sweetmeats, came first, then different kinds of vegetables; after them a course of meat, venison, and birds of all kinds, and we finished with sweet drinks, preserves, and fruit.

When dinner was over, my friend, in concert with her sisters and slave-girls, performed on several musical instruments with wonderful effect. At last all Sonn Klean's slave-women with their children appeared in a group, one hundred and thirty-two in all, in nice new dresses, all looking particularly happy.

"I am wishful to be good like Harriet Beecher Stowe," — or Stowâ, as my friend persisted in pronouncing that name,— "and never to buy human bodies again, but only to let go free once more, and so I have now no more slaves, but hired servants. I have given freedom to all of my slaves to go or to stay with me as they wish. If they go away to their homes, I am glad; if they stay with me, I am still more glad; and I will give them each four ticals every month after this day, with their food and clothes."

Thenceforth, to express her entire sympathy and affection for the author of "Uncle Tom's Cabin," she always signed herself Harriet Beecher Stowe; and her sweet voice trembled with love and music whenever she spoke of the lovely American lady who had taught her, "even as Buddha had once taught kings," to respect the rights of her fellow-creatures.

During a severe illness which confined me a month or more to my room, I used to receive the most affectionate letters from this dear lady, signed Harriet Beecher Stowe; and when I once more returned to the palace, she took all the credit of my recovery from an illness so fatal as

11*

cholera as due to her intercessions and prayers. In one temple she had vowed that she would save seven thousand lives if mine were granted to her prayers.

I was perplexed and curious to know how she would perform the conditions of such a vow, but she assured me there would be no difficulty about it, and forthwith despatched her servant-women to the market to purchase seven baskets, containing each a thousand live fish, which, with great pomp and ceremony, were set free again in the river, and the seven thousand lives were thus actually saved.

One day, when I was sitting with my friend in her little study, she learned that I had recently lost a very dear relative, and she related to me, in a voice full of the tenderest sympathy and affection, the following Buddhist legend, which I give here as nearly as possible in her own words.

" In the village of Sârvâthi there lived a young wife named Keesah, who at the age of fourteen gave birth to a son ; and she loved him with all the love and joy of the possessor of a newly found treasure, for his face was like a golden cloud, his eyes fair and tender as a blue lotus, and his smile bright and beaming like the morning light upon the dewy flowers. But when the boy was able to walk, and could run about the house, there came a day when he suddenly fell sick and died. And Keesah, not understanding what had happened to her fair lotus-eyed boy, clasped him to her bosom, and went about the village from house to house, praying and weeping, and beseeching the good people to give her some medicine to cure her baby.

" But the villagers and neighbors, on seeing her, said : ' Is the girl mad, that she still bears about on her breast the dead body of her child ? '

" At length a holy man, pitying the girl's sorrow, said to himself : ' Alas ! this Keesah does not understand the law of death ; I will try to comfort her.' And he answered her, and said : 'My good girl, I cannot myself give you any medicine to cure your boy, but I know a holy and wise physician who can.'

" ' O,' said the young mother, ' do tell me who it is, that I may go at once to him ! '

" And the holy man replied, 'He is called the Buddha; he alone can cure thy child.'

" Then Keesah, on hearing this, was comforted, and set out to find the Buddha, still clasping to her heart the lifeless body of her child. And when she found him she bowed down before him, and said: 'O my lord and master, do you know of any medicine that will cure my baby ? '

" And the Buddha replied and said: 'Yes, I know of one, but you must get it for me.'

" And she asked : 'What medicine do you want ? Tell me, that I may hasten in search of it.'

" And the Buddha said : ' I want only a few grains of mustard-seed. Leave here the boy, and go you and bring them to me.'

" The girl refused to part with her baby, but promised to get the seed for him.

" As she was about to set out, the pitiful Buddha, recalling her, said : ' My sister, the mustard-seed that I require must be taken from a house where no child, parent, husband, wife, relative, or slave has ever died.'

" The young mother replied, ' Very good, my lord ' ; and went her way, taking her boy with her, and setting him astride on her hip, with his lifeless head resting on her bosom.

" Thus she went from house to house, from palace to hut, begging for some grains of mustard-seed.

" The people said to her : ' Here are the seeds; take them, and go thy way.'

" But she first asked : ' In this, my friend's house, has there ever died a child, a husband, a parent, or a slave ? '

"And they one and all replied: 'Lady, what is this that thou hast said ? Knowest thou not that the living are few, but that the dead are many ? There is no such house as thou seekest.'

"Then she went to other houses and begged the grains of mustard-seed, which they gladly gave her, but to her questionings one said, 'I have lost a son'; another, 'I have lost a parent'; and yet another, 'I have lost a slave'; and every one and all of them made some such reply.

"At last, not being able to discover a single house free from the dead, whence she could obtain the mustard-seed, and feeling utterly faint and weary, she sat herself down upon a stone, with her baby in her lap, and thinking sadly said to herself: 'Alas! this is a heavy task I have undertaken. I am not the only one who has lost her baby. Everywhere children are dying, parents are dying, loved ones are dying, and everywhere they tell me that the dead are more numerous than the living. Shall I then think only of my own sorrow ?'

"Thinking thus, she suddenly summoned courage to put away her sorrow for her dead baby, and she carried him to the forest and laid him down to rest under a tree ; and having covered him over with tender leaves, and taking her last look of his loved face, she betook herself once more to the Buddha and bowed before him.

"And he said to her: 'Sister, hast thou found the mustard-seed ?'

"'I have not, my lord, she replied, 'for the people in the village tell me there is no house in which some one has not died ; for the living are few, but the dead are many.'

"'And where is your baby ?'

"'I have laid him under a tree in the forest, my lord,' said Keesah, gently.

"Then said the Buddha to her: 'You have found the grains of mustard-seed; you thought that you alone had lost a son, but now you have learned that the law of death and of suffering is among all living creatures, and that here there is no permanence.'

" On hearing this Keesah was comforted, and established in the path of virtue, and was thenceforth called Keesah Godami, the disciple of the Buddha." [*]

The pleasantest of the days that I spent in the city of the " Nang Harm " were those that fell on the first full moons in the months of May, which days are always held as the anniversary of the birth, inspiration, and death of the Buddha. On the morning of the 21st of May, 1864, I was conducted by a number of well-dressed slave-women to the residence of my pupil, the " child wife." [29] Her house was a brick building with a low wall running round it, which took in some few acres of ground devoted to gardens and to residences for her numerous slaves and attendants. I was the first, that morning, to pass between the two brick and mortar lions which guarded the entrance, and after a kindly greeting I took my place at the inner end of the hall or antechamber which gave access to the residence.

The " child wife," a remarkably pretty little woman, dressed in pure white silk, stood in the hall beside a small marble fountain, with her two sons on either side of her. All round the fountain were huge China vases containing plants, covered with flowers, and between them were immense silver water-jars, each large enough to hold a couple of men, and each containing a huge silver ladle. Thirty or more young slave-women were engaged in filling them with cool fresh water drawn from a well in the garden.

The hall was freshly furnished with striped floor-mat-

[*] Professor F. Max Müller mentions this parable, in his lecture on " Buddhist Nihilism," as translated from the Birmese by Captain H. T. Rogers ; but the Birmese text is slightly different from that of the Siamese.

ting, and with cushioned seats for a hundred guests. In the garden opposite the doors of the hall was a circular thatched roof supported on one great mast, like a single-poled tent, and this was the theatre erected for the occasion. In one part was an elevated stage for the mario-nettes, and the whole was very gracefully and prettily ornamented, showing, as did everything around, a desire to please and to entertain. Some fifty women-porters came from an inner court, bearing on their heads massive silver dishes of sweetmeats and choice viands, and placed them along the hall; then came some maidens dressed in pure white, and arranged flowers in small gold vases beside each of the seats designed for the expected guests; and when this was done they took their places behind their mistress.

It was early morning, just seven o'clock. But this en-tire woman's city had been up for hours engaged in the important work of rightly celebrating the great day. The grounds around the house were all in a glow with roses, and the pure silver of the water-jars glistened resplen-dently in the morning sunlight.

The gate was thrown wide open, and into this fairy-like scene, amid flowers and sunshine and fragrance, and the dew still trembling on the leaves, were ushered in the guests, one by one, — a hundred decrepit, filthy, unsightly looking beggar-women covered with dirt and rags and the vilest uncleanliness.

And the "child wife," who might have numbered twenty-five summers, but who looked as if she were only sixteen, blushing with a delicacy and beauty of her own, advances and greets her strange guests with all the more respect and tenderness because of their rags and poverty, leads them gently and seats them on low stools around her sparkling fountain, removes their disgusting apparel, and proceeds with the aid of her maidens to wash them clean with fragrant soap and great draughts of cool water ladled out of the silver jars. What a transformation, when the matted hair was washed and combed and parted and dressed with flowers, and the rags were replaced by new robes of purest white! Then she led them towards the hall, and seated them on the silk cushions before the silver trays, and bowed on her knees before them and served to them the delicacies prepared for them, as if they each one and all deserved from her some special token of her love and veneration. After breakfast the music struck up and the actors and puppets appeared on the stage. The music was particularly good. The royal female bands were assembled for the occasion, and relieved each other in succession; the acting was occasionally interspersed with the plaintive notes of female voices; the priestesses of this beautiful scene, who seemed sometimes deeply moved, collected from within themselves all the charms and joys of love to pour them forth with the inspiration of music at the feet of their lowly listeners.*

* The Siamese are naturally very fond of music, and even persons of high rank think it no disparagement to acquire a proficiency in the art. Whence their great skill in music and in architecture it would be difficult to explain, more especially as their music exhibits great poetical genius and has a remarkably pleasing measure. It might naturally be supposed that they had derived their music from the same source that they have their religion; the softness, the playful sweetness and simplicity of the former, seeming to harmonize in great measure with the humane tenets, the pure morality, and the beauty of the latter.

The music of the Siamese Peguans and of Laos differs from that of most Indian nations in being played upon different keys, a feature which characterizes the pathetic music of certain European, and in particular the Scottish and Welsh nations. There is certainly no harsh or disagreeable sound, no abrupt transition, no grating sharpness; all is soft, lively, sweet, and harmonious to a degree which seemed to me quite surprising. They have certainly arrived far beyond the point of being merely pleased with sound. They have far a higher aim, that of interesting the feelings, of awakening thought or emotion.

Their pieces of music are very numerous; some of the women who perform before the king know by heart a hundred and fifty tunes; their memory and their performance are equally remarkable and surprising.

And at length, as the curtain of the last act dropped, and the prolonged cadence of the voices and the instruments died away, a loud buzz of delight and pleasure broke from the listening crowd of old, decrepit women, who received each a sum of money from their kind hostess, and went on their lonely way rejoicing.

"This," said my friend to me, " I do every year, to show my love and obedience to my dear teacher, the Buddha." And to my unaccustomed heart and eyes it seemed the sight in all the world the most worth gazing upon.

CHAPTER XXX.

THE SIAMESE SYSTEM OF SLAVERY.*

UNDER the late king, his Majesty Somdetch P'hra Paramendr Maha Mongkut, there existed in Siam a mixed system of slavery, in part resembling the old system of English feudal service, in part the former serfdom of Russia, and again in part the peonage of Mexico.

Three fourths of the population of Siam are in this condition of modified slavery, branded with the mark of their owners, or held by their creditors in a form of qualified servitude to work out a debt. The royal family, princes, and chief rulers and magistrates of the country, are the only exceptions to this rule. But even they are obliged to serve the king in times of war, or to provide a fitting substitute.

" Slaves," in the minute subdivisions of the law, are classed under seven different heads : first, prisoners of war ; second, slaves by purchase ; third, slaves by birth ; fourth, by gifts and legacies ; fifth, those who become slaves from gratitude ; sixth, voluntary slaves in times of famine ; seventh, debtors and their children.

But these may all be embraced in three general classes, called Prie, Baw, and Bâtt, that of slaves by birth and attached to the land, of slaves by purchase, and of slaves captured in war.

The prisoners of war and their descendants are composed of the following nations and numbers : Malays,

* For the following statements I am indebted to the late king, who very kindly furnished me with a copy of the Siamese " Slave Laws," from which these pages are translated, as if the system still existed.

Q

fifty thousand; Cochin-Chinese, seventy-five thousand; Peguans, one million; Laotians, twenty-five thousand; and Birmese, fifty thousand. All these, with few exceptions, belong to the kings of Siam. Some few are given to the principal nobles and chiefs who have distinguished themselves in the state; but even these, with their descendants, are held as Baw Chow Chewitt, — the king's slaves. The Cochin-Chinese captured in war, and all their numerous descendants, belong exclusively to the second king, — the first or supreme king having a positive antipathy to that people. They are formed into an army under the command of the second king, to guard his person, palaces, harem, etc.

The Malays and Peguans are employed as sailors and soldiers in company with the native Siamese. These are all branded on the left side a little below the armpit, and they are bound to serve three months in every year; the remaining time they may employ in their own private interests.

The slaves by purchase are divided into two classes, "redeemable" and "irredeemable." The first class must furnish security that they will fulfil the legal requirements of their masters. These can always free themselves by refunding the purchase-money, or can change their masters on procuring payment of the sum due to the old masters.

The second class are chiefly young girls sold by their parents, relatives, or owners; with these no security is either given or taken, because they generally become the wives or concubines of the buyer. As a natural consequence more than four fifths abscond whenever they get an opportunity, and the owner has no redress. Women-slaves are not branded or enrolled as the men-slaves are.

Husbands may sell their wives, parents their children,

and masters their slaves and debtors; but no one can sell an adult man-slave after he is sixteen, or a woman-slave after she has attained puberty, without his or her consent.

Prices of slaves vary according to the appearance, color, strength, physical proportions, and parentage of the person sold, from one hundred and twenty ticals for men, and sixty to a hundred ticals * for women. But if the woman be fair and pleasing in form and feature, she will bring as much as a thousand ticals for the harem of a great noble.

The method of selling one's self is very simple. Every man, on becoming a slave, signs an agreement, of which I give a copy below. This paper his master retains, but is obliged to surrender whenever the slave produces the amount mentioned in it.

"Wednesday, the seventh day of the waning moon of the year 1227 of the little era Choola Sakarat,† I, Khow,

* A tical may be valued at from fifty to sixty cents of the Spanish dollar.

† The Siamese months are lunar months; each is divided into two parts, i. e. Khang Khun and Khang Ram, waxing and waning moon. Six of the months have thirty, and six twenty-nine days. To compensate for the deficiency of the eleven days which are required to make a full solar year, they have an intercalary month of thirty days once in three years, and there being still a loss of about three days in nineteen years, this is supplied by an arbitrary addition of a day to the seventh month of such years as may be selected by the Brahmin astrologers, whose business it is to observe the sun's path in the heavens, and to announce all variations in the calendar. At the very moment of the sun's crossing the equator, they make proclamation of the advent of each new year, accompanied by a burst of music and by the firing of great guns, both from the palace and the city walls.

The Siamese have two cycles, one within the other; the greater is twelve, and the lesser ten years in duration. Every year in each cycle has its own peculiar name. Their sacred era is reckoned from the time of the death of the Buddha (2415). It is denominated Buddha Sakarat. Their civil era is called Choola Sakarat, and is reckoned from the time of its establishment (1233) by P'hra Rooang, a Siamese king of great celebrity.

sell myself to Nai Dang for ticals one hundred and twenty, to be refunded by me, Khow, at the time and hour of being set free."

Such is the bill of sale. But as it generally happens that the parents have also sold themselves, some other security is required, which is given in another paper. The value of anything that the slave may break or destroy is added to the original account.

The masters are bound to furnish their slaves with rice and fish daily, but not with clothes.

The position of the slaves by birth differs in no respect from that of slaves by purchase, with the exception that while the prices of the latter vary, the price of the former is fixed by law for every age, size, and sex, and the owners cannot demand more for them than that which is determined by the law.

The severest punishment for slaves is being made to work in chains. If no improvement takes place from this punishment, the slave is handed over to the king's judges, and is, provided the crime or misdemeanor is proven, incarcerated in the Siamese convict prison, — a punishment to which death itself is preferable.

The principal hardship that the slave suffers is being obliged to marry at the will of his or her owner, and this with a people who are highly susceptible of conjugal affection is often the cause of great suffering to the women.

Then comes the difficulty of lodging a complaint against their masters for an insufficiency of food, and sometimes for an absolute want of clothes, for which latter even the law does not hold the master responsible.

There are four conditions under which a slave is freed from the obligations of servitude, — slaves voluntarily manumitted by their masters; slaves admitted to the priesthood; those who are given to serve the priests; and when the master himself takes the vows of a priest, he is obliged to free all his slaves, as the ecclesiastical court will not otherwise receive him into the priesthood, and he can at no time reclaim them for actual service, unless on quitting the priesthood he repurchases them.

Debtors may be made slaves when they do not pay the interest for money borrowed, and will not work to make good the failure of payment; and in case of death the nearest relative becomes a slave till the original amount, with the interest added, is refunded. The rate of interest in Siam is about thirty per cent, and the poor are unable, unless by labor, to pay such an exorbitant rate.

If the bought or rather the redeemable slave should die in his master's service, — even after a lifetime of labor, — the security must refund the original sum or become a slave in his stead. If a slave be sick, and is attended to during his illness in his master's house, the security is liable for the interest of the slave's purchase-money during the period of illness. When children are sold under the full value, they must not be beaten till they bleed.

When a slave volunteers out of affection for his master or mistress to take his or her place in prison or in torture, one half of his or her purchase-money must be refunded to the security. But if the slave is irredeemable, no part is to be refunded.

If a man sell a slave, and after receiving the money refuse to give him or her up to the purchaser, he shall pay double the sum, — three fourths to the buyer and one fourth into the government or state treasury.

If a buyer disapprove of a slave before three months have elapsed, he may recover his money.

If a master strike his slave so that he die, no claim can be made upon the security, and the master shall be punished according to the law.

Anything that a slave may break can be added, at the will of the owner, to the purchase-money.

If in herding cattle he be negligent, and they be lost, he shall pay for them; if more be given into his charge than he can attend to, he shall pay only half; but if robbers bind him and steal the cattle, he cannot be held responsible.

Any claim against a slave must be made by the owner before he is sold to another party.

If a master or mistress force a female slave to marry one man when she has openly professed a preference for another, half her redemption-money must be remitted.

If a slave go to war instead of his master, and fight bravely, he must be set free at the termination of the battle. If he fight only ordinarily well, half his purchase-money shall be remitted.

If a master repurchase a slave, and he die in his service, he can demand only half the original amount from his security.

If a slave begin to plant rice, he cannot, even if able, purchase his freedom until the harvest is over.

If, when rice is dear, a man sell himself to slavery below the standard value, when rice gets cheap the price must be raised, and the balance paid over by the purchaser.

If a slave injure himself while at his master's work, compensation must be made according to the nature of the injury.

If a slave die in the stead or in the defence of his master, nothing can be demanded from the security.

In all cases of an epidemic, nothing can be claimed from the security.

If a man have several wives, and the lesser sell themselves to the higher wives, or the poorer to the richer, no interest can be claimed on the purchase-money, as they are considered sisters in the sight of the law.

If the slave demand a change of masters, and the master cannot dispose of him, he must take him to the judges to sell; and if they find no purchaser within three days, he must return to his master and be thenceforward Khai-Khat, irredeemable.

If a slave run away, the money expended in apprehending him or her must be added to his original account.

Slaves having children, the children become slaves, and must be paid for according to age.

If a master compel a slave to bear a child against her will, both she and the child are free in the sight of the law, even if irredeemable at first.

If a slave complain against his master, the judges will not file the complaint unless he has first paid his purchase-money, except in cases of murder and treason.

If a slave accuse his master falsely of capital crimes, his tongue and lips shall be cut off. But if the charge be true, he shall receive his freedom, even if Khai-Khat irredeemables.

If a slave make money on his or her own private account, at his or her death it will become the property of the master. But if the money be left to him, it shall go to the nearest relative.

In all cases of doubt between the slave-woman and her master, the law shall protect the mother, and the children must be given to her if she bring the price, under penalty of forfeiting both mother and child.

Two slaves, husband and wife, brother and sister, having their names on the same bill of sale, if one run away, the other shall be charged with the entire debt.

CHAPTER XXXI.

THE ROYAL PROCLAMATIONS.

IN the beginning of the reign of P'rabat Somdetch P'hra Paramendr Maha Chulalonkorn, a new era dawned upon the kingdom of the white elephant.

On the 11th of October, 1868, a royal proclamation of the new and auspicious reign was made in all parts of the vast kingdom and provinces of Siam, and a national holiday was appointed. The multitudinous pagoda bells rang all day, while louder still boomed the cannon, up went the rockets, and aloft streamed the red and white banners of the white elephant. Still higher rose the glad hearts of the princes and chiefs of the people, and low in reverential attitudes, even in the very dust, were bowed the heads of the millions of the enslaved subjects.

Classed with the sod, and of as little account as the earth out of which they obtain so scanty a subsistence, branded as cattle with the mark of their owner, what have they to do with the glad shouts and the loud rejoicings that resound on every side ?

To them it means only a change of owners, and royalty is the name fixed to the other end of the enslaving rod of power : "The right divine of kings to govern wrong."

There can be no auspicious reign or any happy future for the slave.

The royal messages of peace and good-will may find an echo in the freedman's heart and in his home, but they must ever come with a darkening power and as a saddening cloud to the home and the heart of the slave. An irre-

KING OF SIAM.

deemable beast of burden, what has he to hope from an auspicious reign, or the enthronement of a promising sovereign ?

Yet that these millions of enslaved men and women are not brutes or wild beasts, or even devoid of noble and generous emotions, is proved by the most astonishing acts of devotion and self-sacrifice performed by slaves for the masters and mistresses whom they have learned to love.

Any one who from curiosity or with a higher motive may visit the prisons in the city of Bangkok will find, to his great surprise, that nearly one half of the inmates are slaves voluntarily expiating the crimes and wrong-doings of their masters and mistresses, or, as is often the case, mothers, daughters, wives, or sisters enduring all the hardships of a Siamese prison — and words would fail me adequately to describe the amount of suffering which those two words imply — in the place and for the sake of sons, husbands, or unworthy relatives. The strength that is in these slaves to suffer is the strength of love. Love combined with despair gives them the awful and wonderful power of utter self-sacrifice.

The rights which every man should enjoy in his wife, his children, and his own labor, and which should be the most sacred and inviolable rights, are here placed at the mercy of a master, and are oft-times to the slave the very fetters of his galling servitude.

But, since that ever-to-be-remembered 11th of October, 1868, a new empire has arisen out of the ashes of the old. The traditions and customs of centuries are as naught. A fresh start has been made, a young king full of generous impulses and noble purposes reigns ; and how he intends to govern may be gathered from his second royal proclamation to his people on the subject of religion : —

" In regard to the concern of seeking and holding a

12

religion that will be a refuge to you in this life: it is a good and noble concern, and it is exceedingly appropriate and suitable that you, as a nation, and each man individually, should investigate for himself, and according to his own wisdom, which is the right and which the wrong; and if you see any religion whatever, or any body of men professing any religion whatsoever who seem likely to be an advantage to you, — a true religion in accordance with your own wisdom, — hold to that religion with all your heart; hold to it not with a shallow mind, or after slight investigation, or even because of its tradition, saying this is the custom held from time immemorial, but from your own deep faith in its excellence; and do not profess a religion for the truth of which you have not good evidence, or one which frightens men through their fears and flatters them through their hopes.

"Do not be either frightened or flattered into doing what is right and just, and do not follow after fictitious signs and wonders.

"But, when you shall have obtained a firm conviction in any religious faith that it is true, beautiful, and good, hold to it with great joy, follow its teachings alone, and it will be a source of happiness to each one of you.

"It is our will that our subjects of whatever race, nation, or creed, live freely and happily in our kingdom, no man despising or molesting another on account of religious difference, or any other difference of opinions, customs, or manners."

This is the second important message from the young king, who has just ascended the throne of his fathers, to his subjects, both bond and free.

The great old dukes and princes and nobles of the realm feel in their hardened hearts that it is barely gracious, and certainly not at all graceful, in one so young, to ignore all that magnificent past. But the young monarch is true to his early promise, and his next step is quietly to abolish the customary prostrations before a superior, and to inaugurate a new costume for his people, which will enable the wearer, whoever he may be, prince, ruler, chieftain, or slave, to stand face to face with his fellow-men and erect in the presence of his sovereign.

And now let us mark the next step made in the path of progress and freedom by this noble young Buddhist monarch.

Years ago, in the little study in his beautiful palace called the "Rose-Planting House," when a mere boy, on hearing of the death of President Lincoln, he had declared "that if he ever lived to reign over Siam, he would reign over a free and not an enslaved nation; that it would be his pride and joy to restore to his kingdom the original constitution under which it was first planted by a small colony of hardy and brave Buddhists, who fled from their native country, Magadah, to escape the religious persecutions of the Brahminical priests, who had arrived at Ayudia and there established themselves under one of their leaders, who was at once priest and king. They called the spot they occupied "Muang Thai," — the kingdom of the free, — and this kingdom now extends from the northern slopes of the mountains of Yuman in China to the Gulf of Siam.

Nobly has he striven to keep this aspiration of his early boyhood; and as he went, day after day, to take his place at the head of his government, and to the nightly sittings of the Secret Council of the state, he endeavored to hold unflinchingly to his one great purpose.

On the first opportunity that offered he urged the abolition of slavery upon the Prince Regent, his uncle, and the Prime Minister; then again he brought it before the mighty Secret Council, sitting at midnight in the hall of his ancestors. "I see," says the brave young king, "no hope for our country until she is freed from the dark blot of slavery."

The Prince Regent and the Prime Minister, though almost persuaded by the vehement pleading of the young and fearless king, replied: "It is impossible to free a nation of slaves without incurring much risk and danger to the state and to the slaveholders. Under the existing laws, Siam could not abolish her system of slavery without undermining at the same time her whole constitution."

"Well," said the young king, "let it be so; but my slaves, my soldiers, and my debtors are my own, and I will free them at least, whatever my ministers may see fit to do; for my part, no human being shall ever again be branded in my name and with my mark."

What strange words from one so young!

The Secret Council meet again and again to discuss the matter, and at length they decide — for they too have the good of their country at heart — to let the young king have his own way.

Then the royal boy king sends another message summoning the heads of all his people, from every department of his vast kingdom, to appear together in his audience hall, and to receive the royal message.

Standing on the lowest step of his glittering throne, he greets the chief rulers and governors and judges of his people, and utters these remarkable words: "Let this our royal message to our people be proclaimed, and not as if we were doing a great and lordly thing, but our simple duty to our fellow-men and subjects, that from the first day of January, 1872, slavery shall cease to be an institution in our country, and every man, woman, and child shall hold themselves free-born citizens; and further let it be made known, that a tax, according to the circumstances of each and every man, shall be levied on the nation to remunerate the slaveholders for the loss of their slaves."[30]

The effect of this speech upon the listeners can hardly be imagined. It was like the winged words of an angel from heaven, and the young monarch descended from the last step of his throne, having firmly laid the corner-stone on which the greatness of his reign and his nation will forever rest unshaken. But seeing that his astonished hearers remained rooted to the spot, still doubting whether they had heard aright, he added: "We bind ourselves to fulfil our word to our subjects at large, no matter what the cost to ourselves. Go you and proclaim our royal will."

When the wonderful tidings were actually proclaimed, the people listened as though they heard not; at best they distrusted the good report, and received the wondrous words as if they were merely the sounding of brass and the tinkling of cymbals in their ears.

Confidence is a plant of slow growth; but how slow must its revival have been in the place whence it has once been torn up by the roots! So the people turned a deaf ear to the loving messages of their young king, and went on their sad way not a whit happier.

But when the 1st of January, 1872, had actually arrived, and they absolutely found themselves "free" men and women, their patient, loving hearts well-nigh burst asunder with joy.

The glad cries of the ransomed millions penetrated the heart of the universe, and the "Despair" of the nation flapped her dark wings and fell down dead at the golden feet of the royal ransomer.

The prison doors are open, and all the prisoners by proxy and those who were slaves by reason of their great poverty or their greater love find, to their amazement, that the sun of freedom has risen for them, and who shall fathom the depth of their joy ? But the land is full of flower shows, and unfurled standards, and cool fountain displays, fireworks, illuminations, and theatrical exhibitions. The music of thousands of choristers and the glad huzzas of congregated myriads rend the air. Let them dance and laugh and sing ; they have had enough of slavery and too little of freedom, and the great hymn of the nation ascends to the Ruler of kings for the " Ransomed One," " Glory to God in the highest, and on earth peace and good-will towards men."

THE END OF THE ROMANCE.

TEMPLE AND RUINS OF KAMPOOT.

A LEGEND OF THE GOLD AND SILVER MINES OF SIAM.

VELA CHOW, or the Beautiful Dawn, was the only daughter of a very powerful king of Ayudia. She was so wondrously beautiful that the old Brahmins and astrologers who foretold her birth named her, even before she was born, the Beautiful Dawn, as the only appropriate name for her.

Now it happened that, at the time of Vela Chow's birth, there was no moon to illuminate the fair earth, but the golden sun and the green earth enjoyed a much closer and more intimate friendship than they now do, and old age, sickness, and death were unknown to the blessed and undying people of Ayudia.

But as the mighty king Somdetch P'hra Batt, the duke of the golden foot, had reigned nearly three thousand five hundred years without ceasing, he became weary of the cares of state, and thereupon abdicated in favor of his young son, P'hra Batt Bandethâno, a vigorous youth of not more than five hundred years of age, who was even from his childhood an especial favorite of the ruby-faced and warm-hearted monarch P'hra Athiett, i. e. the Sun.

In the course of time, the friendship between these two, Bandethâno and P'hra Athiett, sovereigns of the earth and sky, ripened to such a degree of perfection that the latter was loath to withdraw his bright beaming face from his young friend's kingdom, even to seek his couch for a little rest at night, as had been his custom from time immemorial; thus he beamed forth both night and day

in saffron hues on the fair mountains and lovely valleys
of the invincible city of Ayudia, and the land flourished
in luxuriance and beauty, the fruits and flowers rivalled
those that grew and blossomed in Indra's own garden, and
countless birds of marvellous plumage winged their flight
from distant worlds to build their nests and warble their
exquisite melodies among the proud forests of this favored land. As for the men of this region, they were tall
and stately and of golden mien, like the laughter-loving
Gandharwas of Indra's paradise, and the women were glo-
riously beautiful, fair as silvery clouds, with eyes of wondrous hue ; so that no mortal man could look upon one
of them and not yield his spirit to the sweet frenzy of
inextinguishable love.

Away flew the golden days and nights, and round and
round rushed the radiant chariot-wheels of P'hra Athiett,
and thousands and thousands of years sped away, but he
never relaxed the speed of his swift coursers, nor drew in
his rainbow-tinted reins, nor turned away even for an
instant his glowing eyes from this favored kingdom.

Now, things having gone on in this way for several
thousands of years, yet no sweet slumber had ever closed
the godlike eyes of P'hra Athiett, and all the lovely Dowâstrâs, i. e. the stars, finding themselves totally eclipsed,
their brilliancy and beauty marred by this unceasing
sleeplessness on the part of their sovereign, formed the
wicked and cruel design of revolting against him, and of
taking possession, by some means or other, of his golden
car.

Accordingly, instead of going to sleep, as had hitherto
been their practice during the day, they all plotted together to hide themselves behind the many-tinted curtain
of their monarch's chariot, and to watch his movements,
in order to discover the cause of the singular attraction
that drew him forever towards the earth, while he left his

own vaulted and ethereal hemisphere to the tender mer-
cies of stray suns or wandering comets.

Having ratified with many an oath and many a vow
their wicked compact, the treacherous Dowâstrâs, instead
of going to bed like the dutiful children of a kind and
beneficent ruler, only pretended to sleep, but all the while
kept opening and shutting and blinking their bright, in-
quisitive little eyes, winking at one another and peering
behind the golden curtains of the royal chariot at their
unconscious master, who, fully believing that all his subjects were sound asleep, grew brighter and brighter, while
over his round, genial face there beamed forth a smile of
ineffable radiance as he approached the earth. At this
very moment the rebellious Dowâstrâs, wondering at the
blissful face of their monarch, peered out from behind the
rainbow-hued drapery of the celestial chariot and turned
their penetrating eyes towards the earth, where, to their
astonishment, they beheld the matchless form and the
divinely beautiful face of Vela Chow, who was lulling
her wearied father to rest with the music of her sweet
voice.

"Ah! ah!" laughed the wicked Dowâstrâs, "now we
have found out the secret."

As soon as she had soothed her father to sleep, the
lovely Vela Chow, all unconscious of what was happen-
ing around her, sauntered forth among the unfrequented
woods and dells, making the voiceless hills and rocks re-
echo her merry notes in melodious sounds; now culling
rare wild flowers to wreathe round her lovely brow, now
bathing her little feet in the cool crystal waters of a purl-
ing brook that murmured gently through the mountain
caves and caverns, and anon raising her glad heart in
thanksgiving and praise to the great, beneficent, and glorious P'hra Athiett.

At length she sat herself down in the deep solitude to

12 *   R

rest; and as she listened to the gentle zephyrs that fanned
her yellow tresses or rustled amidst the topmost boughs
of the "green-haired" forest trees, the birds plucked for
her the ripest and the sweetest fruits, and some dropped
them at her side, and others, less timid, hovered around her,
holding them in their tender bills, each fluttering against
the other and striving to be the favored one to whom she
would open her sweet mouth to be fed; and while the
many-hued birds were thus rivalling each other in their
delicate attentions to the lovely maiden, it chanced that a
gorgeous butterfly, more glorious than any she had ever
before seen, alighted on a neighboring flower. Up sprang
Vela Chow, and away she flew after it, from flower to
flower, from shrub to tree, until at last the tantalizing butterfly flew so high in the air that the eager damsel could
do no more than raise her fair face and sparkling eyes to
follow its airy flight through the bright sky. Just at
this moment P'hra Athiett's golden chariot was coming
over the hill, and he smiled a smile of such ineffable delight when he caught sight of her, that he dazzled the
eyes of the poor little maiden; and as she could no longer
see the beautiful butterfly, she was obliged to relinquish
all idea of capturing it. So she retraced her disconsolate
steps to her lonely mountain stream, and plunged into its
waters, in the hope of finding therein refreshment and for-
getfulness of her cruel disappointment.

But P'hra Athiett was not to be thus baffled; so he
noiselessly climed higher and higher, and approached
nearer and nearer, and smiled so much more warmly than
ever, that he once more quite overpowered the weary
maiden, who suddenly vanished from his sight, sought refuge in her favorite mountain cavern, and there fell sound
asleep.

For a moment poor P'hra Athiett was disconcerted,
and a great pain, like a dark heavy cloud, shot up from his

heart and overspread his bright, happy face, and he knew
not what to do ; but the next, he broke forth into a more
joyous smile than ever, for he was just as foolish as he
was old, and had been on the lookout all these thousands of years, night and day, hoping to catch a glimpse
of this incomparable maiden; the moment he did so, he
fell desperately in love with her, and he could not make
up his mind to perform his journey without one more
look at her sweet, pure face; therefore, instead of going
on his way through the sky, he changed his course, and
drove at a furious rate down the mountain-side towards
the cavern, alighted from his chariot, and crept softly
into the cave where the lovely Vela Chow slumbered, and
smiled upon her with such rapturous tenderness that the
sleeping maiden's heart was penetrated and completely
captivated.   She opened her beautiful eyes with a joyful
sense of a new and delicious emotion upon P'hra Athiett,
who beamed upon her so lovingly and with such irresistible pleadings in his godlike eyes, that she could not
refuse to return his affection, and they there and then exchanged vows of eternal friendship and love.

But alas ! while the all-unconscious and happy lovers
were thus fondly conversing together, and P'hra Athiett
was painting in glowing words the beauty of his heavenly
dwelling-place, the wicked Dowâstrâs in all haste rushed
to the mountain-side, drove off the golden chariot, and
unharnessed the swift-winged coursers.   Having thus cut
off his retreat, they raised a shout of triumph, deposed
their infatuated monarch, and established a republic
among themselves, permitting neither stray suns nor wandering comets to have anything to do with their government.

Poor P'hra Athiett, who was now about to conduct his
sweet happy bride to his celestial kingdom, found, to his
consternation and grief, that his golden chariot had van-

ished. He bowed his head, and his great joyous face became suddenly overcast; all its light and glory departed, while large tears like mountain torrents rolled from his godlike eyes, and streamed upon the earth, and were there and then transformed into nuggets of the purest gold.

Then the mountains, pitying his sufferings, opened their hearts, and revealed to him a secret passage by which he might regain his heavenly abode.

P'hra Athiett bade a sad adieu to the lovely Vela Chow, and, with promise of speedy return, set out, shedding golden tears all along the way, in search of his missing chariot. And as for the unhappy Vela Chow, the moment she lost sight of her beloved P'hra Athiett, she drooped her fair head in unspeakable sorrow, and followed him with aching heart and faltering step all the way, searching for the lost chariot, and shedding abundantly her bright beautiful tears, which, as they fell upon the rocky sides of the mountains, changed their flinty arteries into veins of the purest and most precious silver.

Thus the grief of these two godlike hearts served to enrich the country with endless wealth.

At the end of twelve hours, however, the wicked stars repented of their cruel conduct, and a fresh compact was made between the republican Dowâstrâs and the godlike lover P'hra Athiett, wherein it was expressly agreed that for a fortnight in every month he should pick up his beautiful bride at the mouth of the cavern and take her with him to his celestial home; but that for the rest of the month she should unveil her matchless face, and reveal her exquisite beauty to the Dowâstrâs, and rule over them in the sky, — for they all, it seems, had also fallen desperately in love with her, — and it was distinctly stipulated that P'hra Athiett should never attempt to approach her while she reigned as their queen and mistress in the heavens; and to distinguish her in her new regal character, the Dowâstrâs changed her name from "Vela Chow" to "Rupea Chandra," — the Silver Moon.

To all this P'hra Athiett readily assented; for he was impatient to regain his chariot, and to bear away his lovely bride.

But it is said that even to this day, while Vela Chow is presiding in queenlike splendor over the jealous Dowâstrâs, P'hra Athiett is foolish enough at times (for now and then he cannot restrain his affection) to attempt to kiss her. When all the Siamese, fearing lest he should again be dethroned, turn out *en masse*, and shout, and fire cannons, and beat drums, to warn him of the impropriety of his proceedings; which in the space of two or three hours — this being the time, it is said, that sound takes to travel to the sun and moon — generally produces the desired effect of recalling the monarch to himself.

Thus are the gold and silver mines, and the lunar and solar eclipses, accounted for in the Siamese legends; and annual pilgrimages are still made to the cavern where the lovely Vela Chow plighted her troth to P'hra Athiett.

Cambridge : Electrotyped and Printed by Welch, Bigelow, & Co.

Textual Notes

(For the information about actual Siamese people I am completely indebted to David Wyatt, who identified them for me. He also provided many other facts about nineteenth-century Siam.)

1. The actual origins of the Siamese are obscure.

2. This theory, frequent in the nineteenth century, is now discredited.

3. Ayudia, or Ayudhya, the first capitol of Siam (as Bangkok was the third), was founded in 1351 and sacked and burned by the Burmese in 1767.

4. The "popular river festival" was probably Loy Krathong. It is still a popular Thai festival, held at the end of the rainy season.

5. Bangkok, a comparatively young city, was founded in 1782 by the new king, Rama I.

6. There are no accurate ways to know the nineteenth-century population of Nang Harm. There were certainly several thousand people living within the inner wall, possibly the 9,000 Leonowens estimates. Some years later, when the population of Nang Harm had decreased, Malcolm Smith in *A Physician at the Court of Siam* estimated its numbers at 3,000 (p. 57).

7. Betel is a kind of nut nineteenth-century Siamese were fond of chewing. It turns the teeth black. Malcolm Smith claimed in *A Physician at the Court of Siam* that the present of a betel box from the king was a sign of high favor (p. 79).

8. Lady Thieng or Lady Thiang, the head wife, was a nobleman's daughter though not of royal blood. She was one of King Mongkut's first concubines and the mother of ten of his children, four sons and six daughters. One of her functions was to be the keeper of the palace

keys. For a list of the royal children see *Ratchasakunwong* [Royal family] (8th rev. ed.; Bangkok: Cremation of Sanon Bunyawiriphan, 1969).

9. Princess Ying Yonwalacks was King Mongkut's eldest daughter, and the first child born to him after his accession to the throne.

10. Thomas George Knox became the British consul in Bangkok in 1866, succeeding Sir Robert Schombergk. Prior to becoming consul, he held the consular position of interpreter. Knox had two daughters by a Siamese wife (whom he left in Siam when he went back to England and retired). One of his daughters, Caroline Knox, married Anna Leonowens's son, Louis, in August 1884.

11. Mohammedans in Thailand were not automatically under British protection.

12. Chow Chom Manda Ung was the daughter of a powerful nobleman, Chaophraya Nikonbodin. He held one of the most important ministerial positions in Siam, the minister of the north, from 1849 to 1863. His daughter was a concubine of Rama III, King Mongkut's elder half brother, who reigned before Mongkut. Chow Chom Manda Ung had only one child, Princess Butri, the last child of Rama III. Princess Brittry or Butri was not Mongkut's half sister, but rather his first cousin. She had a literary reputation and had taught Prince Chulalongkorn to read and write. As King Rama V, Chulalongkorn gave her high rank and the new title of Princess Worasutsuda (see David Wyatt, *The Politics of Reform,* p. 36).

13. The story of the Rajpoot and his daughter, which I believe to be fictional, extends from chapter 7 to 14. Its mythic style seems at least as much Indian as Siamese. Its material may have been adapted from tales Leonowens heard in her earlier life in India, interwoven with what she knew of customs in Siam.

14. The correct spelling is Laotian.

15. Pitchaburee is described under the name Bijrepuree or Petchabury in chapter 22, p. 175. One result of the different alphabets used for Thai and for English is that a Thai word, when translated into English, is given various spellings. King Mongkut had a vacation palace at Phetburi or Petchabury, which has now been restored.

16. The story of Choy and her lover, while almost certainly an invention in its particulars, was probably based on a real incident that occurred in 1859, three years before Leonowens arrived. It is likely she would have been told what happened by both her American missionary acquaintances and her women pupils in Nang Harm. The incident is briefly mentioned in the 1860 *Bangkok Calendar* (see note 22 to my Introduction).

17. Sir Robert Schombergk was the British consul in Bangkok beginning in 1857. He would have been consul at the time of the 1859 incident described in the *Bangkok Calendar*.

18. See Leonowens' note on p. 157 for *P'hoodth thô*.

19. Chiengmai, or Chiang Mai, is the major city of northern Thailand, and second only to Bangkok in size and importance.

20. The second king was Chudamani, Mongkut's younger brother, who as the second king had his palace in Chiang Mai. When he became seriously ill he returned to Bangkok to die in January 1866.

21. The Reverend Dan Beach Bradley was an American medical missionary who spent many years in Siam. The *Bangkok Recorder* was a semimonthly journal in English, published by Dan Beach Bradley and the American missionaries during 1865 and 1866.

22. The Laotians spoke northern Thai, a different language from the Siamese.

23. The alphabet of the northern Thai language was also different from the Siamese, or Thai, alphabet.

24. Monsieur Lamache was drillmaster of the king's soldiers.

25. "Hidden Perfume" was Sonn Klean, one of the king's concubine mothers. Her son, Prince Kreta-Bhinniharn, would have a distinguished career, including serving as the minister of public works and the Siamese ambassador to London.

26. William Bradley records that Robert Hunter (Jr.), private secretary to the king, drank too much, and died by falling off his dock and drowning after a drunken spree in 1865. His father, Robert Hunter,

who left Siam in 1844, was a Scotsman who had come to Bangkok in the 1820s, married a native Portuguese woman named Angelina, and sent their eldest child, Robert, to school in England. Did his son do the same thing with his children?

27. Birmah, or Burma, the traditional enemy of Siam, is on the northwest border of Thailand.

28. The steamer from Singapore to the port of Bangkok took about five days.

29. The "child wife" may be Lady Talap, who had two royal children.

30. The young king, somewhat at the mercy of his powerful prince regent, was to find that change required more than a proclamation. Slavery did not "cease to be an institution" in Thailand until the turn of the century.

Selected Bibliography

Athenaeum. Review of *The English Governess.* December 24, 1870. Review
    of *The Romance of Siamese Harem Life.* February 15, 1873.

Atlantic Monthly. Vol. 25. April, May, June 1870.

Bangkok Recorder: A Semi-Monthly Journal. Bangkok: American Mission-
    ary Association, 1865–66.

Bixby, Olive Jennie. *My Child-Life in Burmah; or, Recollections and Incidents.*
    Boston: W. G. Corthell, 1880.

Bowring, Sir John. *The Kingdom and People of Siam.* 2 vols. London: J. W.
    Parker and Son, 1857. Reprint, Kuala Lumpur: Oxford Univer-
    sity Press, 1969.

Bradley, Dan Beach. *The Bangkok Calendar.* Bangkok: American Mission-
    ary Association, 1859–69.

Bradley, William L. *Siam Then: The Foreign Colony in Bangkok before and
    after Anna.* Pasadena, Calif.: William Carey Library, 1981.

Bristowe, W. S. *Louis and the King of Siam.* New York: Thai-American
    Publishers, 1976.

Cary, Caverlee, "Anna Leonowens' Memoirs and the Problems of Auto-
    biography." Graduate history paper, Cornell University, 1988.

Castleman, Jill A. "The Making of a Myth: Anna Leonowens and Thai-
    land." Undergraduate history paper, Cornell University, 1985.

Chula Chakrabongse, Prince of Thailand. *Lords of Life: The Paternal Mon-
    archy of Bangkok, 1782–1932.* London: Alvin Redman, Ltd., 1960.

Cort, Mary Lovina. *Siam: or, The Heart of Farther India.* New York: Anson
    D. F. Randolph & Co., 1886.

Feltus, George Haws, ed. *Abstract of the Journal of Rev. Dan Beach Bradley,
    M.D.* Published by Rev. Dan F. Bradley. Cleveland: Pilgrim
    Church, 1936.

Frankfurter, Dr. O. "King Mongkut." *Journal of the Siam Society,* 1 (1904):
    191–206.

Great Britain, Foreign Office in Siam: Correspondence 1867–1948. Microfilm.
    Kew, Richmond, Surrey: Public Record Office, 1984.

Griswold, A. B. *King Mongkut of Siam.* New York: Asia Society, 1961.

Knight, Ruth Adams. *The Treasured One: The Story of Rudivoran, Princess of
    Siam.* New York: E. P. Dutton, 1957.

Kukrit Pramoj, M. R. *Si Phaendin, Four Reigns*. Trans. Tulachandra. 2 vols. Bangkok: Duang Kamol, 1981.

Kukrit Pramoj, M. R., and Seni Pramoj, M. R. *A King of Siam Speaks*. Bangkok: The Siam Society, 1987.

Landon, Margaret. *Anna and the King of Siam*. New York: The John Day Company, 1943. Reprints: Garden City, N. Y.: Garden City Publishing Co., 1945; London: G. G. Harrap & Co., 1945; New York: The John Day Company, 1947. Reprinted in a shortened version as *Anna and the King*. London: G. G. Harrap & Co., 1945.

Leonowens, Anna Harriette. *The English Governess at the Siamese Court: Being Recollections of Six Years in the Royal Palace in Bangkok*. Boston, Mass.: Fields, Osgood, & Co., 1870. Reprints: Boston: J. R. Osgood & Co., 1873; New York: Roy, 1954; London: Arthur Barker, 1954; Singapore: Oxford University Press, 1988.

———. *The English Governess at the Siamese Court: Being Recollections of Six Years at the Royal Palace in Bangkok*. Philadelphia: Porter & Coates, 1870. Reprinted as *Siam and the Siamese*. Philadelphia: Henry T. Coates, 1897.

———. *The English Governess at the Siamese Court: Being Recollections of Six Years in the Royal Palace in Bangkok*. London: Trubner & Co., 1870. Reprinted as *The Original Anna and the King of Siam*. Bangkok: Chalermnit, 1979.

———. *The Romance of the Harem*. Boston: J. R. Osgood, 1873. Reprinted as *Siamese Harem Life*—London: Arthur Barker, 1952; New York: E. P. Dutton, 1953.

———. *The Romance of the Harem*. Philadelphia: Porter & Coates, [1873].

———. *The Romance of Siamese Harem Life*. London: Trubner & Co., 1873.

———. *Life and Travel in India: Being Recollections of a Journey before the Days of Railroads*. Philadelphia: Porter & Coates, 1884. Reprint, Philadelphia: Henry T. Coates, 1897.

———. *Life and Travel in India: Being Recollections of a Journey before the Days of Railroads*. London: Trubner & Co., 1884.

———. *Our Asiatic Cousins*. Boston: D. Lothrop, 1889.

Mattini Rubrin, M. "The Role of Thai Women in Dramatic Arts and Social Development Problems Concerning Child Prostitution in Thailand: A Case Study, Accompanied by a Video-tape on the Lives of Child Prostitutes." *Internation Conference on Thai Studies*. Bangkok: Thai Studies Program, Chulalongkorn University, 1984.

Minney, R. J. *Fanny and the Regent of Siam*. London: Collins, 1962.

Moffat, Abbot Low. *Mongkut, the King of Siam*. Ithaca, N.Y.: Cornell University Press, 1961.

Nation. Review of *The English Governess,* 12 (Mar. 9, 1871, 161–62).
Review of *The Romance of the Harem,* 16 (May 15, 1873, 337–38).

New York Times. Review of *The English Governess,* December 10, 1870,
p. 2.1. Review of *The Romance of the Harem,* February 14, 1873,
p. 9.2. See also October 20, 1874, pp. 4–7; March 3, 1875, pp. 6–
7; August 8, 1970, p. 25.7.

Records of the United States Consulate in Bangkok. 1856–1912. Washington:
National Archives and Records Service, 1960.

Smith, Malcolm. *A Physician at the Court of Siam.* London: Country Life
Ltd., 1946. Reprint, Singapore: Oxford University Press, 1982.

Untitled Photograph Album. John M. Echols Collection, Lock Press, Cornell
University.

Vikrom Koompirochana. "Siam in British Foreign Policy 1855–1938: The
Acquisition and Relinquishment of British Extraterritorial
Rights." Ph.D. diss., Michigan State University, 1972.

Wyatt, David K. *The Politics of Reform in Thailand: Education in the Reign of
King Chulalongkorn.* New Haven: Yale University Press, 1969.

———. *Thailand: A Short History.* New Haven: Yale University Press,
1982.

Young, Ernest. *The Kingdom of the Yellow Robe: A Description of Old Siam.*
London: Archibald Constable, 1898. Reprint, Singapore: Oxford University Press, 1982, 1986.